VISUALBASIC
for applications

JEFFREY A. STIPES • TIMOTHY N. TRAINOR
Muskegon Community College • Muskegon, Michigan

Editor	Desiree Faulkner
Proofreader	Susan Capecchi
Indexer	Nancy Fulton
Text and Cover Designer	Jennifer Wreisner
Desktop Production	Jennifer Wreisner

Publishing Team—George Provol, Publisher; Janice Johnson, Director of Product Development; Tony Galvin, Acquisitions Editor; Lori Landwer, Marketing Manager; Shelley Clubb, Electronic Design and Production Manager.

DEDICATION

We would like to dedicate this book to the next generation: Matthew Alan Stipes and Thomas Wendell Maurer.

Acknowledgments—The author and publisher wish to thank the following reviewer for his technical and academic assistance in testing exercises and assessing instructions: Ken Slovak, Slovak Technical Services, Inc.

Text: ISBN 0-7638-1704-X
Order Number: 01587

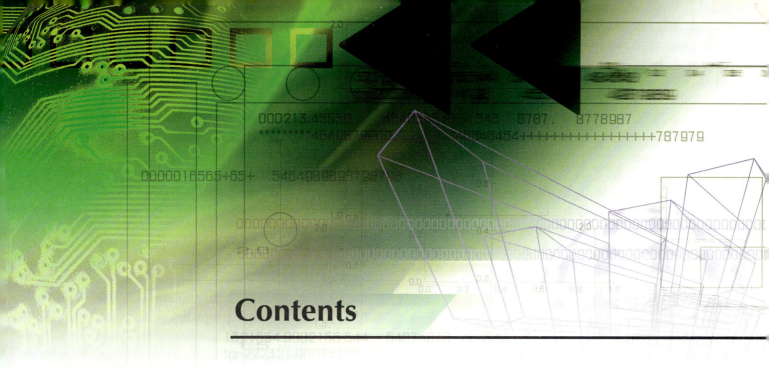

Contents

Chapter 2
CREATING AND CALLING PROCEDURES 33

Chapter 3
DEVELOPING SLIDE SHOWS USING VBA 63

Chapter 4
BUILDING CUSTOM DIALOG BOXES 91

Chapter 5
LINKING TABLES TO WORKBOOKS USING AUTOMATION **121**

Chapter 6
CREATING HYPERLINKS AND CUSTOM TOOLBARS.....................................**151**

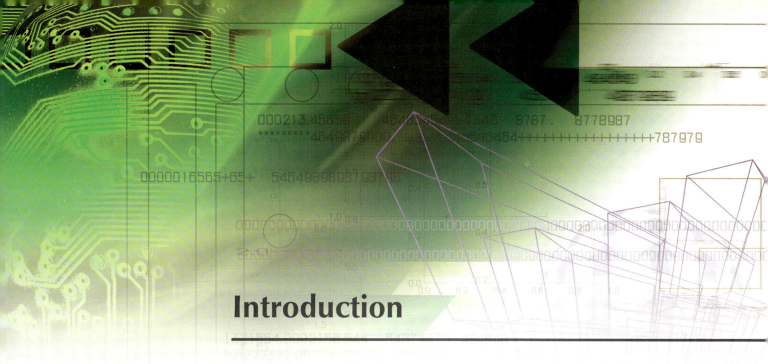

Introduction

Visual Basic for Applications (VBA) is the macro language common to all Office suite products. Knowing VBA can make your application or work more productive. Microsoft's implementation of VBA has remained constant across Office 97, Office 2000, and Office XP. If you learn VBA in the context of one application, you can use it with any application. As Microsoft has expanded its base of software partners, VBA has become the macro language of choice for a wide variety of software packages.

Office users fall into several categories. Some use the related application software for basic tasks, such as writing letters or budget planning. As these people increase their level of use, they start to identify repetitive or cross-application tasks they want to accomplish. For example, they may wish to print different versions of a report with new headers or want to insert a variety of Excel charts in different Word documents. At this time, they start to explore using wizards and the macro recorder to accomplish simple enhancements of their applications. Up to this point, users do not need to know how to modify the VBA code produced by these tools.

However, many users want to go to the next step. This leads people into customizing the VBA procedures created by wizards or the macro recorder. To move forward they need to develop some programming skills and a basic understanding of object-based and event-driven VBA code. Some may consider a new vocation if they find they like to program.

Finally, the truly motivated user can take VBA coding to a level that facilitates complete cross-application integration. This VBA code can execute Access queries that generate dynasets to be imported into Excel workbooks or Word documents and automates Office applications in ways that were unheard of for users just a few years ago. This book investigates all these possibilities.

ORGANIZATION AND SCOPE

The chapters in this text lead you step-by-step through the development stages needed to become skilled at VBA coding. A breakdown of software applications, concepts, and skills by chapter follows.

Chapter 1: Macros and Visual Basic Editor
    Application: Word
    Concepts: Programming structures (sequence, selection, and iteration) and variables
    Skills: Macro recorder, Visual Basic Editor, and using input boxes

Chapter 2: Creating and Calling Procedures
    Application: Excel
    Concepts: Objects, properties, events, and procedure calls
    Skills: Placement of controls, setting object properties, and writing a procedure from scratch

Chapter 3: Developing Slide Shows Using VBA
    Application: PowerPoint
    Concepts: Using VBA as a developer's tool
    Skills: Importing Word outlines, setting slide designs, and utilizing an existing UserForm

Chapter 4: Building Custom Dialog Boxes
    Application: Excel
    Concepts: Form design, passing parameters, and modular design
    Skills: Event programming (interface and tasks) and using additional controls

Chapter 5: Linking Tables to Workbooks Using Automation
    Application: Access and Excel
    Concepts: Automation, error handling, and data access across applications
    Skills: Object library references, remote query execution, and import and validate data sets

Chapter 6: Creating Hyperlinks and Custom Toolbars
    Application: Access and Word
    Concepts: Custom toolbars, import user selected data, and reference Internet sites
    Skills: Building and converting Access macros into VBA code and active application integration

Each chapter furthers your understanding of VBA and its impact on Office applications by the progressive development of critical concepts. Each tutorial not only includes the actions that need to take place, but the resulting response to help you stay on track. To help you address and anticipate problems, Alternatives, Tips, and Pitfalls are provided in the margin of the text. You will find the figures in this book can be used to help debug errors in your VBA code. The following instructional aids are incorporated into each chapter:

Chapter Features

- Objectives: Identify skills taught in the chapter
- Tutorial Steps: Actions you need to take to accomplish a specific task and the related response (when appropriate) produced by the computer
- Next Steps: Set of actions that reinforce the previous tutorial steps that you do on your own

End-of-Chapter Review Features

- Key Terms: List of important terminology introduced in the chapter, allowing you to communicate effectively when talking to others about VBA concepts
- Review Questions: List of important concepts you need to know when writing and debugging VBA procedures
- Check Your Understanding: Ten fill-in and multiple choice questions to test your knowledge of key points introduced in the chapter

End-of-Chapter Assessments

- Last Step: The final task challenges you to apply VBA to conclude the chapter's case study
- Debug: VBA code with errors you are asked to correct, requiring an understanding of the overall structure and concepts behind VBA coding schemes
- New Challenge: Applying your VBA knowledge to a new task as an enhancement of the work already completed on the chapter's case study
- Internet Topic: Prompts you to use Internet resources to research a VBA-related topic
- Discussion Topic: Designed to draw your attention to current VBA-related topics
- In addition, there are three culminating Performance Assessments provided at the end of the text.

GETTING STARTED

To use this book you need a personal computer with access to Microsoft's Office XP Professional with Word, Excel, PowerPoint, and Access along with an Internet browser such as Microsoft's Internet Explorer. These applications need to have Visual Basic help installed. Office 2000 can be used as an alternative, however, it will be necessary to install the text converter to accomplish the PowerPoint material covered in chapter 3. The data files needed to complete the chapter tutorials and end-of-book projects are available online at the Internet Resource Center (IRC) located through EMCParadigm's home page at www.emcp.com. Before you begin working through the textbook, it is necessary to download these files to a 3.5-inch floppy disk. To download the student data documents complete the following steps.

1. Insert a formatted 3.5-inch disk in the floppy disk drive.
2. Connect to the Internet and go to www.emcp.com.
3. At the EMCParadigm home page, click on _College Division_.
4. In the Quick Links Task Pane at the right side of the screen, click on _Internet Resource Centers_.
5. In the Computer Applications section, click _Visual Basic for Applications_.
6. In the Visual Basic for Applications box that displays, click the _Student_ link.
7. Click the _Student Data Files_ link.
8. Click _Student Data Files_.
9. At the File Download dialog box, make sure the _Save this program to disk_ option is selected and then click OK.
10. At the Save As dialog box, click the down-pointing triangle at the right side of the Save in list box.
11. At the drop-down list that displays, click the drive where your disk is located and then click Save.
12. At the Download complete dialog box, click Open.
13. At the WinZip Self-Extractor dialog box, click the Browse button next to the Unzip to folder text box.
14. At the Browse for Folder dialog box, select the drive where your disk is located and then click OK.
15. Click Unzip.
16. At the message saying the files were unzipped successfully, click OK.
17. Close the WinZip Self-Extractor dialog box and then close the browser.

Your data disk should contain the following files in the designated folders:

Root folder (directory)	Documents contained in folder
b-spruce folder	b-books.htm bluefade.gif b-spruce.gif split2.gif
b-spruce.htm	
booklogo.gif	
c2-sales.xls	
c4-chart.xls	
c5-sales.xls	
c6-order.doc	
dstalker folder	dauthors.htm disbns.htm dtitles.htm holmes.gif tubes.gif
dstalker.htm	

jayhawk folder	author.htm books.gif ickya.gif isbn.htm jauthor.htm jisbn.htm jtitle.htm logo.gif order.htm title.htm
jayhawk.htm	
line.gif	
moonbeam folder	kc_ent.gif mbooks.htm moon.gif
moonbeam.htm	
print.bmp	
salesbymonth.xls	
slb-inv.mdb	
SLBpresentations folder	Beam.pot booklogo.gif Competition.pot Digital Dots.pot Franchise.doc Profile.pot SlideDesigns.frm SlideDesigns.frx

The following is a list of data documents that you will be required to open in order to successfully complete each chapter.

Chapter	Data Document	
1	booklogo.gif line.gif	
2	c2-sales.xls salesbymonth.xls	
3	salesbymonth.xls SLBpresentations folder	
4	c4-chart.xls print.bmp	
5	c5-sales.xls slb-inv.mdb	
6	b-spruce.htm dstalker.htm jayhawk.htm moonbeam.htm c6-order.doc slb-inv.mdb	b-spruce folder dstalker folder jayhawk folder moonbeam folder
Performance Assessments	salesbymonth.xls slb-inv.mdb	

TIPS FOR SUCCESS

Before you begin, review these tips to ensure your success in this course.

- Always save your work before testing any VBA procedure you write or record.
- Do not work from the figures. Use them as a reference and for help in debugging your code.
- Most mistakes will be a result of typos you made when entering the code—look for typos first.
- When working with external files it is essential to reference the correct drive and path.
- When an error occurs, always reset the Visual Basic Editor's Code window before making the corrections.
- When your code still does not work, make sure to look for a message or input box behind an open window. Use the Alt + Tab key combination to bring this box to the front.
- Write down the EXACT wording displayed by error messages. Your instructor will be able to provide assistance by reading the exact error message.

ACKNOWLEDGEMENTS

The authors would like to express our deep appreciation for the support and help given to us by the following people at EMC/Paradigm Publishing: Desiree Faulkner, Tony Galvin, Janice Johnson, Bill Connell, and John Collins. We are also greatly indebted to Ken Slovak for his invaluable technical suggestions. Finally, a project of this magnitude would not get done without the support of our significant others: Karen Stipes and Diane Krasnewich.

Jeffrey A. Stipes
Timothy N. Trainor

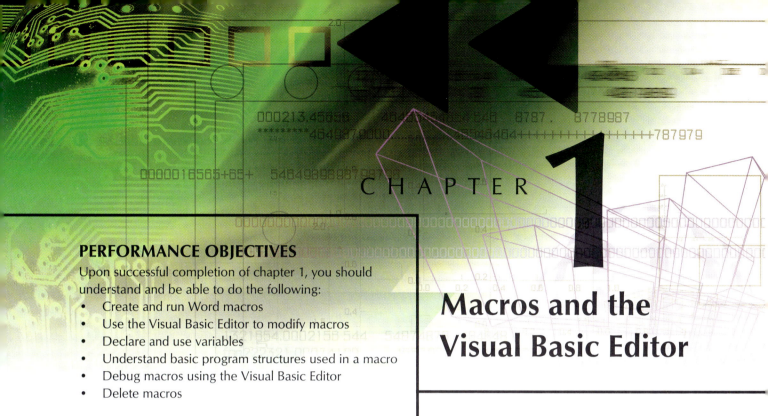

Macros and the Visual Basic Editor

PERFORMANCE OBJECTIVES

Upon successful completion of chapter 1, you should understand and be able to do the following:
- Create and run Word macros
- Use the Visual Basic Editor to modify macros
- Declare and use variables
- Understand basic program structures used in a macro
- Debug macros using the Visual Basic Editor
- Delete macros

This chapter is going to use **Visual Basic for Applications (VBA)** commands that are a part of Microsoft's Office Suite to introduce you to common programming concepts. Simply stated, a **computer program** is the set of instructions you can activate or key into the computer's memory that control computer operations. For example, you will use VBA instructions to automatically add a logo to a Microsoft Word document. This **macro** is a sequence of instructions that are grouped together to automate a task. VBA macros are an example of a computer program.

For years, Microsoft's major applications (Word, Excel, and Access) have contained internal development tools. These tools allow users to customize and automate application tasks. Until the early 1990s, these internal tools were specialized macro languages that were unique to each application. A macro language allows an application user to construct a sequence of instructions that can be executed easily, thus automating repetitive tasks like inserting custom graphic headers into a word processing document or adding data rows to spreadsheet projects. By the mid 1990s these internal development tools started to incorporate common instructions associated with the BASIC programming language. BASIC was originally developed in the 1960s at Dartmouth College as a tool to train students in computer programming. The acronym BASIC stands for Beginners All Purpose Symbolic Instruction Code. Just as the personal computer has evolved into a powerful tool, so has the BASIC programming language.

Today's version of BASIC, called Visual Basic (VB), is one of the world's most popular rapid-application development tools for creating Windows-based software applications. Visual Basic allows programmers to focus on the application task rather than the technical aspects of programming in a Windows environment. In the 1994 release of Excel 5.0, Microsoft replaced its internal macro language with Visual Basic for Applications (VBA). This powerful tool was built on the resources of VB and extended VB's features and flexibility into Excel. In short order, the Office 97 Suite emerged with VBA as the integrated development environment for Word, Excel, Access, and PowerPoint. Today's VBA in Office XP is built on the current version of VB. It incorporates the latest tools for adding *graphical interfaces* (custom dialog boxes) and *event driven programming* (program responds to actions such as the click of a mouse) to customized applications prepared with the Office XP Suite.

Microsoft's objective of providing a standardized *integrated development environment* (*IDE*) for its applications has not gone unnoticed by other major application developers. As a result, Microsoft now licenses the current version of VBA to non-Microsoft applications. You will find VBA as the IDE in AutoCAD (drafting), CorelDRAW (graphic design), Peachtree Office Accounting (accounting), and ArcView (geographical information systems). These four are just a few of the many non-Microsoft licenses of VBA.

Macros are created by recording each keyboard entry or mouse action using the macro recorder tool or by entering the commands using the Visual Basic Editor. You record or write a macro to repeat activities you commonly perform when using Office applications. Creating a macro can improve your productivity in a variety of situations:

- Speed up routine editing and formatting.
- Make commonly used dialog box options easier to activate.
- Automate complex combinations of commands and menu selections.
- Combine several tasks.

A macro can be associated with a single document, workbook, slide presentation, or database. When you want to use a macro in a variety of Word documents or Excel workbooks, you store it in Word's Normal template (normal.dot) or Excel's Personal Macro workbook. These macros are only available on the PC you were using when they were saved as they are not specific to any document or worksheet.

SETTING THE CASE STUDY

In order to show you how to use VBA, the following case study will be used throughout the text. You are the owner/operator of a small used book store called *Second Look Books*. Microsoft's Word, Excel, PowerPoint, and Access help you track the books you buy and sell, print book orders, and write memos.

You will need to download student data files from the Internet Resource Center to a disk in order to finish the tutorial and exercises in this chapter. For more information, refer to the Introduction, the inside front cover of the text, or ask your instructor. The first macro you are going to create will add the Second Look Books logo as shown in figure 1.1 to the active Word document. Holding the Alt key while pressing the L key activates the macro. Since we want to limit the use of this macro to a single document, the macro is stored as part of the chapter 1 Word document memo.doc.

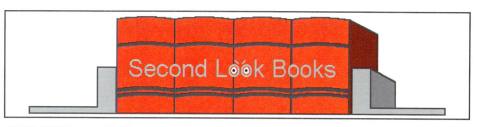

FIGURE 1.1 The Second Look Books Logo

1. Start your computer.
   ➤ *Displays the Windows desktop.*
2. Insert your student data disk into the disk drive.
3. Open a Word application window.
   ➤ *Displays a new Word document similar to figure 1.2.*

At this point you need to double-check several Word display settings to make sure your application window looks the same as those used in the following figures. In this book, clicking refers to pressing the left mouse button once. If the right mouse button is to be used, the text will say to right-click.

4. If necessary, close any open task panes.
5. Click the <u>V</u>iew menu and, if necessary, change the view to <u>P</u>rint Layout, and then turn the Ruler off by clicking <u>R</u>uler from the menu as shown in figure 1.2.
6. Right-click on an open area of a toolbar and, if necessary, turn on the Standard and Formatting toolbars also shown in figure 1.2.
7. Click <u>F</u>ile and then click Save <u>A</u>s.
   ➤ *Word opens the Save As dialog box.*
8. Save the active document on your student data disk and name it memo.doc .

ALTERNATIVE

Click <u>V</u>iew and then point to <u>T</u>oolbars.

View Drop-down Menu

Clicking the chevron displays the remaining menu options.

Toolbar Pop-up Menu

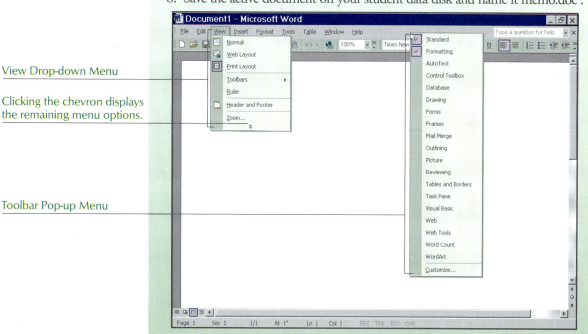

FIGURE 1.2 New Document Window Displaying View and Toolbar Menus

MACRO RECORDING

There are two ways to create a macro. The easiest way is to have Word or any Office application record every keystroke and mouse selection involved with a specific task. The other way is to use the Visual Basic Editor to key in the commands. Next, turn on Word's Record New Macro feature to create the InsertLogo macro.

PITFALL

An invalid procedure error is generated if you use a space in a Macro name.

1. Click the Tools menu, point to Macro, and then click Record New Macro.
   ➤ *The Record Macro dialog box opens similar to the one at the bottom of figure 1.3.*
2. Delete default name by typing **InsertLogo** using no spaces into the Macro name text box.
   ➤ *The macro name InsertLogo replaces the default name.*
3. Click the down-pointing triangle next to the Store macro in list box.
   ➤ *The list box opens.*
4. Select the *memo.doc (document)* option.

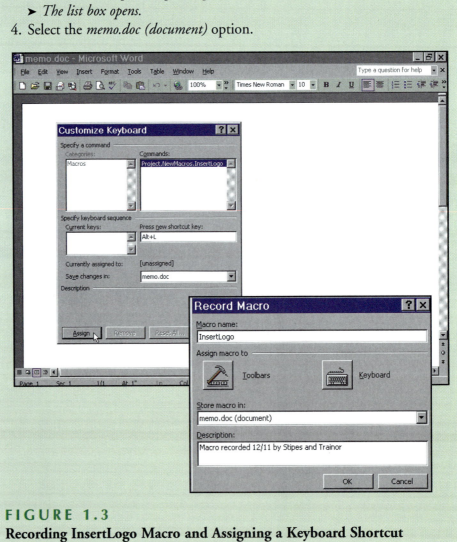

FIGURE 1.3
Recording InsertLogo Macro and Assigning a Keyboard Shortcut

Launching a Macro

It is time to plan ahead regarding how you want to **execute** (run) the new macro. Traditionally **keyboard shortcuts** are assigned to each macro. To run the macro with a keyboard shortcut, the user holds down the Ctrl or Alt key while pressing a key that has been assigned to the macro. You are going to assign the L key to the InsertLogo macro and press the keyboard shortcut Alt + L to execute it.

Another way to run a macro is to place a button for it on a menu or toolbar. Moving the screen pointer over the button and clicking executes the associated macro. You will use this method in chapter 6.

1. Click the Keyboard button in the Record Macro dialog box.
   ➤ *Word opens the Customize Keyboard dialog box with the insertion point flashing in the Press new shortcut key text box.*
2. Hold down the Alt key and press the L key.
   ➤ *The key combination Alt+L appears in the text box as shown in figure 1.3.*
3. Click the down-pointing triangle next to the Save changes in option and select memo.doc from the drop-down menu as shown in figure 1.3.
4. Click the Assign button.
   ➤ *Alt + L moves to the Current keys list box.*

Macro Properties

When working with Office applications, macros, icons, documents, paragraphs, workbooks, a column of cells, data tables, and so on, are all **objects**. Every object has **properties**. These properties include the font used in a document, the numeric format of a worksheet cell, or the name assigned to a macro. You can examine an object's properties by right-clicking on the mouse when pointing at the object.

As shown in the Commands list box in figure 1.3, the InsertLogo macro is assigned the name Project.NewMacros.InsertLogo. This default name indicates that the InsertLogo macro is assigned to the NewMacros module within the Memo project. This hierarchy of objects (project, module, and macro) within an Office application is discussed in chapter 2.

The InsertLogo Macro

The InsertLogo macro inserts the booklogo.gif and line.gif files that you downloaded to your student data disk to the open document, adds your name, and inserts a blank line. Do not worry if you make a few minor mistakes; you can correct them in the Editing Macros section that follows. If you need to start over, click the Stop button on the Stop Recording toolbar (see figure 1.4) and then repeat the steps above starting with the Macro Recording section.

Once you begin recording, every keyboard entry and mouse selection is recorded until you click the Stop Recording or Pause button on the Stop Recording toolbar.

Stop Recording —————— Pause

F I G U R E 1.4 Stop Recording Toolbar

PITFALL

When recording a Word macro you do not have mouse control in the document.

1. Start recording by clicking on the Close button in the Customize Keyboard dialog box.
   ➤ *Word returns to the document and displays the Stop Recording toolbar as shown in figure 1.4.*
2. Press Enter.
   ➤ *Adds a blank line to the document.*
3. Press the Up Arrow key once.
   ➤ *The insertion point moves up to the first line.*
4. Click the Center align button on the Formatting toolbar.
5. Click Insert, point to Picture, and then click From File.
   ➤ *The Insert Picture dialog box displays.*
6. Use the Look in list box to identify the disk drive where your student data disk is located, usually drive A.
7. Select *booklogo.gif* from the File name list box.
8. Click the Insert button.
   ➤ *Second Look Books logo is centered in the first line.*
9. Press Enter.
10. Click Insert, point to Picture, and then click From File.
    ➤ *The Insert Picture dialog box displays.*
11. Insert line.gif into the document.
    ➤ *A line is centered under the logo as shown in figure 1.6.*
12. Press Enter.
13. Click Format and then Font.
    ➤ *The Font dialog box opens.*

PITFALL

Do not make Font or Size selections from the Formatting toolbar, as they will not be recorded.

14. At the Font tab select the Arial font, Regular font style, a point size of 11, and then press the Enter key to close the dialog box.
15. Click the Bold button on the Formatting toolbar. **B**
16. Key **Owned and Operated by Your Name**, substituting your own name.
17. Click the Bold button on the Formatting toolbar.
18. Press Enter.
19. Press the Down Arrow key once.
    ➤ *The insertion point moves down to the next line.*

TIP

If the small Stop Recording box disappears, click Tools, point to Macro, and then click Stop Recording.

TIP

To add a keyboard shortcut to a macro: Click Tools and then Customize. Click the Keyboard button in the Customize dialog box. Scroll down the Categories list box to Macros and select it, and then select your document from the Save changes in drop-down menu. Define and assign the shortcut. Do not forget to resave your document.

Stop Recording

The InsertLogo macro is now complete and you need to stop the macro recorder.

1. Click the Stop Recording button on the Stop Recording toolbar (see figure 1.4).
   ➤ *The Stop Recording toolbar disappears.*
2. Click File and then Save.
   ➤ *Document changes and the macro are saved to disk.*

Macro Security and Viruses

The macro is now a part of memo.doc. When you open any Office Suite file that contains a macro, the macro is either enabled or disabled based on the current macro security level. Office applications provide a three-level macro security feature. If the security level is set to High, any unrecognized (unsigned) macros in a document are automatically disabled. The Medium level notifies users of the presence of a macro(s) in a file and requires them to select Enable or Disable before continuing. Figure 1.5 shows both the Security dialog box and the virus warning message when a medium security level is active. The Low level, not recommended, enables all macros without user notification.

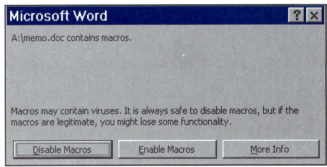

FIGURE 1.5
Macro Security Dialog Box and Virus Warning Message

This macro security is in place because a *macro virus*, like other computer viruses, can be acquired from outside sources and can erase files or potentially damage equipment. If a file contains macros you created, click the Enable Macros button. If no known macros are associated with the file, click the Disable Macros button and check to see if your computer system and files are infected by using up-to-date antivirus software.

Before continuing, you should check the current macro security level and set it to medium if necessary by completing the following steps.

1. Click Tools, point to Macro, and then click Security.
   ➤ *The Security dialog box opens as shown in figure 1.5.*
2. At the Security Level tab, click the Medium option button.
   ➤ *Medium security level is selected.*
3. Click OK.

Running A Macro

You can execute the new macro by holding down the Alt key and pressing the L key or by clicking the Run button in the Macros dialog box. However, before doing so you should remove the logo from Memo.doc. This will give you a clean page for testing the macro.

Testing a Macro

Before using a new macro it should be tested at least once to make sure it is working properly. More sophisticated macros and computer programs that perform several operations should have every feature tested. Testing a new macro creates a situation where you need to repeat the same step over and over as you test and debug it. In this case we want to clear the logo before running (testing) the macro again. Since we will run the macro several times, this presents an opportunity to create a macro that automates several commands that you, as the macro developer, repeatedly use when writing or testing VBA code. In Next Step 1-1, you will create the ClearDoc macro that deletes all the graphics and text from the active document by incorporating the following actions:

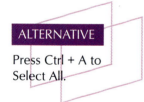

1. Click the Edit menu and then click Select All.
   ➤ *Every graphics and line of text is highlighted.*
2. Press the Delete key.
   ➤ *Clears document.*

You are now ready to run the InsertLogo macro. If it does not work exactly as expected, you can make corrections in the next section on Editing Macros.

3. Hold down the Alt key and press L.
   ➤ *The Second Look Books logo is added to the top of the document as shown in figure 1.6.*
4. Use the File menu's Print option to print a copy of memo.doc.

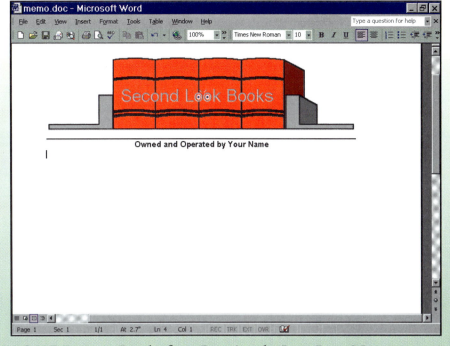

FIGURE 1.6 **Results from Running the InsertLogo Macro**

Next Step 1-1

Create a new macro named ClearDoc and store it in memo.doc. Assign Alt + C as the keyboard shortcut. The ClearDoc macro should do the following:
1. Select everything in the active document.
2. Delete the selection.

EDITING MACROS

The Visual Basic Editor displays a macro's VBA statements and allows you to change them. Each statement contains object names and a command that uses a specified **syntax** or sentence structure. Syntax for VBA statements includes rules for punctuation, spacing of words, word order, and spelling. Each **statement** identifies one executable action the computer can perform.

1. Click <u>T</u>ools, point to <u>M</u>acro, and then click the <u>M</u>acros.
   ➤ *The Macros dialog box opens as shown in figure 1.7.*
2. Select InsertLogo from the <u>M</u>acro name list box and then click the <u>E</u>dit button.
   ➤ *The Visual Basic Editor displays the InsertLogo macro as shown in figure 1.7.*
3. If necessary, maximize the Code window within the Editor's window.
   ➤ *When the Code and Editor windows are maximized, there are two Restore buttons in the top right corner of the VB Editor window (see top of figure 1.7).*

ALTERNATIVE

Hold down Alt and press F8 to open the Macro dialog box.

Macros and the Visual Basic Editor   **9**

The Visual Basic Editor can display several windows at the same time. These windows are discussed in chapter 2. At this time the Editor's window should be maximized. Any other windows in the Editor should be closed.

4. If necessary, close the Project and/or Properties window(s) in the Visual Basic Editor.

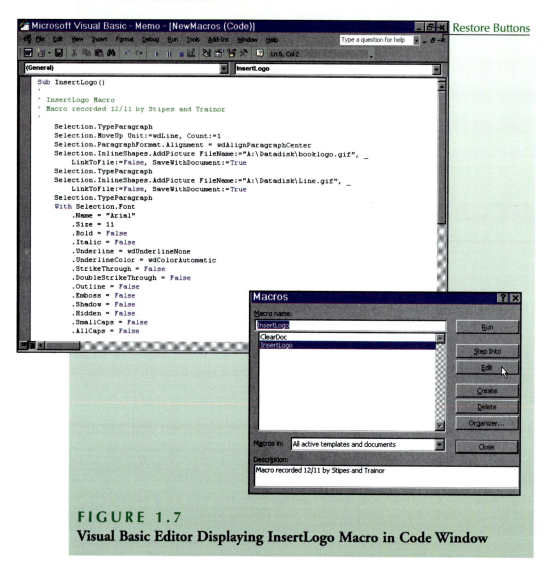

FIGURE 1.7
Visual Basic Editor Displaying InsertLogo Macro in Code Window

Using the Editor's Code Window

The macro statements shown in figure 1.7 appear in the Editor's Code window. To help keep objects organized within templates and documents, macros are classified as *sub procedures* and are stored within a module. In this case the InsertLogo sub procedure (macro) begins with Sub InsertLogo () and ends with End Sub.

Notice the statements Sub and End Sub appear in dark blue. Words displayed in blue are **keywords** associated with specific VBA statements. As a general rule, you should not use these words out of context. Upon closer inspection of figure 1.7 you will notice some text is displayed in green while other text is in black. The Editor ignores comments, also called *remarks*, that start with a single quote mark and displays them in green. They only serve to document the author's name, the creation date, and annotate selected statements. The VBA statements the computer executes are in black and blue.

Using Help

Trying to distinguish between methods and objects can be very confusing. When in doubt use the Editor's online help as a resource. Pressing the F1 key with part of a VBA statement highlighted displays a context sensitive help screen with related information. To find out more about the Type-Paragraph method using VBA's Help function, complete the following steps.

1. If necessary, scroll down the Code window until you see the Sub InsertLogo() sub procedure.
2. Highlight *TypeParagraph* in the Selection.TypeParagraph statement in the first line of code.
3. Press the F1 key.
   ➤ *The Editor displays the TypeParagraph Method help screen as shown in figure 1.8. (NOTE: The Help screen in figure 1.8 was maximized to improve readability.)*
4. Close the Help screen.

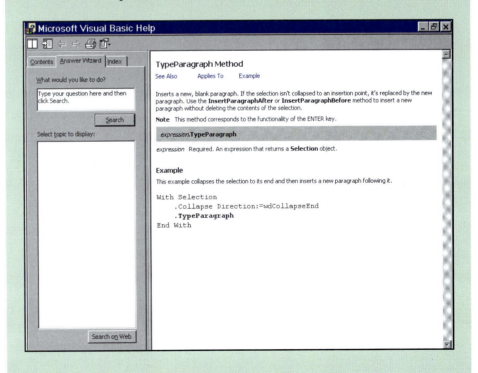

FIGURE 1.8 TypeParagraph Method Help Screen

Visual Basic Statements

You are going to delete the last Selection.TypeParagraph statement from the macro. This VBA statement includes a reference to an object (Selection) and a command (TypeParagraph). Another name for command is **method**. Methods identify preset actions the computer can perform. Selection is an object because it identifies the current insertion point in the active document or a selected block of text. When the computer executes the TypeParagraph method, it inserts a hard return at the selected point in the active document.

Deleting a Statement

The Visual Basic Editor uses the same keys, menus, and buttons that Word uses to edit text. The blinking insertion point indicates where new text is added, while the arrow keys move the insertion point to new locations within the macro. To delete a statement, select the text you wish to remove and press the Delete key.

When the InsertLogo macro runs, it inserts two blank lines under the logo. Only one blank line is needed and it should maintain the default font name and font size used by the document. By deleting the last Selection.TypeParagraph statement from the macro, only one blank line appears under the logo. Since you will be jumping between Word and the Visual Basic Editor, it will save time if you horizontally tile the screen using these windows. Before splitting the screen you should close any other programs listed in the taskbar.

1. Select the Selection.TypeParagraph statement located two lines above the End Sub statement.
   ➤ *The statement will be highlighted as shown in figure 1.9.*
2. Press Delete.
   ➤ *The Selection.TypeParagraph statement is removed from the Code window.*
3. Check that the remaining code matches the code found in figures 1.7 and 1.9. If not, make the necessary corrections.

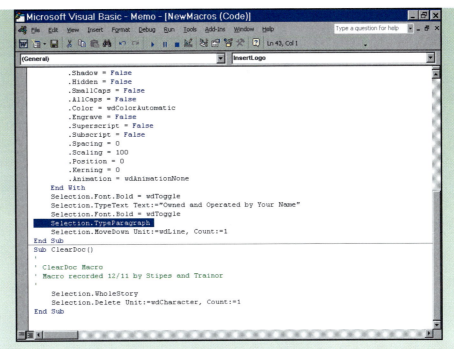

```
Microsoft Visual Basic - Memo - [NewMacros (Code)]
File   Edit   View   Insert   Format   Debug   Run   Tools   Add-Ins   Window   Help        Type a question for help
                                                                                              Ln 43, Col 1
(General)                                              InsertLogo
            .Shadow = False
            .Hidden = False
            .SmallCaps = False
            .AllCaps = False
            .Color = wdColorAutomatic
            .Engrave = False
            .Superscript = False
            .Subscript = False
            .Spacing = 0
            .Scaling = 100
            .Position = 0
            .Kerning = 0
            .Animation = wdAnimationNone
        End With
        Selection.Font.Bold = wdToggle
        Selection.TypeText Text:="Owned and Operated by Your Name"
        Selection.Font.Bold = wdToggle
        Selection.TypeParagraph
        Selection.MoveDown Unit:=wdLine, Count:=1
    End Sub
    Sub ClearDoc()
    '
    ' ClearDoc Macro
    ' Macro recorded 12/11 by Stipes and Trainor
    '
        Selection.WholeStory
        Selection.Delete Unit:=wdCharacter, Count:=1
    End Sub
```

FIGURE 1.9 Selection.TypeParagraph Selected for Deletion

4. Except for Word and the Visual Basic Editor, close all programs listed on the taskbar by right-clicking the associated button and selecting <u>C</u>lose from the shortcut menu.

> ➤ *Only the Word and Visual Basic Editor buttons appear on the taskbar.*

5. Right-click on an open area of the taskbar.

> ➤ *The taskbar's shortcut menu opens.*

6. Select the Tile Windows <u>H</u>orizontally option.

> ➤ *The Word and VB Editor windows are tiled horizontally on the screen as shown in figure 1.10. At this time neither the VB Editor window or the Word window is active.*

7. Click on the Word Title bar.

> ➤ *The Word window becomes the active window.*

8. Run the InsertLogo macro.

> ➤ *The Second Look Books logo, your name, and one blank line are added to the document.*

TIP

If more than two windows are horizontally tiled, close the extra window(s) and repeat the last two actions.

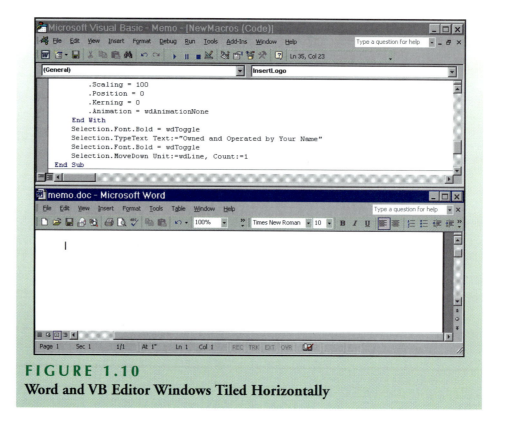

FIGURE 1.10
Word and VB Editor Windows Tiled Horizontally

Toggling Object Properties

Currently your name is displayed in a bold font because the statement
Selection.Font.Bold = wdToggle turned on the bold property. As previously
mentioned, Selection is the present location of the insertion point in the document. Font.Bold is a new property of the Selection object. The bold property is
either on or off. In the InsertLogo macro, the wdToggle toggles the bold property, i.e., reverses its on/off status.

The value associated with wdToggle is supplied by Word's object library. Labels,
like wdToggle, associated with values from an object library are called **intrinsic con-
stants**. When a statement containing the intrinsic constant wdToggle is executed,
the computer switches the selected object property on if it is off. If the property is
currently on, then it is switched off. The first two letters indicate which object
library the intrinsic constant comes from; *wd* for Word, *xl* for Excel, *ac* for Access,
and *vb* for Visual Basic. Each **object library** contains a variety of objects commonly
used within the related application. Word's object library, for instance, is used for
centering paragraphs, formatting borders, defining page size, changing the document view, and so on.

1. Click on the Editor's Title bar.
   ➤ *The editor becomes the active window.*
2. If necessary, scroll down the Code window to bring the first
   Selection.Font.Bold = wdToggle statement into view.

Modifying Statements

Macros are usually created using the macro recorder because it is easier than keying each statement using the VB Editor. However, if changes need to be made to a macro it is much easier to modify statements using the VB Editor than to rerecord the macro. Modifying a macro is as easy as editing any Word document. To print the owner's name in italics instead of bold, complete the following steps.

1. Replace the word Bold with **Italic** in first Selection.Font.Bold = wdToggle statement.
   ➤ *The statement now appears as Selection.Font.Italic = wdToggle.*
2. Click on the Word Title bar.
3. Run the ClearDoc macro.
   ➤ *This clears the logo from Memo.doc.*
4. Run the InsertLogo macro.
   ➤ *Your name appears in italics under the logo.*

Catching Compiler Errors

The statements you see in the Code window are translated into the computer's binary machine language, one at a time, when you run the macro. The translating program is called a **compiler**. If you make any typographical errors that cannot be translated, the compiler halts execution when it gets to the statement with the error. As shown in figure 1.11, an error message pops up and the untranslatable syntax is highlighted in the Code window. Once the error is corrected, you reset the macro and run it again. To demonstrate these debugging steps we are going to have you misspell italic as shown in figure 1.11.

1. Click on the Editor's Title bar.
2. Misspell italic by adding an extra "a" in the Selection.Font.Italic = wdToggle statement.
   ➤ *The statement with misspelling appears as Selection.Font.Itaalic = wdToggle.*
3. Click in the Word application window.
4. Run the ClearDoc macro.
5. Run the InsertLogo macro.
   ➤ *The execution stops, the error is highlighted in the Code window, and an error message is displayed as shown in figure 1.11.*
6. Click OK in the error message box.

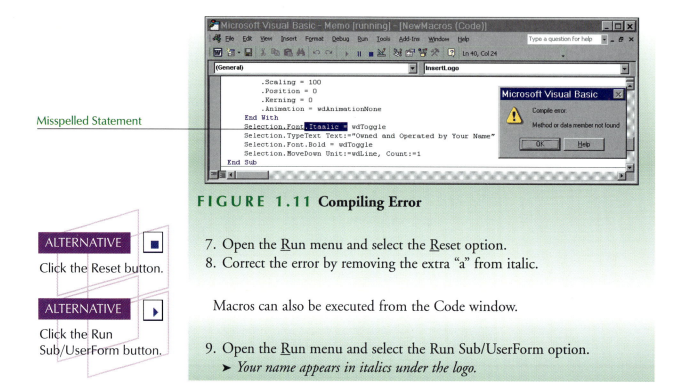

FIGURE 1.11 Compiling Error

Misspelled Statement

ALTERNATIVE ■

Click the Reset button.

ALTERNATIVE ▶

Click the Run Sub/UserForm button.

7. Open the Run menu and select the Reset option.
8. Correct the error by removing the extra "a" from italic.

Macros can also be executed from the Code window.

9. Open the Run menu and select the Run Sub/UserForm option.
   ➤ *Your name appears in italics under the logo.*

Next Step 1-2

1. Change bold to italic in the other Selection.Font.Bold = wdToggle statement.
2. Change font size from 11 to 18 in the .Size = 18 statement.
3. Run the InsertLogo macro to verify that it is working correctly.
4. Print a copy of memo.doc after the macro works properly.

Adding Statements

The easiest way to add a new statement to a macro is to copy one like it, paste it where it is needed, and modify it accordingly. After working with the Visual Basic Editor for a while you begin to remember commonly used statements and can just key them in as needed. Until then, the Help function will remind you of available objects and methods.

Like Word, the VB Editor displays the line and column number associated with the current position of the insertion point. These line and column indicators are found in on the right side of the Editor's Standard toolbar as noted in figure 1.12. If the indicators are not visible, extend the Standard toolbar to the right. The line number references that follow require that the InsertLogo macro be the first macro in the Editor. Depending upon screen resolution, how you recorded your macro, and edits made to it, it is very likely that your line numbers may not exactly match the indicated line numbers in the text. Because of this, the line number references provided should be viewed as general reference points (within 2 to 3 lines) of the actual position of the edit.

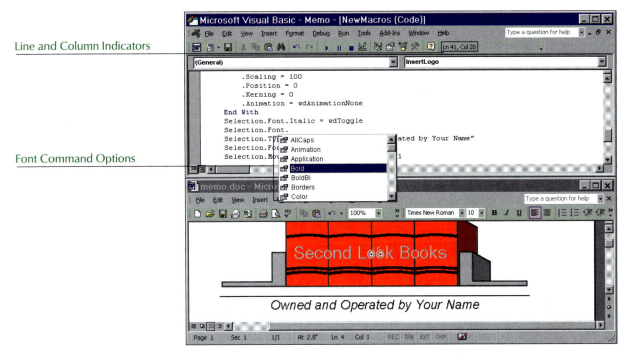

Line and Column Indicators

Font Command Options

FIGURE 1.12 Inserting a Font Command

1. Click in the Code window behind the first wdToggle (line 40).
   ➤ *Insertion point is flashing to the right of the "e" in wdToggle.*
2. Press Enter.
   ➤ *A blank line is created under the first Selection.Font.Italic = wdToggle statement.*
3. Key **Selection.** including a period at the end.
   ➤ *The Editor displays a list of methods that can work with the Selection object.*
4. Key **Font.** including a period at the end.
   ➤ *The Editor displays a list of methods that work with the Font command (see figure 1.12).*
5. Double-click on Bold in the list box.
   ➤ *The word Bold is inserted into the statement.*
6. Complete the line by keying **= wdToggle** with no period at the end.
   ➤ *The line should read Selection.Font.Bold = wdToggle.*

Next, you will copy this statement below the next instruction as shown in figure 1.13. The second statement toggles the bold property off. Doing so is considered a good programming practice. As you format text it is a good habit to turn off features after they have been used. When two features are turned on at the same time it is also good practice to turn the features off in the reverse order in which they were turned on. In other words, we have turned on the italic font property and then the bold font property. Therefore, we need to copy the Selection.Font.Bold = wdToggle statement to a line that precedes the statement where you toggle off the italic feature. Figure 1.13 illustrates how the bold statements are nested within the italic statements. **Nested statements** are a set of VBA code that start and finish a specific feature or task in the reverse order in which the statements were introduced. The nesting structure of these types of statements helps assure a beginning and close to the related actions.

7. Highlight the Selection.Font.Bold = wdToggle statement.
8. Click <u>E</u>dit and then <u>C</u>opy.
9. Move the insertion pointer in front of the "S" in the second Selection.Font.Italic = wdToggle.
10. Click <u>E</u>dit and then <u>P</u>aste.
   ➤ *The Selection.Font.Bold = wdToggle statement is copied in front of Selection.Font.Italic = wdToggle.*
11. Press Enter.
   ➤ *The middle portion of the InsertLogo macro should appear as shown in figure 1.13.*

outside nest

inside nest

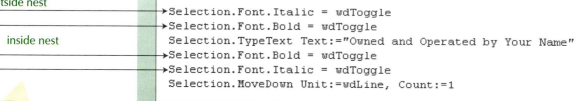

```
Selection.Font.Italic = wdToggle
Selection.Font.Bold = wdToggle
Selection.TypeText Text:="Owned and Operated by Your Name"
Selection.Font.Bold = wdToggle
Selection.Font.Italic = wdToggle
Selection.MoveDown Unit:=wdLine, Count:=1
```

FIGURE 1.13 **Nested Statements**

12. Run the ClearDoc macro.
13. Run the InsertLogo macro.
   ➤ *Your name appears in bold italics under the logo.*

TIP

If the statements do not line up along the same tab as shown in figure 1.13, use the Tab or Delete keys to align them.

Adding Remarks

The Macro Recorder automatically starts every macro with remark statements that identify the creation date and macro author. In this case, the macro author is assumed to be the name of the person or organization with which the application software is registered. As mentioned earlier, remark statements are displayed in green within the Code window. Remarks start with a single quote. When a remark is attached to the end of an executable VBA statement, key a single quotation mark and then your comments.

1. Click after the "h" in the first Selection.TypeParagraph statement (line 6).
2. Press the spacebar and key **'Maintain default font name and font size** with no period at the end.
   ➤ *This adds remarks to the end of the statement as shown in figure 1.14.*

Added remark

```
Sub InsertLogo()
'
' InsertLogo Macro
' Macro recorded 12/11 by Stipes and Trainor
'
    Selection.TypeParagraph 'Maintain default font name and font size
    Selection.MoveUp Unit:=wdLine, Count:=1 'Press Up Arrow key
    Selection.ParagraphFormat.Alignment = wdAlignParagraphCenter
    Selection.InlineShapes.AddPicture FileName:="A:\Datadisk\booklogo.gif", _
        LinkToFile:=False, SaveWithDocument:=True
    Selection.TypeParagraph
    Selection.InlineShapes.AddPicture FileName:="A:\Datadisk\Line.gif", _
        LinkToFile:=False, SaveWithDocument:=True
    Selection.TypeParagraph
    With Selection.Font
        .Name = "Arial"
        .Size = 18
        .Bold = False
        .Italic = False
        .Underline = wdUnderlineNone
        .UnderlineColor = wdColorAutomatic
        .StrikeThrough = False
        .DoubleStrikeThrough = False
        .Outline = False
        .Emboss = False
        .Shadow = False
        .Hidden = False
        .SmallCaps = False
        .AllCaps = False
        .Color = wdColorAutomatic
        .Engrave = False
        .Superscript = False
        .Subscript = False
        .Spacing = 0
        .Scaling = 100
        .Position = 0
        .Kerning = 0
        .Animation = wdAnimationNone
    End With
    Selection.Font.Italic = wdToggle
    Selection.Font.Bold = wdToggle
    Selection.TypeText Text:="Owned and Operated by Your Name"
    Selection.Font.Bold = wdToggle
    Selection.Font.Italic = wdToggle
    Selection.MoveDown Unit:=wdLine, Count:=1 'Press Down Arrow key
End Sub
```

FIGURE 1.14 InsertLogo Macro with Remarks

Next Step 1-3

Your name and today's date must be included in the first comment lines. Using figure 1.14 as a model, add the following remarks at the end of the indicated lines in the InsertLogo macro.

Line 7:   'Press Up Arrow key
Line 45:   'Press Down Arrow key

Printing a Macro

Now is a good time to save and print the InsertLogo and ClearDoc macros. You want to print the code for the active module using the File menu's Print option.

1. Click the Save button. 🖫
2. Click <u>F</u>ile and then click <u>P</u>rint.
   ➤ *The Print dialog box is displayed.*
3. Verify that the Current <u>M</u>odule option button and <u>C</u>ode check box are selected and then click OK.
   ➤ *The Editor prints the InsertLogo and ClearDoc macros.*

PROGRAM STRUCTURES

Take a close look at the macro code for InsertLogo shown in figure 1.14. This same code could be found in a Visual Basic program. You have become a computer programmer by creating it. As a programmer you should understand that no matter how complex a program or macro becomes, the program logic is represented in one of three ways:

- *sequence* of statements
- *iteration* (repetition) of a sequence until some condition is met
- *selection* of one sequence versus another sequence

Sequence of Statements

The InsertLogo macro is a sequence of instructions that are followed one at a time. It is the simplest example of a computer program because you start it, each statement is executed once, and it stops. It produces the same results every time it is run.

Iteration of a Sequence

Once a programmer has written a sequence of code, it can be used over again within the same program or macro. For example, in a payroll program the sequence of code to compute an employee's pay and print a paycheck is used over and over again for each employee. The instructions are used again while the name, hours worked, and other data changes. Repeating a sequence of statements is called a **program loop**. VBA statements that incorporate program loops come in pairs:

- For and Next
- Do and Loop

The first statement identifies the beginning of the loop and usually the condition for repeating it. The other instruction is placed after the last statement in the loop and identifies the point at which the computer jumps back to the first statement. Figure 1.17 illustrates the For/Next loop you are going to add to the InsertLogo macro.

1. Position the insertion point at the end of Selection.TypeParagraph (line 11).
2. Press Enter and key **For intCounter = 1 to 3** with no period at end.
   ➤ *The For statement is added as line 12 as shown in figure 1.17.*
3. Move the insertion point at the end of the second Selection.Font.Italic = wdToggle (line 45).
4. Press Enter and key **Next intCounter** with no period at end.
   ➤ *The Next statement is added at the end of the macro as shown in figure 1.17.*

To help word wrapping work properly when repeating these statements, you need to add a space after the owner's name as shown in figure 1.17. The space is added by positioning the insertion point in front of the second double quote in line 43 and pressing the spacebar.

5. Move the insertion point inside the last quotation mark.
6. Press the spacebar.
   ➤ *The program will now print a space after the owner's name (see figure 1.17).*
7. Run the ClearDoc macro.
8. Run the InsertLogo macro.
   ➤ *The line and your name appear three times under the logo.*

Obviously repeating your name three times is a little redundant. However, the For/Next loop does provide an opportunity to explore other program structures.

Variables

This For/Next loop uses a variable named intCounter to keep track of the number of times the macro loops between the For and Next statements. A **variable** is a location in the computer's memory where data values are stored and changed as the program executes. The **variable name**, in this case *intCounter*, identifies the memory location assigned to the variable. Each name can be up to 255 characters in length and must start with a letter. Typically a three-letter lowercase **tag** is used as a prefix to the variable name to identify its data type. In this example, *int* stands for an integer or whole number. Other naming rules for user-defined variables are listed in figure 1.15. When running InsertLogo, intCounter is initially assigned the value 1. Each time the loop is completed, intCounter is increased by 1. When intCounter is greater than 3, the loop is completed and execution moves on to the statements following the For/Next loop.

When a programmer declares a variable, they tell VBA the variable's name and what type of data it will be expected to contain. To accomplish this task a Dim statement is entered in the procedure (macro) where the variable will be used, followed by the variable's name. After the variable name an As statement is added, then the data type identification completes the declaration statement.

The declaration statement *Dim intCounter As Integer* creates a storage location in the computer's memory named intCounter to store whole numbers (integers). Other naming conventions, rules, and some basic data types for user-defined variables are listed in figure 1.15.

User Defined Variable Names
> First character must be a letter
> Maximum number of characters is 255
> Unacceptable characters (space, . ; ! @ # $)
> Tag – three-letter prefix identifies data type

User Defined Variable Types (basic list) and Related Tag
> Integer (int)   – Whole numbers
> Single (sng)   – Floating Point numbers
> String (str)   – Text
> Date (dtm)   – Date and Time
> Currency (cur)   – Monetary values

FIGURE 1.15 Syntax Rules for VB Variable Names

TIP

A shortcut way to use the Auto Fill-In box is to click on the desired selection as soon as the box appears.

1. Move the insertion point behind the last blank remark line (the single apostrophe) in line 5.
2. Press Enter and type **Dim intCounter As Integer** with no period at the end.
   > ► *As soon as you keyed the space after the key word As, the Auto Fill-In box opened. The box highlights fill-in matches as you type. When the one you want is highlighted, pressing Enter will complete the statement.*

Selection of a Sequence

The If statement is considered one of the most important statements in any programming language. It performs selected actions based on a condition established by the programmer. Which action to take is determined by testing to see if the condition is true or false. For instance, in a payroll program an If statement can check the hours an employee worked to see if these hours are greater than 40. If the condition is true, overtime pay is computed. If the condition is false, overtime pay is set equal to 0.

A condition is composed of two values and/or variables separated by one of the comparison operators identified in figure 1.16. The condition is located between the keywords If and Then (see figure 1.17). The statement that follows Then is executed when the condition is true. In its simplest form the If, condition, Then, and action are placed on a single line.

```
Comparison Operator    Condition Tested
        =                   Equal To
        <                   Less Than
        >                   Greater Than
        <=                  Less Than or Equal To
        >=                  Greater Than or Equal To
        <>                  Not Equal To

If Shift = 2 Then ShiftPremium = .25

If Hours >= 70 Then Print "Get a Life!"

If Hours > 40 Then
        Overtime = (Rate*40) + ((Hours − 40) * (Rate * 1.5))
Else
        Overtime = 0
End If
```

FIGURE 1.16 **Comparison Operators**

The If statement in figure 1.17 is in a block format and contains the optional Else clause. The statement following Else is executed when the condition is false (actually a computer scientist would say the condition is "not true"). An End If statement on a separate line must follow the Else option when using the block form. When the condition is false and the Else option is not available, execution continues to the next statement without doing anything.

The plan for InsertLogo is to leave the For/Next loop in the macro. You will use an If/Then statement to print the owner's name the first time the loop is executed. An Else option will set the font size to 1 to make the spacing between lines shorter. It is not necessary to reset the font size; it is done to show you the syntax associated with the Else option.

1. Place the insertion point at the end of the third Selection.TypeParagraph (line 16).
2. Press Enter and key **If intCounter = 1 then** (no period at the end).
3. Move the insertion point to the end of the second Selection.Font.Italic = wdToggle (line 47).
4. Press Enter, key **Selection.Font.Size = 4**, and then press Enter.
5. Key **Selection.TypeParagraph** and then press Enter.
6. Key **Else** and then press Enter.
7. Key **Selection.Font.Size = 1** and then press Enter.
8. Key **End if** (no period at the end).
   ➤ *The If statement takes up 35 lines as shown in figure 1.17.*

Finally, you will use the Tab key to indent statements in the loop as well as the Then and Else options. It is considered good programming practice to indent the true and false actions in block If statements and statements nested in program loops. Indenting these program structures makes it easier to identify and follow the related program logic.

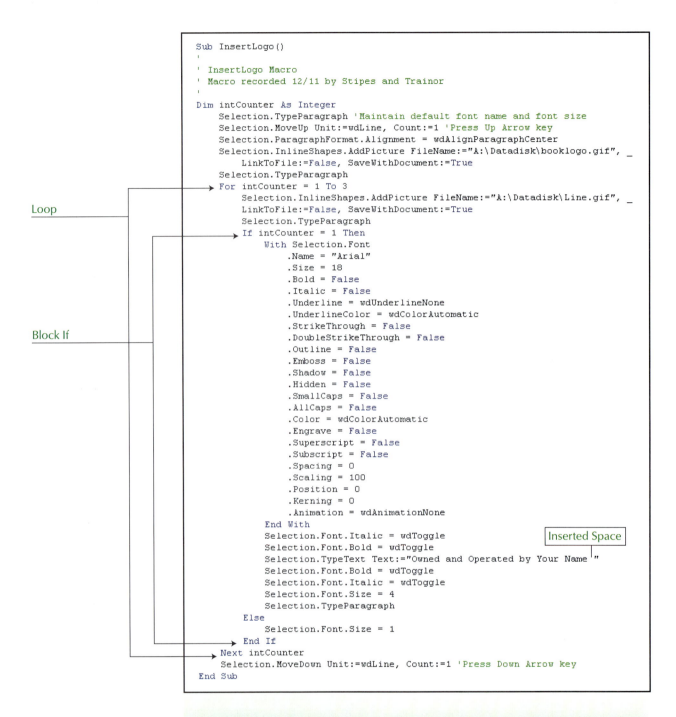

Loop

Block If

Inserted Space

```
Sub InsertLogo()
'
' InsertLogo Macro
' Macro recorded 12/11 by Stipes and Trainor
'
Dim intCounter As Integer
    Selection.TypeParagraph 'Maintain default font name and font size
    Selection.MoveUp Unit:=wdLine, Count:=1 'Press Up Arrow key
    Selection.ParagraphFormat.Alignment = wdAlignParagraphCenter
    Selection.InlineShapes.AddPicture FileName:="A:\Datadisk\booklogo.gif", _
        LinkToFile:=False, SaveWithDocument:=True
    Selection.TypeParagraph
    For intCounter = 1 To 3
        Selection.InlineShapes.AddPicture FileName:="A:\Datadisk\Line.gif", _
        LinkToFile:=False, SaveWithDocument:=True
        Selection.TypeParagraph
    If intCounter = 1 Then
            With Selection.Font
                .Name = "Arial"
                .Size = 18
                .Bold = False
                .Italic = False
                .Underline = wdUnderlineNone
                .UnderlineColor = wdColorAutomatic
                .StrikeThrough = False
                .DoubleStrikeThrough = False
                .Outline = False
                .Emboss = False
                .Shadow = False
                .Hidden = False
                .SmallCaps = False
                .AllCaps = False
                .Color = wdColorAutomatic
                .Engrave = False
                .Superscript = False
                .Subscript = False
                .Spacing = 0
                .Scaling = 100
                .Position = 0
                .Kerning = 0
                .Animation = wdAnimationNone
            End With
            Selection.Font.Italic = wdToggle
            Selection.Font.Bold = wdToggle
            Selection.TypeText Text:="Owned and Operated by Your Name "
            Selection.Font.Bold = wdToggle
            Selection.Font.Italic = wdToggle
            Selection.Font.Size = 4
            Selection.TypeParagraph
        Else
            Selection.Font.Size = 1
        End If
    Next intCounter
    Selection.MoveDown Unit:=wdLine, Count:=1 'Press Down Arrow key
End Sub
```

FIGURE 1.17

InsertLogo Macro with For/Next Loop and If Statements

TIP

In the VB Editor select a group of lines and use the Tab key to indent the entire selection.

10. Using figure 1.17 as a model, press the Tab key to indent the statements within the For/Next loop one tab stop.

11. Use the Tab key to indent the Then and Else options two tab stops.

12. Run the ClearDoc macro.

13. Run the InsertLogo macro.

   ➤ *Your name and the logo appear with one line above the owner's name and two lines under it.*

14. Save memo.doc.

DEBUGGING TOOLS

In a perfect world your macros would work the first time and every time. Since this is not the case, the VB Editor provides a set of debugging tools that help you track down and correct errors. You will run into two types of errors: syntax and logic. A **syntax error** is a spelling error or mistake in the statement's word order that the compiler cannot translate. The compiler displays an error message box when it encounters this type of error. You encountered a syntax error when you were asked to misspell italic (see figure 1.11).

Unfortunately, a macro can contain other errors besides those of syntax. A compiler cannot find **logic errors**. This type of error is syntactically correct and translatable but produces the wrong results. If a programmer accidentally multiplied an employee's pay rate by their employee number, the statement could be translated and executed. However, the results would be incorrect (a logic error) because the hours worked, not the employee number, should be used to calculate pay. Another example of a logic error would be using a plus sign (+) when a minus sign (-) is needed.

Step-by-Step Macro Execution

Quite often you can spot a logic error by watching the macro execute one statement at a time. The Editor's Step Into debugging tool lets you control how fast the macro executes. If the Code window is tiled horizontally with the Word application window (see figure 1.18), you can use the Step Into feature to watch the macro run step-by-step in Word while the next line is highlighted in the Code window.

Pointer

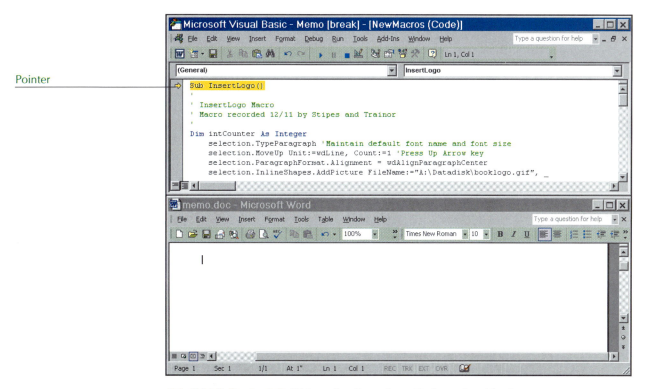

F I G U R E 1 . 1 8 Using the Step Into Debugging Tool

At this time the InsertLogo macro should be running without errors. You will use it to explore several of the debugging tools provided by the Editor.

1. Run the ClearDoc macro.
2. Make sure the insertion point is flashing in the InsertLogo macro in the Code window.
3. Open the <u>D</u>ebug menu and select the Step <u>I</u>nto option.
   ▶ *The Editor highlights the first line in InsertLogo and places an arrow in the margin next to it as shown in figure 1.18.*

The arrow in the left margin is a *pointer*. It points at the next executable statement. In other words, it points at the line you are going to run when you select Step <u>I</u>nto or press F8.

4. Press F8.
   ▶ *The Editor skips over comments, highlights the first executable state-ment, and then moves the pointer to the margin next to it.*
5. Use F8 to step through the execution of InsertLogo.
   ▶ *The Word application window shows the results of executing each state-ment. Watch the buttons on the toolbars as the different formatting tog-gles are used.*

Reset Macro

You can stop the step-by-step execution of the macro at any time by clicking on the <u>R</u>eset option from the <u>R</u>un menu or the Reset button. You will notice that the Reset button looks like the Stop Recording button (see figure 1.4). Resetting the macro when using the Step <u>I</u>nto option turns off the line high-light and removes the pointer from the margin. The next time you run the macro, regardless of where you stop, execution will start at the beginning.

ALTERNATIVE

Click the Reset button.

1. If necessary, open the <u>R</u>un menu and select the <u>R</u>eset button.
2. Run the ClearDoc macro.

Next Step 1-4

1. Use the Editor to remove the Else and Selection.Font.Size = 1 from the InsertLogo macro.
2. Before the second Select.TypeParagraph statement (line 12) insert the following statement that sets the font size to 4:
   Selection.Font.Size = 4
3. Test the macro and correct any errors.
4. Print the code for the InsertLogo macro.

CUSTOM INPUT

For people working in an office it might be useful to create another macro that inserts the date and the traditional To: and From: memo headings. It could be used with a personalized letterhead or after the logo is inserted. This memo macro (see figure 1.19) also provides the opportunity to show you how to handle user input from the keyboard. In this case the user is asked to enter the names of people receiving the memo.

Next Step 1-5

Record a new macro, name it Memo, and store it in memo.doc. Assign Alt + M as the keyboard shortcut. The Memo macro should do the following after you have noted the default font and size:
1. Add 1 blank line.
2. Set the font to Arial 12 bold.
3. Use the Insert menu's Date and Time option to add the date in a *Month ?, 200?* format and set it up to update automatically.
4. Add 3 blank lines after the date.
5. Key **To:** with a space at the end.
6. Add 1 blank line.
7. Key **From:** and *your name*.
8. Turn off bold and return to default font you identified in step 1.
9. Add 1 blank line.

InputBox(prompt, title) Function

The InputBox function is used to accept input from the keyboard and assign the input to a variable. When the function executes it creates a dialog box similar to the one found at the top of figure 1.19. This example displays "Who should receive this memo?" as the *prompt* and "Memo Heading" in the Title bar. The InputBox function shown in the Code window of figure 1.19 sets the variable strMemoTo equal to the keyboard entry (Joe Smoe) the user typed into the dialog box. The parentheses after the function name contain the prompt and title in double quotes.

1. Display the Memo macro in the Visual Basic Editor's Code window.
2. Make sure your name and today's date are included in the remarks.
3. Add a blank line under the remarks.
4. Press Tab, key **Dim strMemoTo As String**, and then press Enter.
5. Key **strMemoTo = InputBox ("Who should receive this memo?", "Memo Heading")**.
   ➤ *The VBA code should look like figure 1.19.*

Many of the preset codes used as part of the macro recording do not set new values. To make the code easier to read, you are going to delete several of these lines from the With.Select.Font statement. In most cases there will be two With.Select.Font statements in your macro from which code can be removed without adverse effect.

6. Delete all the lines from and including .Italic = False to Animation = wdAnimationNone in every With.Selection.Font statement in the Memo macro.
   ➤ *The end results should look like figure 1.19.*

The input data is incorporated into the memo by adding the variable name MemoTo at the end of the Selection.TypeText statement that adds the text To: to the memo.

7. Position Insertion point at the end of Selection.TypeText Text:="To:".
8. Key **& strMemoTo** with no period at the end.
   ➤ *The VBA code should look like figure 1.19.*
9. Run and debug the macro.
10. Save and print the Memo macro.

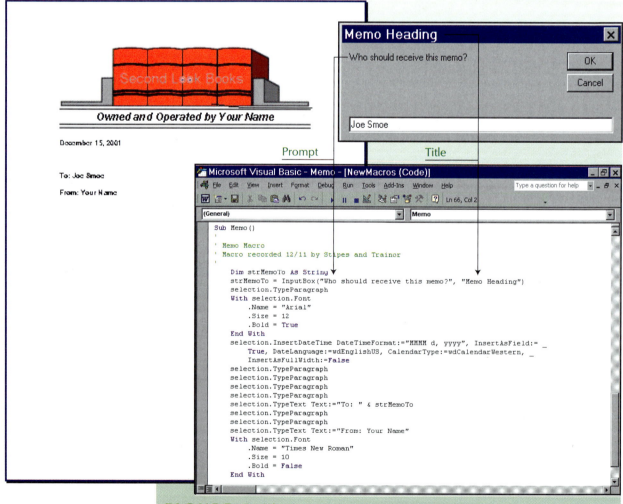

FIGURE 1.19
Memo Heading Dialog Box, InputBox Function Code, and the Memo Macro

DELETING A MACRO

Deleting a macro removes the related VBA statements from the Code window. Periodically macros you don't use should be deleted to keep the storage size of the related disk files at a minimum. This is especially true for macros assigned to the Word's Normal.dot template or Excel's Personal Macro workbook. The easiest way to delete a macro is by using the Macro dialog box.

1. Click Tools, point to Macro, and then click Macros.
   ➤ *The Macros dialog box displays.*
2. Select ClearDoc and click Delete.
   ➤ *A message box asking if you are sure you want to delete the macro will appear.*
3. Click Yes.
   ➤ *ClearDoc is removed from the list of macro names.*

CLOSING VISUAL BASIC EDITOR

This is the end of chapter 1. Before closing the Editor, run the InsertLogo and Memo macros one more time. Finish the memo by describing the computer system you will be using to learn VBA.

1. Close the Visual Basic Editor.
2. Run the InsertLogo macro.
3. Run the Memo macro.
4. Input your instructor's name when prompted by the Memo Heading dialog box.
5. Under the From option, key the answers to the following questions:
   What brand of computer are you using?
   What type of processor does it have?
   How much main memory is there?
   How much hard disk storage is available?
6. Save the document.
7. Print the document.
8. Close Word.

REVIEW QUESTIONS

On a blank sheet of paper provide a short answer for the following questions.

1. Define the key terms.
2. Identify four situations where running a macro could improve productivity.
3. What are two ways you can create a macro?
4. Describe three ways you can execute a macro.
5. What should be done if you suspect a file is infected with a macro virus?
6. When and how many times do you test a new macro?
7. What colors does the Visual Basic Editor use to display keywords, remarks, and executable statements?
8. Which resource would you use to identify an object, method, or property within a Visual Basic statement?
9. How do you delete a VBA statement from a macro?
10. What is the easiest way to create a macro?
11. What is the easiest way to change a macro?
12. In what order should program features be turned off?
13. What type of information is included in a Remark statement?
14. Identify the three basic program structures and give a VBA example of each.
15. Identify the six comparison operators and describe the testing conditions in which each is used.
16. What type of statement should be indented?
17. What type of error does the compiler find?
18. How is the Inputbox funtion used?
19. How do you remove a macro?

CHECK YOUR UNDERSTANDING

Indicate the correct term or choose the correct answer for each item.

1. The specific structure used in creating a program statement is called the statement's ___Syntax___.
2. Comments used in a procedure to describe its purpose are called ___Remarks___.
3. The three-letter prefix in a variable name is referred to as a(n) ___tag___.
4. Attributes of an object, such as its font, format, or name, are ___properties___ of the object.
5. A program error that produces undesired results yet does not prevent the procedure from executing is called a(n) ___logic___ error.
6. The program structure called iteration refers to
   a. step-by-step instructions.
   b. a set of instructions that are repeated.
   c. a variable declaration.
   d. a conditional evaluation.

7. Which of the following is *not* a variable type?
   a. String
   b. Date
   c. Percent
   d. Currency
8. User input can be incorporated into a procedure by use of a(n)
   a. input box.
   b. set of nested statements.
   c. selection structure.
   d. method.
9. Select from the following the best variable name for a storage location for the number of books purchased by a customer.
   a. int#OfBooks
   b. strNumberOfBooks
   c. curNumberOfBooks
   d. intNumberOfBooks
10. Which of the following statements identifies when the contents of the curBalanceDue variable exceeds $1,000?
   a. If curBalanceDue = 1000 then
   b. If curBalanceDue <> 1000 then
   c. If curBalanceDue <= 1000 then
   d. If curBalanceDue > 1000 then

EXERCISES

Complete the following exercises.

Last Step

Modify the Memo macro you created as part of the chapter 1 tutorial to include a Subject line. Use an input box to accept the subject after the user has input the name of the person receiving the memo. The text Subject: and the input information should appear after a blank line that follows the memo's From line. Print the macro and the resulting Word document.

Debug

The LinedName macro was developed to create two horizontal lines above and below the text "Second Look Books". The macro's output should resemble the output shown below.

Second Look Books

There are three coding errors in the LinedName macro code that will prevent its correct execution. Identify and correct these errors.

```
Sub LinedName()
    Dim intCounter as String
    For intCounter = 1 to 4
        Selection.InLineShapes.AddPicture FileName:="A:
        Line.gif", _LinkToFile:=False, SaveWithDocument:=True
    Selection.TypeParagraph
    If intCounter = 3 Then
        Selection.TypeText Text:="Second Look Books"
        Selection.TypeParagraph
    Next intCounter
    End If
End Sub
```

Second Look Books

Internet

Go to Microsoft's Visual Basic for Applications Web site located at http://msdn.microsoft.com/vba and then click *Licensing Partners*. Identify six software developers with different application focuses (i.e. retail, accounting, etc.) and the product for which they license VBA.

New Challenge

Second Look Books sponsors a Quarterly Readers Club. Since everyone in the community is welcome to attend, Name tags can not be made ahead of time.

Develop a macro that will prompt, via an InputBox, for the attendee's name and then print the name tag as specified below.

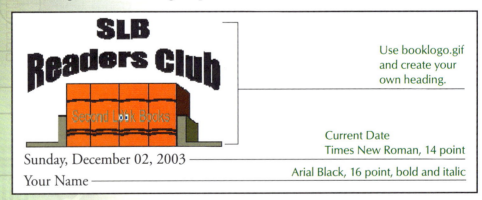

Use booklogo.gif and create your own heading.

Sunday, December 02, 2003 ——————
Your Name ——————

Current Date
Times New Roman, 14 point

Arial Black, 16 point, bold and italic

Discussion

Do you think a non-Microsoft software application that is licensed to include VBA actually has a greater sales attraction to prospective users than a competitive application that does not include VBA? Explain the thinking behind your answer.

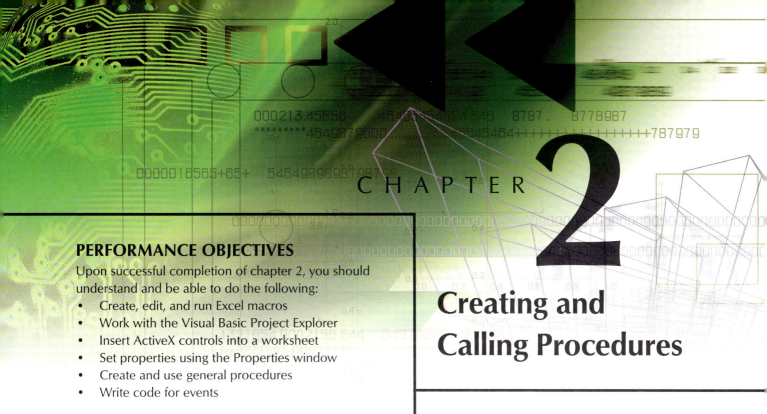

CHAPTER

2

Creating and Calling Procedures

PERFORMANCE OBJECTIVES

Upon successful completion of chapter 2, you should understand and be able to do the following:

- Create, edit, and run Excel macros
- Work with the Visual Basic Project Explorer
- Insert ActiveX controls into a worksheet
- Set properties using the Properties window
- Create and use general procedures
- Write code for events

Microsoft's Office Suite provides powerful financial analysis tools with the resources of its Excel spreadsheet software. For example, worksheets and charts used by Second Look Books monitor performance and are constantly updated as the fiscal year progresses. Using macros to carry out complex and repetitive sequences of actions quickly and easily enhances user productivity in areas such as inserting new data and printing reports. In this chapter you will create a macro that facilitates data entry and the printing of a sales report.

Early macro languages for spreadsheets did nothing more than imitate popular command driven user interfaces. For example, the macro entry FCW 25 (**F**ormat **C**olumn **W**idth) would automate the setting of a worksheet's column width to 25 characters wide. This keystroke-based approach is difficult to read and completely out of place with today's graphical interfaces. Microsoft then responded with a new macro language made up of an extensive set of function-based commands, like LOAD and ADD, that were independent of the user interface. Unfortunately, the language was unique to Excel, making it unacceptable for people using a suite of software applications.

Visual Basic for Applications (VBA), on the other hand, is a general-purpose language that is independent of the application. VBA enables the user to automate in single macro commands that manipulate and integrate data used by other applications. Later in this book you will run a macro using Excel that opens an Access database, runs a query, and imports the results of the query into an Excel worksheet. VBA macros integrate procedures and methods from Excel tasks as well as operations in other Office applications by communicating with their object libraries. The capabilities of Office applications and other non-Microsoft applications are available to VBA through their object libraries. You have already changed an object's properties in chapter 1 when you manipulated the status of the bold property using the wdToggle constant from Word's object library. Figure 2.1 illustrates this relationship.

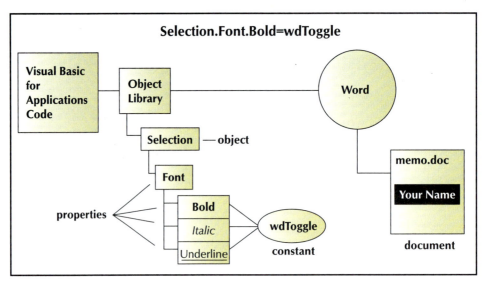

FIGURE 2.1 Relationship Between the Object Library and VBA Code

Since Visual Basic for Applications is an extension of Microsoft's Visual Basic programming language, anyone who understands Visual Basic will be familiar with VBA code. Likewise, learning Visual Basic for Applications provides you with an introduction to programming concepts used by Visual Basic, Visual C++, and other object-based programming languages.

SECOND LOOK BOOKS' SPREADSHEET

As the owner of Second Look Books, you evaluate sales trends weekly. To accomplish this, a book classification system is used to organize sales data. This system has six categories: Computer, History, Mystery, Romance, Science Fiction, and Western. Monitoring sales in these classifications helps you when ordering new books, pricing, advertising, and making promotional decisions. The c2-sales.xls workbook that you downloaded onto your data disk contains the 2003 Sales worksheet. You will use this worksheet to analyze weekly sales for Second Look Books.

TIP

If Excel appears on the taskbar, click it.

1. Open Excel.
   ➤ *Excel opens with a default workbook.*
2. If necessary, close the New Workbook Task Pane.
3. Click the File menu and then click Open.
   ➤ *Excel displays an Open dialog box.*
4. From the Look in list box select the disk drive and file folder that contains your data disk.
5. Select *c2-sales.xls* and then click Open.
   ➤ *The c2-sales workbook opens as seen in figure 2.2.*

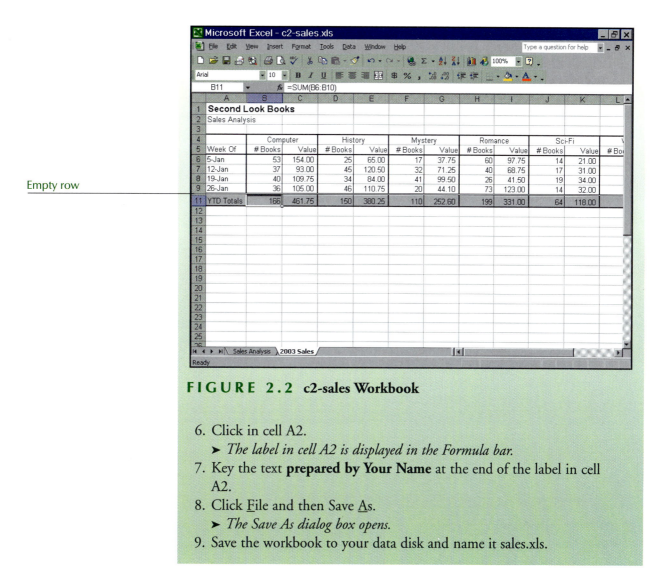

Empty row

FIGURE 2.2 c2-sales Workbook

6. Click in cell A2.
   ➤ *The label in cell A2 is displayed in the Formula bar.*
7. Key the text **prepared by Your Name** at the end of the label in cell A2.
8. Click File and then Save As.
   ➤ *The Save As dialog box opens.*
9. Save the workbook to your data disk and name it sales.xls.

You will work with the sales.xls workbook for the remainder of this chapter. If you have difficulty and need to recreate sales.xls, use the c2-sales.xls file and repeat steps 4-9.

Adding Weekly Sales Data

The sales analysis worksheet contains a breakdown by classification of each week's sales by number of books sold and the value of those sales. The starting date of each week is always Sunday. The reference B6:B10 inside the SUM function (see the Formula bar in figure 2.2) identifies a range of cells. A range is a group of adjoining cells defined by the upper left cell address and the lower right cell address. This range is the SUM function's argument. In this case, the range identifies all of the cells to be used in the year-to-date (YTD) totals displayed in row 11.

Once the sales numbers for a week are compiled, they are entered into the worksheet. This is done by inserting a row under the last week's sales for the new data. While it is difficult to append a new row to the end of a range, it is easy to expand a range by inserting a new row inside the range. Therefore, upon close inspection of the worksheet, you will notice row 10 is reduced in height. This was done to help carry forward cell formatting by inserting a new row within a range that ends with a blank row. Reducing the height of the cells eliminates the visual effect of a blank row of cells. Since the cells in this row contain no data they can be included in the SUM() functions used in row 11 and not adversely affect the result of the calculation. By including this empty row in the year-to-date formula (see figure 2.2) when inserting a new row, Excel automatically updates the range reference in the SUM() function.

Inserting a New Row

The sales data for the week of February 2 needs to be entered into the worksheet. You are going to manually work through this task to become familiar with the process and then in Next Step 2-1 these tasks will be recorded and saved as the InsertNewRow macro. In the following steps you will be asked to use a special key sequence that locates the last row of data in the worksheet. This key sequence consists of the End key and the Down Arrow key. Nothing happens until the second key, the Down Arrow, is pressed, at which point the cell pointer jumps to the last row of data.

1. Click in cell A6.
2. Press the End key on the keyboard and then press the Down Arrow key.
   ➤ *The cell pointer moves to cell A11.*
3. Press the Up Arrow key once.
   ➤ *The cell pointer moves to cell A10 (the narrow row discussed earlier).*

   This technique of positioning the cell pointer is used to locate the insertion point for the new row, regardless of how many weeks of data the worksheet contains.

4. Click Insert and then click Rows.
   ➤ *A new row is inserted and the old row 10 becomes row 11.*

   You can click on any of the Year To Date totals in row 12 and confirm that the range referenced in the SUM() function has been updated to include the cells in row 11.

Adding Weekly Totals

The weekly totals formulas in columns N and O need to be copied into the new row. If necessary, use the horizontal scroll arrow to bring columns N and O into view.

1. Click on cell N9 then click the Copy button. ⧉
2. Click on cell N10 then click the Paste button. ⧉
   ➤ *The value 0 is displayed in cell N10.*
3. Copy and paste the formula from cell O9 to cell O10.
   ➤ *Cell O10 displays 0.00.*
4. Press the Esc key.
   ➤ *The copy selection indicator, the dotted line box, is released.*
5. If necessary, use the horizontal scroll button to bring column A back into view.
6. Click in cell A10.
7. Enter the following sales data for the week of February 2 in row 10.

A10	2/2/03
B10	48
C10	128
D10	50
E10	131.25
F10	25
G10	60
H10	57
I10	96.25
J10	23
K10	35.5
L10	7
M10	23.5

   ➤ *The totals in cells N10 and O10 are 210 and 474.50, respectively.*
8. Save the workbook.

CREATING A MACRO TO INSERT A NEW ROW

As you have seen, the procedure necessary to prepare the worksheet for the entry of a new week's data is time-consuming and complex. This is an instance where a macro is useful.

1. Click the Tools menu, point to Macro, and then click Record New Macro.
   ➤ *The Record Macro dialog box opens similar to figure 2.3.*

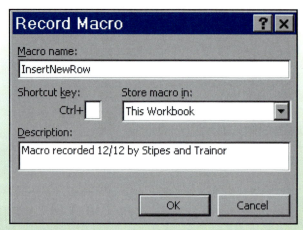

FIGURE 2.3 **Record Macro Dialog Box**

2. Delete the default name by keying **InsertNewRow**, using no spaces, in the Macro name text box.
   ➤ *The Macro name* InsertNewRow *replaces the default name.*
3. Key your name in the Description text box.
4. Confirm that the Store macro in selection is *This Workbook* and then click OK.
   ➤ *The Stop Recording toolbar appears.*

Next Step 2-1

Repeat the steps used previously in the Inserting A New Row and Adding Weekly Totals sections as follows:
1. Select cell A6.
2. Move the selector to bottom of the data range in column A.
3. Position the pointer and insert a new row.
4. Position the pointer and then copy the total formulas in columns N and On to the new row.
5. Release the selection indicator.
6. Locate the cell pointer in column A of the new row.
7. Click the Stop Recording button.

At this point the macro recording is done and the worksheet is ready for sales data.

Running and Testing the Macro

In the process of recording the insert row macro, you have prepared the worksheet for the February 9 sales data. Before entering this data it would be wise to confirm that the macro works as expected.

1. Right-click on the row 11 header.
   ➤ *The entire row is highlighted and a shortcut menu appears.*
2. Click <u>D</u>elete.
   ➤ *Row 11 is deleted from the worksheet.*
3. Click the <u>T</u>ools menu, point to <u>M</u>acro, and then click <u>M</u>acros.
   ➤ *The Macro dialog box opens.*
4. Make sure the InsertNewRow macro is selected in the <u>M</u>acro name list box and then click the <u>R</u>un button.
   ➤ *A new row is inserted into the worksheet, total formulas are copied, and the cell pointer is located in column A.*
5. Enter the following sales data for the week of February 9.

A11	**2/9/03**
B11	**47**
C11	**130.25**
D11	**60**
E11	**158.25**
F11	**35**
G11	**79.75**
H11	**40**
I11	**66.5**
J11	**14**
K11	**24.25**
L11	**9**
M11	**29.5**

   ➤ *The totals are 205 and 488.50.*
6. Save the workbook.
7. Run the InsertNewRow macro to prepare the worksheet for the next week's data.
   ➤ *The inserted row is in the WRONG LOCATION.*

The new row has been inserted between February 2 and February 9 data rather than below the February 9 row. The InsertNewRow macro must be modified so it inserts the new row below the last data row regardless of that row's location in the worksheet.

8. Delete the new row.

USING THE VISUAL BASIC EDITOR

The problem with the InsertNewRow macro is that the macro recorder uses absolute cell positioning. As a result the macro will always insert a new row 11 into the worksheet. Modifying the macro to correct the problem is done with the Visual Basic Editor.

1. Click <u>T</u>ools, point to <u>M</u>acro, and then click <u>M</u>acros.
   ➤ *The Macro dialog box is displayed.*
2. With the InsertNewRow macro selected, click the <u>E</u>dit button.
   ➤ *The Visual Basic Editor opens.*

When you worked with the Visual Basic Editor in chapter 1, you used the Code window. What you see in figure 2.4 is the Visual Basic Editor's Code window on the right containing the InsertNewRow macro, and the Project Explorer window on the left. Complete the following actions to make your screen look similar to figure 2.4.

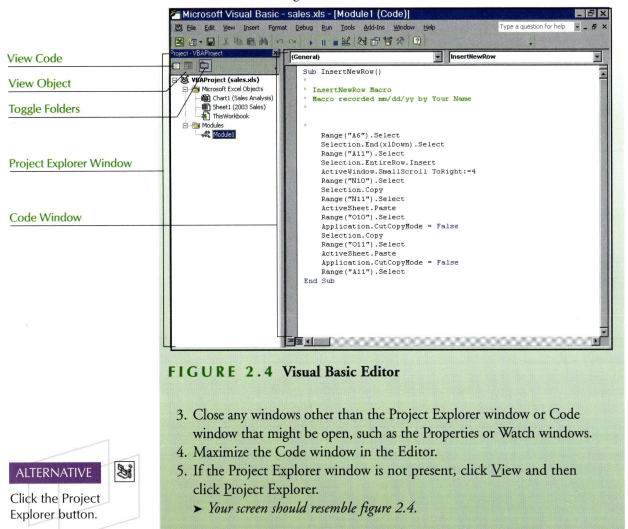

FIGURE 2.4 Visual Basic Editor

3. Close any windows other than the Project Explorer window or Code window that might be open, such as the Properties or Watch windows.
4. Maximize the Code window in the Editor.
5. If the Project Explorer window is not present, click <u>V</u>iew and then click <u>P</u>roject Explorer.
   ➤ *Your screen should resemble figure 2.4.*

Project Explorer

All the VBA code associated with a workbook or document is stored as a **project**. When new components are added, such as code modules containing macros, they automatically becomes part of the workbook project. The **Project Explorer** identifies and displays various objects and modules associated with a project. The Project Explorer window has three buttons—View Code, View

Object, and Toggle Folders—all of which are labeled in figure 2.4. The Toggle Folders button displays or hides the project folder icons.

1. Click the Toggle Folders button.
   ➤ *Project folders, similar to those in Windows Explorer, are displayed or hidden.*
2. If the folder icons are not visible, toggle them on.
   ➤ *The folder icons appear.*
3. If necessary, open each folder by clicking on the plus sign preceding the folder icon.
   ➤ *The display should look similar to figure 2.4.*

The VBAProject (sales.xls) project referenced in the Project Explorer window has two folders. One is labeled Microsoft Excel Objects and the other is labeled Modules. The object folder has three objects: Chart1 (Sales Analysis), Sheet1 (2003 Sales), and This Workbook. The Modules folder contains one module titled Module1. Visual Basic code can be located in any of these locations. Module1 was created to store the InsertNewRow macro when you recorded it. Each time a workbook is opened and a macro recorded, Excel creates a new module for it and all subsequent macros recorded during that session.

Since there is no way for you to control where the recorder puts a new macro, a project may contain a number of modules. Having macros in multiple modules may be confusing to you, but it is not a problem for Excel. Should you forget where a macro is stored, use the Macro dialog box to open the macro for editing and Excel will automatically take you to the appropriate module. The Project Explorer may also reference a project titled VBAProject (PERSONAL.XLS). This is a workbook where worksheets and procedures can be stored so they are available to all other workbooks. If nothing is stored in the PERSONAL.XLS workbook, you will not see a reference to it in the Project Explorer.

Since modules contain only code, the View Object button is inactive when a module is selected. The workbook is an object that references the workbook as a whole. Like each of the individual sheets, the workbook has its own code page and worksheet.

1. Click on Sheet1 (2003 Sales) in the Project Explorer window.
   ➤ *The Sheet1 object is highlighted.*
2. Click the View Code button.
   ➤ *The Code window for Sheet1 is opened, but contains no code.*
3. Click the View Object button.
   ➤ *The 2003 Sales worksheet window is opened.*
4. Click the Microsoft Visual Basic button in the taskbar.
   ➤ *This returns you to the Visual Basic Editor window.*

EDITING THE INSERTNEWROW MACRO

The InsertNewRow macro code contains five objects: Range, Selection, ActiveWindow, ActiveSheet, and Application. Six methods (SmallScroll, EntireRow, Select, Insert, Copy, and Paste) are used and three properties (ScrollColumn, End, and CutCopyMode) are set. Users with 17" monitors will not have any scroll statements since scrolling will not be necessary to view column O. As a result, these users will not have an ActiveWindow object in the macro. Notice that the arguments of the Range objects in figure 2.4 contain specific cell references to rows 10 and 11. This explains why the new row is always inserted as row 11.

Offset(row, column) Property

Correcting the problem requires that all Range().Select statements, except for the one that initially places the cell pointer in cell A6, be modified with the Offset() property. This property requires positive/negative row and column arguments to relocate the cell pointer relative to its current position. For example, Selection.Offset(1,0) moves the cell selector down one row. Manipulating the cell pointer with this technique eliminates the need for any ActiveWindow.Scroll statements. As a result, these statements need to be deleted. The scroll statements in your macro may differ from those in figure 2.4 depending upon whether you used the scroll bar or arrows to adjust the view.

Next Step 2-2

1. Display the code for the InsertNewRow macro in the Code Window.
2. Modify the InsertNewRow macro using the offset coordinates and line deletions identified in the Replace with column. The modified macro should look similar to figure 2.5.

Statement	Replace with	Description
Range("A6").Select		selector at cell A6
Selection.End(xlDown).Select		selector to YTD Totals row
Range("A11").Select	**Selection.Offset(-1, 0).Select**	selector up 1
Selection.EntireRow.Insert		insert new row at selector location
ActiveWindow.Small Scroll ToRight:=7	Delete Scroll arrow statement if present	selector up 1, right 13
Range("N10").Select	**Selection.Offset(-1, 13).Select**	
Selection.Copy		copy to clipboard

Range("N11").Select	Selection.Offset(1, 0).Select	selector down 1
ActiveSheet.Paste		paste from clipboard
Range("O10").Select	Selection.Offset(-1, 1).Select	selector up 1, right 1
Selection.Copy		copy to clipboard
Range("O11").Select	Selection.Offset(1, 0).Select	selector down 1
ActiveSheet.Paste		paste from clipboard
Application.CutCopy Mode = False		release selection
ActiveWindow.Scroll Column = 1	Delete Scroll button statement if present	
Range("A11").Select	Selection.Offset(0, -13).Select	selector left 13

3. Print the macro code for InsertNewRow.
4. Compare your printout with figure 2.5 for accuracy and correct any mistakes you find. If you want to test the macro again, delete the inserted blank row before doing so.

ActiveCell Object

The final modification to the macro is to have it enter the date that begins the new week. Since the data cells in column A contain a Date format, this is a simple process of using the date from the cell above and adding 7 to it. The current position of the cell pointer is referenced with the ActiveCell object. The contents of this object can be modified via its FormulaR1C1 property that uses a row/column notation. Setting this property equal to R[-1]C+7 will capture the date from the cell above the active cell and add the value 7 to it. The result is the start date of the next week.

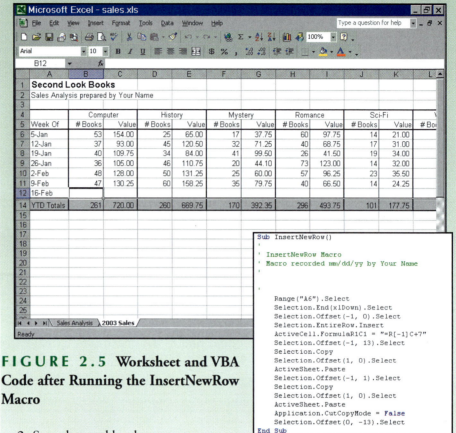

TIP

Setting uses brackets [ ], not parenthesis ( ).

PITFALL

It is very easy to miss one of the two equal (=) signs, thus causing an error.

1. After the Selection.EntireRow.Insert line add the line **ActiveCell.FormulaR1C1 = "=R[-1]C+7".**
   ➤ *Edited macro should look like code in figure 2.5.*

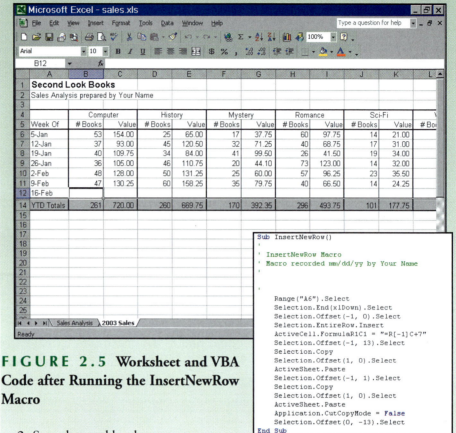

FIGURE 2.5 Worksheet and VBA Code after Running the InsertNewRow Macro

2. Save the workbook.
3. Return to Excel via the Excel button on the taskbar and then test the macro.
   ➤ *The new row for the week of February 16 sales data is inserted as shown in figure 2.5.*
4. Use figure 2.5 to debug the macro, if necessary.
5. Enter the following sales data for the week of February 16.

B12	**53**
C12	**159.5**
D12	**49**
E12	**122**
F12	**16**
G12	**37**
H12	**57**
I12	**92.25**
J12	**20**
K12	**34.5**
L12	**3**
M12	**10**

   ➤ *The totals are 198 and 455.25.*
6. Save the workbook.

Printing a Year to Date Report

Now it is time to turn your attention to printing the worksheet. If the data in the worksheet was static there would not be any reason to automate printing. However, new data is added each and every week causing the sales analysis to constantly change. You are going to create a sub procedure that selects the data in the worksheet regardless of the number of weeks. Then the page orientation is set to landscape, fitting the output on a single page, and the sales analysis is printed.

INSERTING A PROCEDURE

As a Visual Basic for Applications programmer, it is important that you understand the difference between macros and procedures. A **procedure** is a set of VBA code statements that accomplish a specific task. It is a broad term that applies to any code that lies between a Sub and End Sub statement or Function and End Function statement. All macros are procedures; however, not all procedures qualify as macros. Any code created with the Macro Recorder or the Visual Basic Editor which can be run from the Macros dialog box, is a macro procedure. Macros cannot accept arguments (data) from other procedures. Sub and function procedures, on the other hand, have the ability to accept arguments from other procedures. A **sub procedure** is distinguished from a function procedure, usually shortened to just **function**, by the simple fact that functions return data while sub procedures do not.

In many cases the most efficient way to create a procedure is to use the macro recorder to code the task. Once recorded, the macro procedure can easily be modified to a sub procedure with the Visual Basic Editor. However, the macro recorder often includes a lot of unnecessary code in the macro. You encountered an example of this in chapter 1 when using the Font dialog box to change the font size. The macro recorder includes every Font property, whether it had been changed or not, as part of the With.Select.Font statement.

Users trying to create easy to read (and edit) macros can often write it faster than it takes to record it, due to the extent of editing necessary. Consider that the PageSetup dialog box contains over 20 properties that the macro recorder will capture when you modify one property. Since we only need to reset three of these properties, as shown in figure 2.6, it is easier to code the procedure in the Visual Basic Editor rather than edit out over 20 property statements. Figure 2.6 compares code recorded by the macro recorder and the actual code that is necessary.

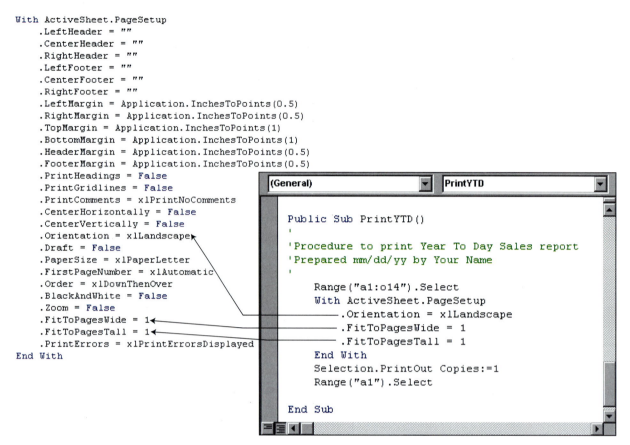

```
With ActiveSheet.PageSetup
    .LeftHeader = ""
    .CenterHeader = ""
    .RightHeader = ""
    .LeftFooter = ""
    .CenterFooter = ""
    .RightFooter = ""
    .LeftMargin = Application.InchesToPoints(0.5)
    .RightMargin = Application.InchesToPoints(0.5)
    .TopMargin = Application.InchesToPoints(1)
    .BottomMargin = Application.InchesToPoints(1)
    .HeaderMargin = Application.InchesToPoints(0.5)
    .FooterMargin = Application.InchesToPoints(0.5)
    .PrintHeadings = False
    .PrintGridlines = False
    .PrintComments = xlPrintNoComments
    .CenterHorizontally = False
    .CenterVertically = False
    .Orientation = xlLandscape
    .Draft = False
    .PaperSize = xlPaperLetter
    .FirstPageNumber = xlAutomatic
    .Order = xlDownThenOver
    .BlackAndWhite = False
    .Zoom = False
    .FitToPagesWide = 1
    .FitToPagesTall = 1
    .PrintErrors = xlPrintErrorsDisplayed
End With
```

Code window:

(General)   PrintYTD

```
Public Sub PrintYTD()
'
'Procedure to print Year To Day Sales report
'Prepared mm/dd/yy by Your Name
'
    Range("a1:o14").Select
    With ActiveSheet.PageSetup
        .Orientation = xlLandscape
        .FitToPagesWide = 1
        .FitToPagesTall = 1
    End With
    Selection.PrintOut Copies:=1
    Range("a1").Select

End Sub
```

FIGURE 2.6 Recording Versus Writing Procedures

Eventually we will want the print procedure to generate multiple copies of the sales analysis. This requires the passing of an argument identifying to the procedure the number of copies desired. When we make this modification the macro procedure must be converted to a sub procedure since a macro cannot accept an argument.

1. Open the Visual Basic Editor.
2. In the Project Explorer window, double-click *Module1*.
   ➤ *Module1 is active in the Code window.*
3. Click Insert and then Procedure.
   ➤ *The Add Procedure dialog box similar to figure 2.7 opens.*
4. Key **PrintYTD** in the Name text box, accept the default Type as Sub, and then click OK.
   ➤ *The new procedure is added to Module1.*

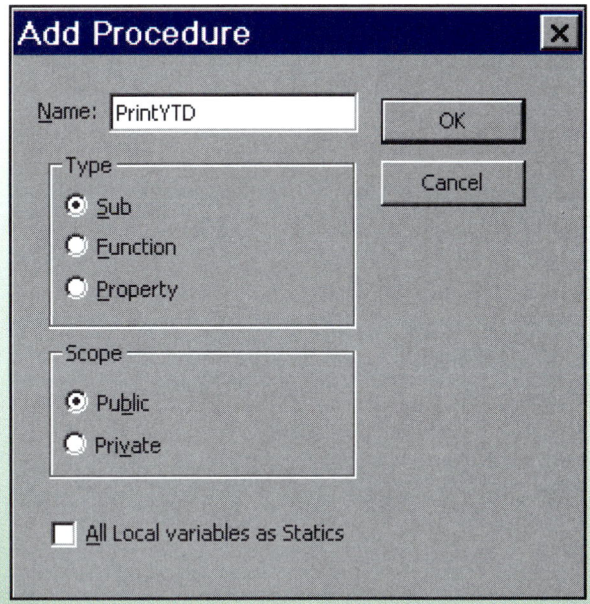

FIGURE 2.7 Add Procedure Dialog Box

Coding the Print Procedure

You are now ready to code, instead of record, the PrintYTD procedure. The cell address argument in the statement Range("A1:O14"). Select (as shown in figure 2.6) identifies the section of the worksheet to print. Once the data to be printed is selected, three properties of the PageSetup object are reset. A print statement is then executed, followed by a range statement that returns the range selection to cell A1.

WITH STATEMENT

To provide the desired look, the Orientation, FitToPagesWide, and FitToPagesTall properties of the PageSetup object must be changed from their default values. When setting multiple properties of an object, a With structure eliminates the need to repeat the common object reference. With statements start by identifying the object; in our case, the object is the PageSetup object of the ActiveSheet. Each property name referenced inside the With structure is preceded by a period. This syntax causes the object to be assumed. The structure is concluded using an End With statement. In figure 2.8 you can see how the simplicity of a With structure improves the readability of the code. It also reduces the amount of code, in this case 98 versus 127 typed characters. These FitToPageWide and FitToPageTall settings maximize the use of an $8^1/_2$ x 11 inch sheet of paper, yet scale the range so it never exceeds a single page.

```
With ActiveSheet.PageSetup
    .Orientation = xlLandscape
    .FitToPagesWide = 1
    .FitToPagesTall = 1
End With
```

```
ActiveSheet.PageSetup.Orientation = xlLandscape
ActiveSheet.PageSetup.FitToPagesWide = 1
ActiveSheet.PageSetup.FitToPagesTall = 1
```

FIGURE 2.8 **With Syntax versus Standard Syntax**

PRINTOUT METHOD

Printing is accomplished by applying the PrintOut method to the selection and hard coding its Copies parameter to specify the number of reports. As a final step, the target selection of cells is released by setting the Range to the single cell A1.

1. Return to the Visual Basic Editor.
2. Key the following code between the Public Sub PrintYTD() and End Sub statements.

```
'
'Procedure to print Year To Date Sales report
'Prepared mm/dd/yy by Your Name
'

        Range("A1:O14").Select
        With ActiveSheet.PageSetup
                .Orientation = xlLandscape
                .FitToPagesWide = 1
                .FitToPagesTall = 1
        End With
        Selection.PrintOut Copies:=1
        Range("A1").Select
```

➤ *Procedure matches figure 2.6.*

The PrintYTD sub procedure currently qualifies as a macro and therefore can be run from the Macros dialog box. Its macro status will not change until you modify it to accept an argument passed by another procedure.

3. Save the workbook.
4. Run the PrintYTD procedure from the Macros dialog box and debug, if necessary.
    ➤ *One copy of the Year To Date Sales Analysis prints.*
5. Print the code for the PrintYTD procedure.

Using Range Names

The PrintYTD macro currently references the range of cells from A1 to O14. Once sales data for the next week is inserted, this range will no longer be correct. To print sections of a worksheet that constantly change requires a reference that updates as the worksheet data expands and contracts. **Range names** are user-defined names assigned to a single cell or group of cells. These names can then be used to reference the selection rather than the row/column address. The advantage to using a range name is that Excel automatically accounts for rows/columns added to or deleted from the range. Range names are defined from the Insert menu's Name option. This menu option can also be used to identify what range name assignments exist in a worksheet.

1. Return to the 2003 Sales worksheet.
2. Click in cell A1, making it the active cell.
   ➤ *Cell A1 is highlighted.*
3. Click <u>I</u>nsert, point to <u>N</u>ame, and then click <u>D</u>efine.
   ➤ *The Define Name dialog box opens similar to one shown in figure 2.9.*

Excel assumes you want to use the label in cell A1 as the name of the range and adapts it for use. Since blank spaces are not allowed in a range name, the underscore character is typically entered in their place. You will delete this name and enter the name Print_Area and assign the range A1:O14 to the name.

4. Delete the default name, Second_Look_Books, from the Names in <u>w</u>orkbook text box.
   ➤ *The text box clears.*
5. Key **Print_Area**.
6. Click the Return to Worksheet button at the end of the <u>R</u>efers to text box.
   ➤ *The Define Name dialog box is reduced and cell A1 is highlighted by a marquee box.*

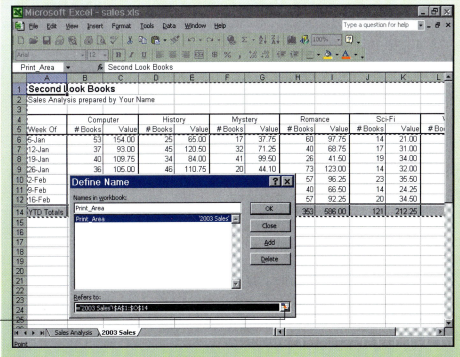

Return to Worksheet Button

FIGURE 2.9 Define Name Dialog Box

Selecting ranges can be done in a variety of ways. Most commonly used is the click-and-drag method or directly typing in the reference. Both methods have their drawbacks. Any time the target range exceeds the viewable area of the screen, the click-and-drag method becomes a challenge. Keying the cell range, as we all know, lends itself to typographical errors (typos). A typo in a cell range reference can produce a very undesirable outcome.

The most reliable way to select cell range references is the *Click-Shift-Click method*. This process starts by clicking in either one of the upper or lower corners of the desired range. Then use the scroll bars to bring the diagonal corner into view; this will not alter the active cell. Finally, while holding the Shift key down, click on the diagonal cell. The entire range will be selected.

1. Using the horizontal scroll bar, bring cell O14 into view.
2. While holding down the Shift key, click on cell O14.
   ➤ *The range of cells from A1 to O14 is highlighted by a marquee box and the dialog box refers to '2003 Sales'!$A$1:$O$14.*
3. Click the Return button at the end of the Define Name – Refers to text box. 🔁
   ➤ *The Define Name dialog box appears and the range name Print_Area refers to cells A1:O14 as shown in figure 2.9.*
4. Click the OK button.
   ➤ *The dialog box closes and the marquee box disappears.*
5. Save the workbook.

Before you can test your work, the PrintYTD procedure must be modified to reference the Print_Area range name as shown in figure 2.10. Once this edit is completed, add a new row and then print. If the printout includes the totals row, delete the new row and print again. These tests will determine if the range name is updating as the worksheet is expanded and reduced.

1. Open the Visual Basic Editor.
2. Modify the PrintYTD procedure as follows (see figure 2.10):
   Change Range("A1:O14").Select to Range("**Print_Area**").Select

```
Public Sub PrintYTD()
'
'Procedure to print Year To Day Sales report
'Prepared mm/dd/yy by Your Name
'
    Range("Print_Area").Select
    With ActiveSheet.PageSetup
        .Orientation = xlLandscape
        .FitToPagesWide = 1
        .FitToPagesTall = 1
    End With
    Selection.PrintOut Copies:=1
    Range("a1").Select

End Sub
```

FIGURE 2.10 Using a Range Name in the PrintYTD Macro

3. Return to Excel.
4. Insert a new row and then print.
5. Delete the inserted row and then print.
6. If the printouts are correct, save the workbook, otherwise debug, retest, and then save.

EMBEDDED CONTROL OBJECTS

Using the Macro dialog box is cumbersome. Keyboard alternatives, though efficient, are not intuitive and need to be documented for the user. ActiveX controls provide an easy to use tool for running macros or procedures. By adding a command button to the 2003 Sales worksheet, it provides the user with a quick and intuitive way to insert a new row in the 2003 Sales worksheet. Once in place, this **control object** (graphical feature that contains properties, methods, and events) can be coded to respond to a mouse action controlled by the user.

An **ActiveX control** is a Microsoft sponsored graphic object, such as a command button or check box, which is placed in a document, worksheet, slide show, form, or report to activate a software resource. Figure 2.12 shows the command button you are going to add to the 2003 Sales worksheet. Visual tools, like buttons or boxes, enhance user interaction because they are universally recognized and easy to use. Each control responds to a large variety of user-generated actions, called **events**, such as a mouse click or double click. Controls allow users to change object properties or run a macro that automates a task.

Inserting an ActiveX Control

The ActiveX control objects available to an Office Application can be found in the Control Toolbox. This Toolbox is activated from the <u>V</u>iew menu, at the Toolbars side menu and displays as in figure 2.11.

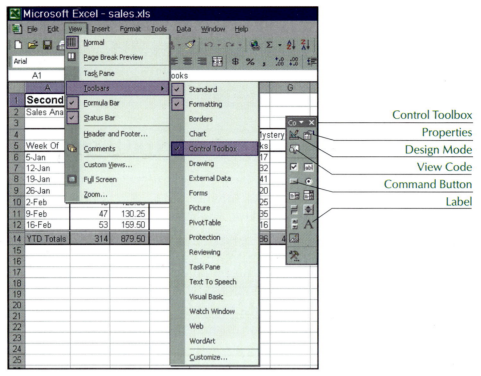

FIGURE 2.11 Control Object Toolbox

1. Activate the Excel window.
2. Click <u>V</u>iew, point to <u>T</u>oolbars, and then click Control Toolbox.
   ➤ *The Control Toolbox toolbar opens (see figure 2.11).*

The Control Toolbox has three critical buttons—Design Mode, Properties, and View Code—all of which are labeled in figure 2.11. Controls can be added, deleted, and modified only when the Design mode is active. Controls respond to the user only when the Design mode is not active.

TIP

You can remove the Exit Design Mode button by clicking on the associated close button. When it is closed, the Design Mode button in the Control Toolbox acts as a toggle.

3. Click the Design Mode button.
   ➤ *The Exit Design Mode button (see figure 2.12) appears, indicating the mode is active.*
4. Click the Command button in the Toolbox.
   ➤ *The screen pointer changes to a crosshair pointer.*
5. Position the crosshair pointer in the upper left corner of cell E1 and then click.
   ➤ *CommandButton1, of default size, is embedded into the Sales worksheet. Note the entry in the Formula bar as shown in figure 2.12.*

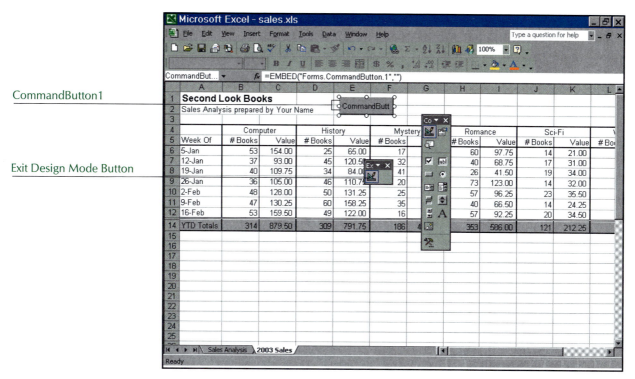

FIGURE 2.12 Command Button Embedded in the Sales Worksheet

Setting Object Properties

Every control object has a comprehensive set of properties that can be set with code or from the Properties window. In chapter 1, you set the bold property of a text object with the InsertLogo macro. This property was set at **Run mode**, meaning that it was set when the macro's code was executed. The **Property window** is a comprehensive list of an object's properties that can be set at design time; it provides a second way to view and/or set properties. **Design mode** is when controls are added to the worksheet or other objects. Embedded ActiveX objects cannot execute code when the design mode is active.

1. Click CommandButton1.
   ➤ *Sizing handles appear and the embedded object is referenced in the Formula bar.*
2. Click the Properties button located in the Toolbox (see figure 2.11).
   ➤ *The Properties window opens.*
3. Select the Categorized tab.
   ➤ *The Properties window looks similar to figure 2.13.*

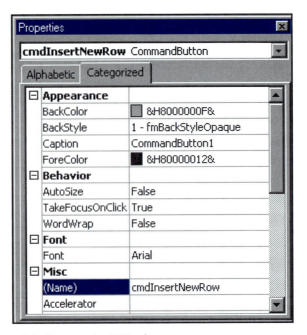

FIGURE 2.13 **Properties Window**

In the Properties window, the option box at the top of the window contains a list of all objects in the active worksheet. The list box below it provides access to all the design time properties and displays their current settings. The two tabs, Alphabetic and Categorized, are alternative display formats for the properties list. Alphabetic is an A-Z listing of the properties while Categorized organizes the properties into logical classifications such as Appearance, Behavior, Font, and so on. For the beginning VBA programmer, using the categorized list is suggested.

NAME PROPERTY

A control is referenced by its name property. Changing the name property to be more descriptive is good programming practice. Typically, the customized name starts with a three-letter tag (see figure 2.14) that identifies the control type followed by a word or words that describe its action. Spaces are not allowed in object names. If a sub procedure is coded for an event the control recognizes, Visual Basic uses the name property and event as the procedure name. If you are going to change a control name, it is important to make the change before assigning any code to the control. Changing a control's name property after the code is assigned will cause the control to loose its reference to the code.

Next, you will change the Command button's name to cmdInsertNewRow and then code its click event. Visual Basic will assign this procedure the name cmdInsertNewRow_Click.

Tag	Control	Tag	Control
cbo	Combo Box	lst	List Box
chk	Check Box	opt	Option Button
cmd	Command Button	scr	Scroll Bar
img	Image Box	spn	Spin Button
lbl	Label	txt	Text Box

FIGURE 2.14 Typical Tags for Controls

1. Select CommandButton1 in the option box in the Properties window.
   ➤ *The Property window resembles figure 2.13.*
2. In the Misc section, delete the (Name) property setting, CommandButton1, found in the right column.
3. Key **cmdInsertNewRow**.
   ➤ *The command button (Name) displays cmdInsertNewRow.*

CAPTION PROPERTY

The caption property of a control is the label or description that appears on the control itself. The default setting of the caption typically provides the programmer with two pieces of information. The first part of the caption identifies the type of control followed by a number that makes the caption unique from any other controls of the same type. The command button you just placed in the worksheet has the default caption CommandButton1. If a second command button were added, it would have the default caption CommandButton2. It is vital that the caption property be changed to something that makes the control's function clear to the user.

TIP

If the new caption does not fit in the command button, drag the sizing handles to widen the button until the caption fits.

1. In the Appearance section, delete the Caption property setting, CommandButton1, found in the right column.
2. Key **Insert New Row**.
   ➤ *The command button caption now displays Insert New Row.*

ACCELERATOR PROPERTY

The accelerator property is used to assign a keyboard alternative to a control. Keying the letter *i* as the value of the accelerator property activates the command button from the keyboard by pressing Alt + i. Furthermore, if the selected letter for the accelerator key is present in the caption, it is underlined in the way Windows traditionally identifies alternative keys options.

1. In the Misc section, key **i** in the empty Accelerator text box, located under the Misc category.
2. Save the workbook.

CODING ACTIVEX CONTROL OBJECT EVENTS

The presence of the Insert New Row button provides users with an easy and intuitive way to prepare the worksheet for the addition of new sales data. All they need to do is click on the button with their mouse. This command button, like every other object, has a predefined set of events that it can detect, such as a single or double mouse click. By coding a sub procedure for any or all of these events, we can assign actions the user can execute. As mentioned earlier, you will code the cmdInsertNewRow command button's click event. This procedure must reside in the module where the associated control is located. Since the only place the user can click on this button is in the 2003 Sales worksheet, the sub procedure is private and therefore will not appear in the Macros dialog box. Procedures fall into two classifications, public and private. A **public procedure** can be executed from any module in the application. **Private procedures**, on the other hand, can only be executed from the module in which they reside.

There are two ways to code the Insert New Row button to prepare the worksheet for new data. One option would be to relocate the code you wrote for the InsertNewRow procedure in Module1 into the button's click event procedure. Because the InsertNewRow procedure is public, the other option is to execute it from the Sheet1 (2003 Sales) module. Keeping the InsertNewRow procedure public and simply coding the command button to access it is a better approach. If the print code were moved from its public procedure to the command button's private event procedure, future access to the code from other modules would not be possible.

Call Statement

Executing one procedure from another is a common programming practice. If the procedure is private, then only the procedures within the same module have access to it. But if it is public, like the InsertNewRow procedure in Module1, it can be run from any module in the project. A Call statement is used to run one procedure from another. Therefore the code Call InsertNewRow can be used from anywhere in the workbook to run the procedure. Though the keyword Call is optional, its presence clarifies the action being taken.

1. If the Insert New Row command button is not selected, select it now.
   ➤ *Handles appear around the command button.*
2. Click the View Code button in the Control Toolbox.
   ➤ *The Code window opens similar to figure 2.15.*

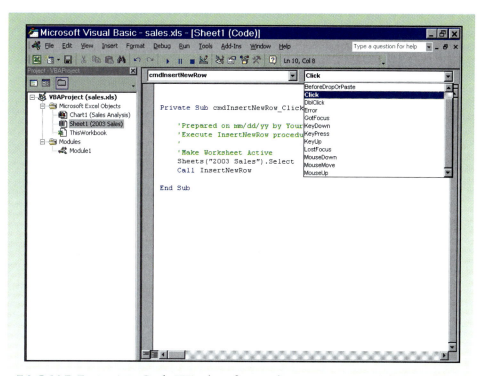

FIGURE 2.15 Code Window for cmdInsertNewRow_Click Event

Using figure 2.15 as a reference, note that the open code window is for Sheet1 (2003 Sales) where the control object resides. The Code window's left combo box provides a list of all objects in the Sales worksheet, while the right one contains a list of all the events the object can recognize.

3. Click the down-pointing triangle next to the event box.
   ➤ *The list of events the command button recognizes opens as shown in figure 2.15.*

Any listed event displayed in bold type has an associated procedure. Currently, none of the events are in bold. The code for the command button's Click event, seen in figure 2.15, executes a call to the public InsertNewRow procedure located in Module1.

4. Close the list of events by selecting *Click* from the drop-down menu.

Notice that VBA automatically defines the procedure as private to the worksheet module.

5. Key the following remarks and code under
   Private Sub cmdInsertNewRow_Click().
   ➤ *The code resembles figure 2.15.*
   'Prepared on mm/dd/yy by Your Name
   'Execute InsertNewRow procedure in Module1
   '
   'Make Worksheet Active Sheets ("2003 Sales").Select
   Call InsertNewRow
6. Activate the Excel window.

The command button will not respond to any of the events it recognizes while the design mode is active. To return to the run mode, click the same button in the Control Toolbox you did to activate the Design mode. The function of this button toggles between Design Mode and Exit Design Mode. This button is only available in two locations, the Visual Basic Button Bar and the Control Toolbox.

TIP

If you have closed the Exit Design Mode tool-bar, click the Design Mode button in the Control Toolbox.

TIP

If the control button does not work as expected, make sure you have coded the Click event and that the Design Mode is not active. Then recheck code against figure 2.15 and retest.

1. Click on the Exit Design Mode button to toggle to Run Time.
   ➤ *The Exit Design Mode toolbar disappears.*
2. Close the Control Toolbox by clicking the close button in its Title bar.
3. Save the workbook.
4. Click on the Insert New Row command button.
   ➤ *A new row for the week of February 23 sales data is added.*
5. Print a copy of the worksheet with the newly added row using the PrintYTD macro.
   ➤ *A copy of the Sales Analysis prints.*

PrintObject Property

Take a close look at the Sales Analysis worksheet you just printed. The presence of the Insert New Row button on the printout detracts from its professional appearance. Setting the control's PrintObject property to False can easily solve this problem.

1. Activate the Design Mode.
2. Set the Insert New Row command button PrintObject property to False.
3. Print a copy of the worksheet with the newly added row.
   ➤ *A copy of the Sales Analysis prints without the command button.*

REVIEW QUESTIONS

On a blank sheet of paper provide a short answer for the following questions.

1. Define the key terms.
2. What resource does VBA use to communicate with other software applications?
3. Where is all the code associated with an Excel workbook stored?
4. How do you display the objects and modules associated with an Excel workbook or Word document?
5. What arguments are required by the Offset property?
6. How can the current position of the cell pointer be referenced?
7. Describe the difference between a macro and a sub procedure.
8. When are With structures typically used?
9. How do range names benefit the Excel/VBA programmer?
10. What advantages do visual tools like command buttons provide?
11. Where do you find an application's ActiveX controls?
12. Identify the resource that provides a comprehensive list of design mode properties.
13. How does run mode differ from design mode?
14. What property is used to assign a keyboard alternative to a control?
15. What tags are used with customized control names?
16. Why are the event procedures of controls placed on a worksheet always private procedures?
17. What term is used to describe code that is designed to be global and independent?
18. Identify the statement used to execute one procedure from another.

CHECK YOUR UNDERSTANDING

Indicate the correct term or choose the correct answer for each item.

1. Controls can be added to a worksheet when the _Design_ mode is active.
2. Click and double-click are both user-initiated _event_'s.
3. A user-defined _range_ name can be assigned to a single cell or group of cells.
4. _ActiveX_ are Microsoft sponsored graphic controls.
5. The _Call_ statement is used to execute one procedure from another.
6. Which of the following is *not* a common tag for customized control names?
   a. obj
   b. txt
   c. cmd
   d. chk
7. What object identifies the current worksheet position of the cell pointer?
   a. CellPos
   b. Locate
   c. RCPosition
   d. ActiveCell

8. Property values are set at design time using the
   a. Property Explorer.
   b. Property window.
   c. Property toolbar.
   d. Property dialog box.
9. What type of procedure does *not* accept or return data?
   a. Macro
   b. Sub
   c. Function
   d. RunTime
10. Which if the following is an example of a control object?
   a. Bold
   b. Margin
   c. Button
   d. Page number

EXERCISES

Complete the following exercises.

Last Step

Add a command button to provide the user a quick way to print a copy of the 2003 Sales worksheet.
1. Locate the button to the right of the Insert New Row button.
2. Set the following properties:

(Name)	cmdPrintYTD
Caption	Print Sales Data
Accelerator	p
PrintObject	False

3. Save the workbook.

Debug

Second Look Books' manager recorded the following macro to print the chart in the Sales Analysis Sheet and added a Print Sales Analysis button to the 2003 Sales worksheet. The button's click event correctly calls the PrintSalesChart macro but then prints a copy of the 2003 Sales worksheet. How would you edit the macro, rather than moving the button, so that it will print the Sales Analysis chart?

```
Sub PrintSalesChart()
'
'PrintSalesChart Macro
'Macro recorded mm/dd/yy by Store Manager
'

'
ActiveWindow.SelectedSheets.PrintOut Copies:=1, Collate:=True
End Sub
```

Internet

Go to the Microsoft Developer Network (MSDN) library Web site found at
http://msdn.microsoft.com/library. Using the site's navigation and search tools,
locate new methods associated with Excel 2002. This information is often associated with Office Solutions Development for Office XP and the associated
VBA Language Reference. Print the new methods by object.

New Challenge

To better understand the customers of Second Look Books it would be advanta-
geous to expand the Sales 2003 worksheet to include the average price of each
book purchased. This information can be easily calculated in column P by
dividing the total value of the books sold in a week (column O) by the number
of books sold in that week (column N). For the first week the formula would
be "=O6/N6". Once the formula is entered in cell P6 the cell should be formatted as Number showing 2 decimal places. Next extend the formula to all the
existing weeks and YTD Totals. Don't forget to add an appropriate column
header.

Once you have added this column of information to the worksheet, modify
the InsertNewRow procedure so it will also update column P each time a new
week is added. Do not be alarmed by the fact that the formula will produce a
division by zero result in the cell (#DIV/O!). This will go away as soon as some
sales data is entered into the new row. You will also need to update the
Print_Area range name to include the added column.

Discussion

It takes a lot of time and effort to create and debug even simple macros and sub
procedures. Describe a situation where you think it is worth it to develop new
VBA code. Include in your answer a description of the user and the type of
application that is involved.

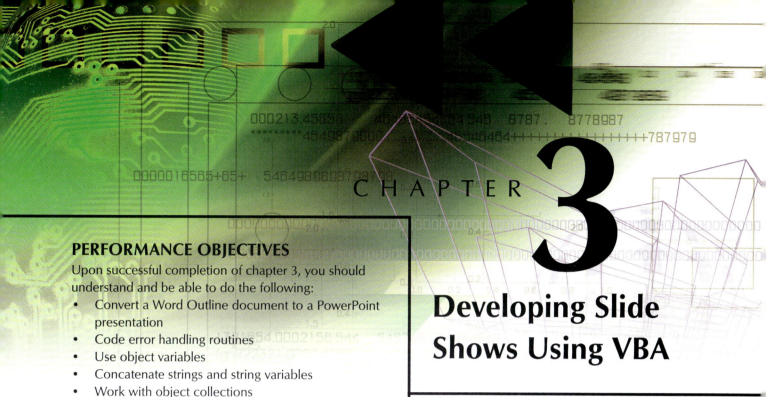

Developing Slide Shows Using VBA

PERFORMANCE OBJECTIVES

Upon successful completion of chapter 3, you should understand and be able to do the following:
- Convert a Word Outline document to a PowerPoint presentation
- Code error handling routines
- Use object variables
- Concatenate strings and string variables
- Work with object collections
- Write code to modify PowerPoint slide format
- Change PowerPoint slide design using VBA
- Import and use a UserForm

Microsoft PowerPoint is by far the most widely used presentation software. A PowerPoint user can easily develop a professional quality slide show for on screen or Web presentation, notes, handouts, and even 35mm slides. These presentations usually contain a mix of text and images plus audio and video clips. Once developed, these slide shows can be used to support a lecture, sales pitch, or specific promotion to a target audience. Second Look Books (SLB) is currently in the process of preparing a PowerPoint presentation to promote franchise opportunities to potential new retail and e-tail (electronic retail using the Internet) bookstore owners.

Like Word and Excel, PowerPoint has a macro recorder and access to the Visual Basic Editor and VBA object libraries. Unlike these other Office applications, macros and VBA procedures with PowerPoint do not create day-in day-out software tools for businesses. PowerPoint utilizes VBA as a development tool for individuals to use as they prepare presentations. It is not used to create macros that presenters will run while making PowerPoint presentations in front of an audience. Therefore, the VBA resources in PowerPoint do not require the broad range of objects and properties found in Word or Excel.

A PowerPoint presentation is similar in many ways to a report you prepare about a specific issue. The primary difference is that the PowerPoint presentation becomes a sequential presentation consisting of the key points, facts, and considerations. As with any report, the process starts with an outline. Microsoft Word has an Outline view specifically intended for this task as shown in figure 3.1. Once the outline is completed using Word, PowerPoint is able to convert it into a slide show presentation. Each first level heading from the outline provides information needed to create a slide containing the data subordinate to that heading.

Second Look Books' franchise marketing team has just finished an outline (see figure 3.1) to promote the organization's three franchise opportunities in retail, e-tail, or both. Your task will be to develop a VBA procedure that further enhances the productivity of this conversion from a Word outline into a PowerPoint presentation. The procedure should prompt the developer for the filename of the outline to convert and then automatically open the specified outline file into a blank presentation, after which the developer will be prompted to enter a presenter's name and select a slide design approved for SLB's presentations.

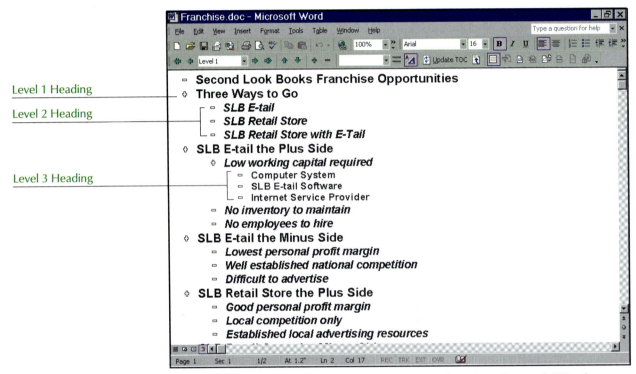

FIGURE 3.1 Franchise Presentation Outline in Microsoft Word

FILE ORGANIZATION

A logical, well thought out file organization always makes a programmer's work easier. In this case, all presentations and their supporting files will be stored in a folder called SLBpresentations. Supporting files include the Word Outline files developed for conversion into a presentation, slide design templates approved for use by Second Look Books, and a predeveloped UserForm for use as a custom dialog box.

Any document created by an Office application maintains a path property that retains a reference to the document's default drive and path. This reference is established when a file is either opened or saved. By keeping all files in the SLBpresentations folder, you are able to create, import, export, and apply resources to your project without ever having to identify a drive/path reference. As a result, any time Windows is not told where to look for or save a file it uses the path property's default path and drive designation.

1. Open Windows Explorer.
2. Locate and display the contents of the SLBpresentations folder that you downloaded to your student data disk (see figure 3.2).
   ▶ *Contents include: 4 PowerPoint template files, 1 Word document, 2 Visual Basic form files, and SLB's logo.*

Folder Contents

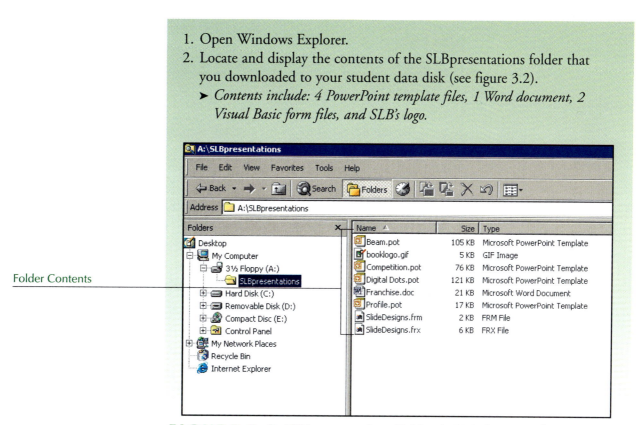

FIGURE 3.2 SLBpresentations Folder in Windows Explorer

You may relocate or copy this folder to any location on your data disk or to other disks provided you move or copy the folder in its entirety. This is as simple as clicking on the SLBpresentations folder and dragging it wherever you desire. But remember, keeping it on a floppy or Zip disk makes it portable.

3. Open Word.
4. Open the Franchise outline document found in the SLBpresentations folder.
   ▶ *Franchise.doc opens similar to figure 3.1.*

Subordinate heading levels in an outline, Heading 2 and Heading 3, are established by moving desired text to the second or third tab stop. When you scroll to the end of the document you will notice that the Retail Store with E-trade franchise options do not have subordinate headings.

CREATING A PRESENTATION

Since PowerPoint does not have a public resource area such as Word's Normal.dot or Excel's PERSONAL Workbook, you will need to create a blank presentation to store your VBA procedures. Once completed, you will use this presentation to create new presentations from Word Outline files.

1. Open PowerPoint.
   ➤ *PowerPoint opens with a default presentation.*
2. From the New Presentations Task Pane, click *Blank Presentation* in the New section.
   ➤ *The New Presentation Task Pane closes and the Slide Layout Task Pane opens as seen in figure 3.3.*
3. Select the Blank layout from the Current Layouts section.
   ➤ *The current slide changes to a Blank layout.*
4. Click File and then Save As.
   ➤ *The Save As dialog box opens.*
5. Save the presentation to the SLBpresentations folder and name it outline-to-ppt.

TIP

Watch for the tool tip that appears to identify the Blank layout when you hold the mouse pointer over a layout image as shown in figure 3.3.

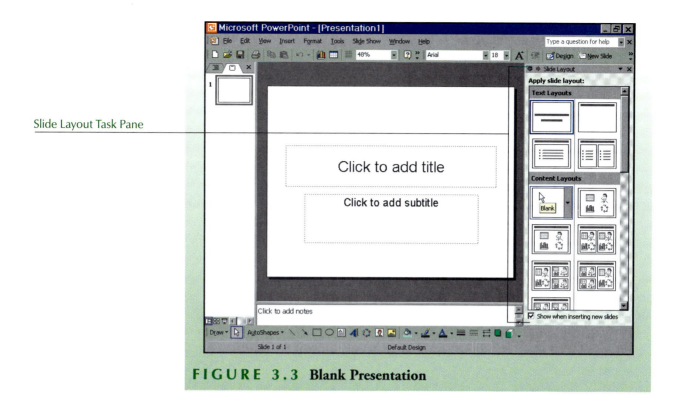

Slide Layout Task Pane

FIGURE 3.3 Blank Presentation

CODE MODULES

Modules are VBA's containers for macros and other procedures that are not associated with any specific object. In chapter 2 the InsertNewRow and PrintYTD macros were in a module, while the command button's click event procedures were in the Sheet 1 (2003 Sales) object. The command buttons were physically located on the worksheet and the click events you coded were specific to each button. However, the InsertNewRow and PrintYTD macros were not attached to any specific object. Any time you record a macro, VBA inserts the macro code into a Public procedure in a module. If a module exists, VBA will either add procedures to it or create a new module for the procedure.

The keyword Public in a procedure that does not receive data defines the procedure as a macro. The keyword Private defines a procedure that is not viewed as a macro. Thus a Private procedure would not appear in the Macros dialog box, preventing it from being executed directly from the application. Since you are starting from scratch with a new presentation and will be coding rather than recording the VBA code, you must manually insert a module (see figure 3.4). Once the module is present you can then insert a procedure in a manner similar to the way you inserted the PrintYTD procedure in chapter 2.

1. Click Tools, point to Macro, and then click Visual Basic Editor.
   ➤ *The Visual Basic Editor opens.*
2. In the Editor, click Insert and then Module.
   ➤ *Module1 is inserted (see the Project window of figure 3.4) and its code window is opened.*

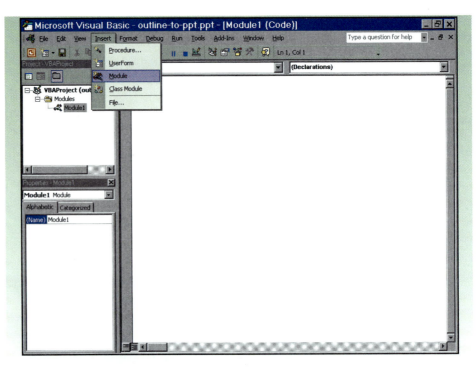

FIGURE 3.4 VB Editor Window with New Module

Now that a module has been inserted into the project you can insert a procedure into the module.

3. Click Insert and then Procedure.
   ➤ *The Add Procedure dialog box opens.*
4. Confirm that the Sub and Public option buttons are selected as seen in figure 3.5.
5. In the Name text box, key **PPTpresentation** and then click OK.
   ➤ *The dialog box closes and the procedure's Sub and End Sub statements are entered into the Code window.*

FIGURE 3.5 Add Procedure Dialog Box

ERROR HANDLING

Before any VBA procedure is put into regular use it must be free of all syntax and logic errors. Despite this, the need for error handling of unexpected actions caused by the user must be considered. In the PowerPoint presentation procedure, you are preparing to convert Word outline files to a PowerPoint presentation. The user will be expected to enter the filename of the desired outline file. If they misspell the filename, the procedure will attempt to open a file that does not exist. This action would generate a runtime error that may halt (crash) your code. Other unexpected errors, such as referencing an open file or a file type that cannot be converted to a slide presentation, might not crash the code but could result in unpredictable outcomes.

To deal with these problems, use the built-in error handling resources of VBA. These error-handling features allow VBA to intercept errors so you can code corrective actions. Programmers call this process of intercepting errors **error trapping**. Incorporating error handling into a procedure is a three-step process. First, VBA error trapping resources must be enabled. Second, a specific location in the procedure must be identified as the point where code execution is transferred if an error is intercepted. Finally, code must be written to respond to the error. Error trapping only applies to the procedure in which it is contained and is disabled when the procedure ends.

Activating Error Handling

The On Error GoTo label statement enables error handling and identifies, via a specific label, the location to branch to when an error is trapped. **Labels** are identifiable markers that can be included in a procedure. The label can be any word or words immediately followed by a colon (:) such as Error_Handler:.

1. Key the following code between the Public Sub PPTpresentation() and End Sub statements.

```
'

'Open Word Outline macro
'Prepared mm/dd/yy by Your Name
'

{blank line}
'Setup error trap
On Error GoTo Error_Handler
```

The handling of an error might simply require alerting the user of the problem. On the other hand, as you will see in chapter 5, it can include error identification and management. VBA has an error object "Err" that enables you to identify the number and description of the error that occurred. The error object's description and number properties provide this information. The description property provides a short description of the problem. In PowerPoint when a specified file cannot be found, is currently open in another application, or is of the wrong type, Err.Description will return the message "PowerPoint could not open the file." The object's number property returns the unique number assigned to this error (-2147467259). The number property is used for error identification in error handlers that attempt to correct the problem.

Prior to the label that identifies where the error handling code resides, there must be an Exit Sub statement. Without this statement execution would fall into the error handling code even when no error occur.

2. Enter one blank line and then key the following code:
   {blank line}
   'CODE CONTINUATION
   {blank line}
   'Exit procedure so error code does not execute
   Exit Sub
   {blank line}
   Error_Handler:
   'Present message box with error description
   MsgBox Err.Description
3. Save the presentation and check your code against figure 3.6.

PITFALL

Failure to include the colon at the end of a label will result in an error.

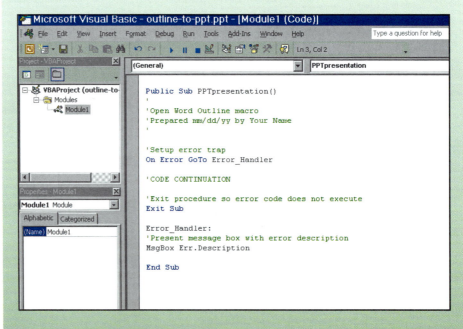

FIGURE 3.6 Visual Basic Editor with Error Handling Code

INPUTTING THE OUTLINE FILENAME

Inputting the Word Outline filename will require a string variable and an input box. Once the user responds to the input box you can test the variable. If the user failed to enter a filename or clicked the Cancel button, the variable will be assigned an empty string. **Empty strings**, sometimes referred to as zero length strings, contain nothing and can be tested for with two quotation marks with nothing between them (""). On the other hand, if the variable is not empty it will be assumed to contain a filename. Before this name can be used to open a file, the appropriate file extension (.doc) must be added to the name. Since we are going to construct the filename, a second string variable used strictly to identify the file extension is advisable.

1. Position the insertion point in the blank line above the CODE CON-TINUATION remark.
2. Key the following code:

```
{blank line}
'Declare variables
Dim strUserResponse As String
Dim strFileName As String
{blank line}
'Prompt for Outline filename
strUserResponse = InputBox("Enter the MS Word Outline
filename.", "File Specification")
{blank line}
'Check for Cancel request
If strUserResponse = "" Then
        Exit Sub
Else
```

CONCATENATION

Concatenation is the combining of two independent strings of text into one. The expression *strFileSpecification = "A:\SLBpresentations\"& "franchise.doc"* combines two literal strings to produce a complete file location and name specification which is then assigned to a string variable. The ampersand (&) is the concatenation operator. Concatenation can connect literal strings to other literal strings or to the text contained in a string variable. You will use this text manipulation technique to construct a complete file specification for the outline filename provided by the user.

PITFALL

When coding concatenation statements, you must include a space before and after the ampersand (&) or VBA will not recognize it as the concatenation operator.

1. Position the insertion point in the blank line above the CODE CON-TINUATION remark.
2. Key the following code:

```
        'Construct the filename
        strFileName = strUserResponse & ".doc"
End If
{blank line}
{blank line}
```

USING OBJECT VARIABLES

If you reference an object more than once in a procedure it is advisable to set a variable name that points to the object. Using a variable name to reference an object is easier to write and understand, plus it is considerably more efficient. An **object variable**, like any other user declared variable, is a named memory location that contains data. In the case of the object variable, the stored data is a reference to the memory location of the specified object. Using an object variable name to reference an object allows VBA to go directly to the object rather than search the computer's memory for the object each time it is used in the code.

As with standard variables, an object variable is declared with a Dim statement and must be assigned an object type. The following declaration statements would declare a PowerPoint application and presentation object variable:

    Dim appPPT As PowerPoint.Application
    Dim prsWordOutline As PowerPoint.Presentation

The naming conventions for object variables also use tags for easy identification of the variable type. Some common objects tags and data types are shown in figure 3.7.

Tag	Data Type	Application
app	Application	PowerPoint (or Word or Excel)
prs	Presentation	PowerPoint
sld	Slide	PowerPoint
wkb	Workbook	Excel
sht	Worksheet	Excel
doc	Document	Word
par	Paragraph	Word

FIGURE 3.7 Typical Object Variable Tags and Corresponding Data Types

Declaring and Assigning Object Variables

In this procedure you will need to reference the PowerPoint application four times. Therefore, an object variable set to the application object will be useful. Once the object variable has been declared, use the Set statement and the CreateObject function to establish a PowerPoint object that is assigned to the variable name.

1. Add the following Dim statement below the other Dim statement near the top of the procedure:
   Dim appPPT As PowerPoint.Application

Object assignment is similar to the variable assignments you made in the earlier chapters but requires the use of the key word Set.

2. Position the insertion point in the blank line above the CODE CONTINUATION remark and enter the following code:
   'Assign an application object variable
   Set appPPT = CreateObject("PowerPoint.Application")
   Set appPPT = PowerPoint.Application
   {blank line}
   {blank line}

Now the object variable has been assigned the memory address of the PowerPoint application and is able to go directly to it rather than searching for its location each time it is referenced. Before exiting the procedure, good programming practice dictates that you release the reference to the object variable by assigning it to the Visual Basic reserve word Nothing.

3. Insert the following code before the Exit Sub statement:
   Set appPPT = Nothing

Opening the Outline File and Setting the Window View

The PowerPoint object variable can now be used to open the Word Outline file in a PowerPoint presentation using the object's Open method. When PowerPoint opens a Word outline file into a presentation, the PowerPoint display defaults to the Handout Master view. Unfortunately, slide layouts and objects cannot be manipulated from this view so you will need to set the view back to Normal before continuing.

1. Position the insertion point in the blank line *above* the CODE CONTINUATION remark. Enter the code to open the file indicated by the user and set the view to normal.
   'Open the designated Outline file and set view to normal
   appPPT.Presentations.Open (strFileName)
   appPPT.ActiveWindow.ViewType = ppViewNormal
   {blank line}
   {blank line}
2. Save your work.
3. Check your work against figure 3.8.

```
Public Sub PPTpresentation()
'
'Open Word Outline macro
'Prepared mm/dd/yy by Your Name
'

'Setup error trap
On Error GoTo Error_Handler

'Declare variables
Dim strUserResponse As String
Dim strFileName As String
Dim appPPT As PowerPoint.Application

'Prompt for Outline filename
strUserResponse = InputBox("Enter the MS Word Outline filename.", "File Specification")

'Check for Cancel request
If strUserResponse = "" Then
    Exit Sub
Else
    'Construct the filename
    strFileName = strUserResponse & ".doc"
End If

'Assign an application object variable
Set appPPT = CreateObject("PowerPoint.Application")

'Open the designated Outline file and set view to normal
appPPT.Presentations.Open (strFileName)
appPPT.ActiveWindow.ViewType = ppViewNormal

'CODE CONTINUATION

'Exit procedure so error code does not execute
Set appPPT = Nothing
Exit Sub

Error_Handler:
'Present message box with error description
MsgBox Err.Description

End Sub
```

FIGURE 3.8 PPTpresentation Sub Procedure

4. Using the Visual Basic Editor, click <u>T</u>ools and then <u>M</u>acros.
   ➤ *The Macros dialog box open as seen in figure 3.9.*
5. With the PPTpresentation macro selected, click the <u>R</u>un button.
   ➤ *File Specification Input Box opens similar to figure 3.9.*

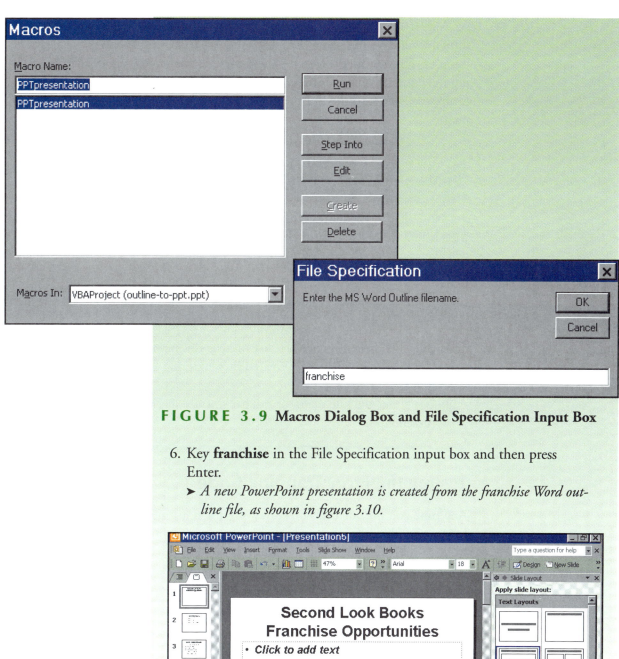

FIGURE 3.9 Macros Dialog Box and File Specification Input Box

6. Key **franchise** in the File Specification input box and then press Enter.

   ➤ *A new PowerPoint presentation is created from the franchise Word outline file, as shown in figure 3.10.*

FIGURE 3.10 Presentation Created from the Franchise Outline

When a new presentation is created, it becomes the active presentation and initially will have the name Presentation#, where # is a sequentially generated number. This number represents the number of new presentations created during the current PowerPoint session. If you wish to store the presentation for future use, save it to the SLBpresentations folder and assign a more descriptive name.

> 7. If a new presentation is not created from the franchise outline file or if any errors occurred, check your code against figure 3.8 for mistakes.

Note that the default, Blank slide layout, has been applied to all the slides. This is fine for Slide(2) through Slide(8). However, Slide(1) of the collection will eventually need to be changed to a Title slide layout.

Next Step 3-2

At this time there is no need to save or keep this newly created presentation.
1. Confirm that your newly created Presentation# is the active presentation.
2. Use either the File menu or taskbar to close it. DO NOT save this presentation.

Testing the Error Trapping Code

Any time you include cancel features or error traps they must be tested. Only by running the procedure and selecting the cancel option can you confirm that it does in fact terminate the procedure without any action being taken. Furthermore, nonexistent outline filenames must be entered in order to confirm that the error trapping code functions correctly and appropriately responds to the error.

1. If outline-to-ppt is not the active presentation, click on the outline-to-ppt button on the taskbar.
   ➤ *The outline-to-ppt presentation becomes the active presentation.*
2. Open the Macro dialog box by pressing Alt + F8.
   ➤ *Macro dialog box opens.*

3. Run the PPTpresentation macro and when the File Specification Input Box opens, misspell the outline filename by keying **franchis**.
   ➤ *The error trap intercepts the error and returns the message box in figure 3.11.*
4. Click OK in the message box.
   ➤ *The procedure terminates without opening a new presentation.*

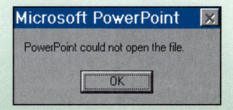

FIGURE 3.11 **Error Message Generated by the Error Handler Code**

Next Step 3-3

Run the PPTpresentation macro and when the File Specification Input Box opens, click the Cancel button to confirm that a new presentation is not opened. If the macro does not terminate without creating a new presentation, debug your code and try again.

COLLECTIONS

Each PowerPoint presentation, Word document, and Excel workbook you develop consists of a number of similar objects. For example, every document you open in Word becomes one of the application's current set of open documents. Furthermore, each paragraph in a document is one of that document's set of paragraphs. It is through these sets of objects that VBA is able to identify and manipulate the properties of specific elements.

PowerPoint presentations and the slides they contain offer an excellent opportunity to develop a better understanding of object programming and collections. A **collection** is a set of similar objects. As with Word and Excel, PowerPoint can have a number of presentations open. The three you see in figure 3.12 would be the current collection of presentations. Each presentation can be referenced by its index value or name. Individual presentations, like the active one in figure 3.12, contain a collection of slides. They also are referenced by index or name. Furthermore each individual slide contains a collection of shapes that consist of all the elements on the slide. In figure 3.12 the title would be Shapes(1) and the subtitle would be Shapes(2).

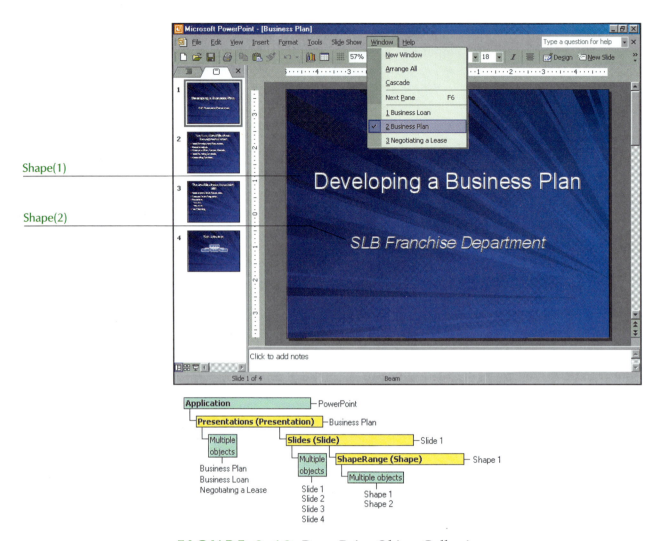

FIGURE 3.12 PowerPoint Object Collections

Manipulating the Objects in a Shape Collection

The final tasks needed to complete the PPTpresentation procedure are as follows:
- Prompt and input the presenter's name.
- Change the layout of the first slide to a Title design.
- Enter the presenter's name in the Title slide's subtitle.
- Apply the SLB default graphic design to all the slides in the presentation.

Using an input box to acquire the presenter's name provides an opportunity to customize the presentation. If the specific presenter is unknown or if a number of individuals might use the presentation then a generic subtitle, SLB Franchise Department, will be used in place of a presenter's name. The application object (appPPT) can manipulate related objects (SlideRange or TextFrame) and properties (Selection or Layout) needed to convert the first slide into a custom Title slide. Applying a Title layout to the first slide establishes both a title and subtitle text area. The first Heading1 entry from the outline (*Second Look Book Franchise Opportunities* as shown in figure 3.1) provides Slide(1) with a title and the user will input the data for the subtitle.

1. Switch to the Visual Basic Editor and the code in the PPTpresentation macro.
2. Position the insertion point in the blank line above the CODE CONTINUATION remark. Continue coding the PPTpresentation procedure as follows under the code that assigns the active PowerPoint window to the Normal view (ppViewNormal):

```
'Prompt for presenter name
strUserResponse = InputBox("Enter presenter's name or leave blank for default.", "Presenter")
{blank line}
'If no presenter, name is assigned a default entry
If strUserResponse = "" Then
        strUserResponse = "SLB Franchise Department"
End If
{blank line}
{blank line}
```

Once the presenter's name or the generic name *SLB Franchise Department* has been assigned to the strUserResponse variable you are ready to customize Slide(1). When a new presentation is created the first slide is always the current slide, which makes any additional slide selection code, in our case, unnecessary.

Setting the application object's ActiveWindow property to the current Selection object, Slide(1), in a With structure will greatly simplify the code. Then it is just a matter of assigning a layout, selecting the TextFrame in the title slide's second shape, and assigning its text property to the strUserResponse variable. Figure 3.13 defines the objects, properties, and methods that you will use in the With structure to customize the first slide.

appPPT	Object variable	Reference to the PowerPoint application
ActiveWindow	Property	References the current document window.
Selection	Property	References the object currently selected in the document window.
SlideRange	Object collection	Represents the slide selection.
Layout	Property	Sets a slides layout.
ppLayoutTitle	Intrinsic constant	Identifies a title slide.
Shapes	Property	Returns a specified element in a collection of shapes.
Select	Method	Acquires an object.
ShapeRange	Object	Represents all currently selected slide objects.
TextFrame	Object	Represents the text frame in the ShapeRange.
TextRange	Object	Contains the text attached to a TextFrame.
Text:	Parameter of TextRange	Assigns text to a frame.
vbCrLf	Intrinsic constant	Moves following text to the next line.

FIGURE 3.13 Objects, Properties, and Methods used in the With Structure

3. Position the insertion point in the blank line above the CODE CON-TINUATION remark. Continue coding the PPTpresentation proce-dure as follows:

```
'Change the first slide to a title slide and
'insert the presenter's name.
With appPPT.ActiveWindow.Selection
    .SlideRange.Layout = ppLayoutTitle
    .SlideRange.Shapes(2).Select
    .ShapeRange.TextFrame.TextRange.Select
    .TextRange.Text = "Presented by " & vbCrLf & strUserResponse
    .Unselect
End With
{blank line}
{blank line}
```

Applying a Design Template

The look of a presentation can significantly affect an audience's response to your message. Today, high quality graphic designs are an integral component of all good presentations. To accommodate the need for this resource, PowerPoint provides an array of professionally designed templates that can be applied to a presentation. To maintain a level of consistency Second Look Books' Marketing Team has selected a template to be used for all presentations. Standards of this nature are not uncommon in well-managed organizations.

One final line of code is needed to apply the design template called "Profile" to the presentation. Template files are saved with a *.pot* filename exten-sion. In order to retain the efficiency of Second Look Books' file organizational structure, a copy of the Profile.pot template is included in the SLBpresentations folder. By applying the template to the ActivePresentation object, all of the slides in the presentation will receive the graphic design.

1. Position the insertion point in the blank line above the CODE CON-TINUATION remark. Continue coding the PPTpresentation proce-dure after the End With statement as follows:

```
'Apply the SLB's default slide design
appPPT.ActivePresentation.ApplyTemplate FileName:="Profile.pot"
```
2. Delete the CODE CONTINUATION remark line.
3. Save your work.
4. Check your code against figure 3.14 and then return to the outline-to-ppt presentation.
5. Run the PPTpresentation macro procedure you just completed.
6. Use the franchise outline file.
7. Key **Your Name** as the presenter.

```
'Open the designated Outline file and set view to normal
appPPT.Presentations.Open (strFileName)
appPPT.ActiveWindow.ViewType = ppViewNormal

'Prompt for presenter name
strUserResponse = InputBox("Enter presenter's name or leave blank for default.", "Presenter")

'If no presenter, name is assigned a default entry
If strUserResponse = "" Then
    strUserResponse = "SLB Franchise Department"
End If

'Change the first slide to a title slide and
'insert the presenter's name.
With appPPT.ActiveWindow.Selection
    .SlideRange.Layout = ppLayoutTitle
    .SlideRange.Shapes(2).Select
    .ShapeRange.TextFrame.TextRange.Select
    .TextRange.Text = "Presented by " & vbCrLf & strUserResponse
    .Unselect
End With

'Apply the SLB's default slide design
appPPT.ActivePresentation.ApplyTemplate FileName:="Profile.pot"

'Exit procedure so error code does not execute
Exit Sub
```

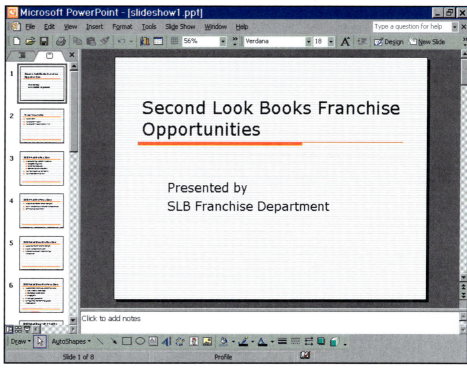

FIGURE 3.14 Slide Manipulation Code

If any errors occur, end the run and return to the VB Editor to debug your code. Do not forget to resave the project if you make any changes or corrections to the procedure.

8. If necessary, close the Slide Layout Task Pane found at the right side of the PowerPoint window.
9. Click File and then Save.
   ➤ *The Save As dialog box opens with the SLBpresentations folder selected and the first slide's title as the suggested filename.*

10. Name the file SlideShow1, select the SLBpresentations folder, and then click Save.
   ➤ *The file is written to disk.*
11. Close the SlideShow1 presentation.

Next Step 3-4

1. Create another copy of the franchise presentation using the generic presenter subtitle as shown at the bottom of figure 3.14.
2. Save this presentation as SlideShow1 informing PowerPoint to replace the previous version.
3. Close SlideShow1.

USERFORMS

UserForms are user created custom dialog boxes that can contain a wide variety of controls and procedures needed to accomplish different variations of a task. Second Look Books' marketing team has recently approved two additional slide design templates for use in presentations. Providing an input box from which to make a design selection would prevent the user from being able to preview each of the three designs before making a final decision. Therefore, a UserForm has been developed and coded to preview and select the approved design templates. Once created, user forms can be exported to a file, then imported into any VBA application for use. This feature allows you to develop a library of UserForms that can then be used in future VBA applications. In chapter 4 you will develop and code your own custom dialog box.

Importing a UserForm

A UserForm can be imported using the Import File option from the VB Editor's File menu. Selecting this option opens the Import File dialog box. From this dialog box, select the desired form and then click Open.

1. Use the taskbar to switch to the Visual Basic Editor if you are not already there.
2. Open the Editor's File menu then select Import File.
   ➤ *The Import File dialog box opens as seen in figure 3.15.*
3. Select the SlideDesigns UserForm and then click Open.
   ➤ *The UserForm named frmSlideDesigns is imported into the PPTpresentation project.*

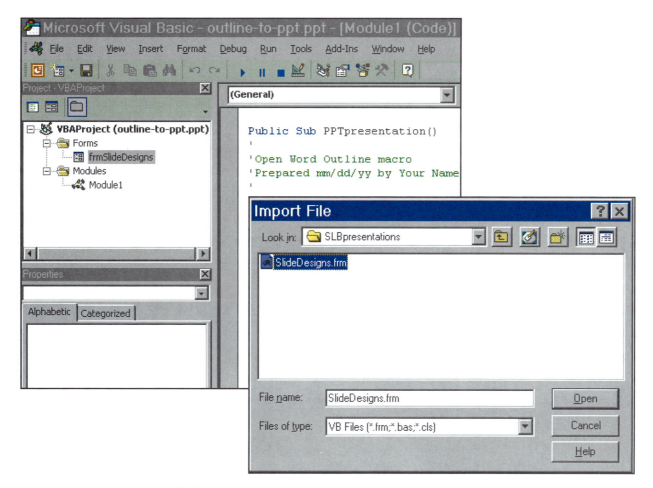

FIGURE 3.15 VBA Project Window and Import File Dialog Box

All UserForms included in a project are identified in the Project Window as seen in figure 3.15. You can view the form or the procedures it contains by clicking on its name in the Project window and then clicking either the window's View Object or View Code button.

PITFALL

If you do not see the frmSlideDesigns UserForm, double-click on the Forms folder in the Project window.

4. Select the frmSlideDesigns UserForm in the Project Window and then click the View Object button.
   ► *The Visual Basics UserForm design window opens as does the Toolbox similar to figure 3.16.*

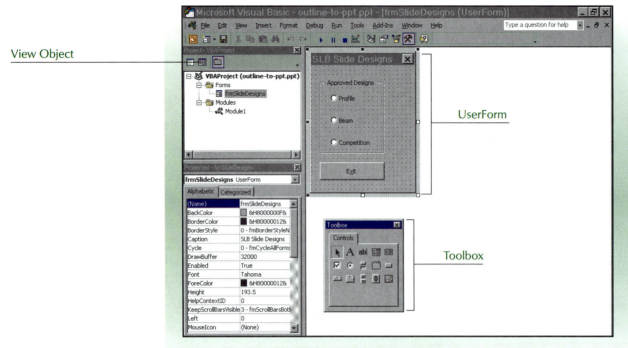

FIGURE 3.16 UserForm Design Window and Toolbox

The UserForm, seen in figure 3.16, contains three option buttons, one for each of the approved designs and an Exit command button. Option buttons provide the user with the ability to make a selection from a group of predefined choices. This control functions in a manner similar to the buttons on your car radio. Selecting any button in the group automatically deselects the previous selection.

The Toolbox and the controls it contains work just like the Control toolbar you used in chapter 2. Control objects in the box are placed on the form in the same manner you placed the command buttons on the 2003 Sales worksheet.

5. Click the View Code button.
   ➤ *The UserForm Code window opens as seen in figure 3.17.*

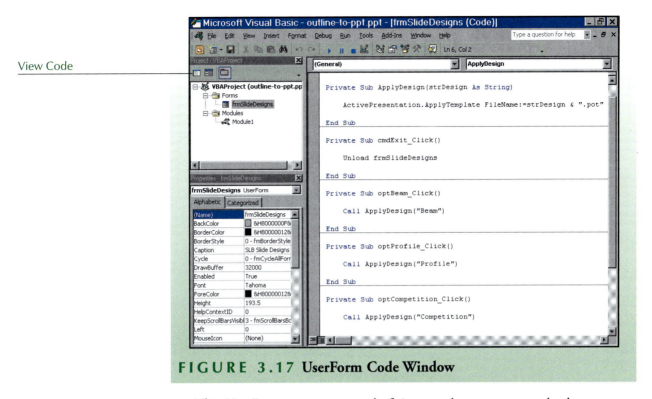

View Code

FIGURE 3.17 UserForm Code Window

This UserForm supports a total of six procedures: one general sub procedure (ApplyDesign), four control object Click event procedures, and one UserForm Activate event procedure. The ApplyDesign procedure is the only procedure that has any effect upon the presentation. When any of the option button click event procedures call it, they pass the filename of the desired template. The ApplyDesign procedure then accepts the passed data into its strDesign variable and sets the presentations template by referencing that design file. The click event for the Exit command button unloads the UserForm from memory and returns execution to the PPTpresentation macro, which promptly terminates, leaving the selected design in place.

Take a close look at the UserForm Activate event procedure shown in figure 3.18–you may have to scroll down the Code window to see it. This event occurs when the form opens. First it sets the Profile option button's value property to True. This assignment causes the button to respond as if the user had clicked it. Thus the Profile design template is applied to the presentation as a default selection. Secondly, the SetFocus method of the Profile option button is executed. This method causes the Profile option button to have the **focus**, which is another way of identifying the active control in a dialog box. You can tell which control has the focus because it is highlighted in some way. For example, the insertion point appears in a text box when it has the focus and a dotted line appears around the caption of any button with the focus.

```
Private Sub UserForm_Activate()

    optProfile.Value = True
    optProfile.SetFocus

End Sub
```

FIGURE 3.18 **Procedure to Set the Profile Template When UserForm is Activated**

Showing a UserForm

UserForms are activated by executing their Show method. This method loads the UserForm into memory and presents it on the user's screen.

1. Display the PPTpresentation procedure in the Code window.
2. Delete the appPPT.ActivePresentation.ApplyTemplate FileName: = "Profile.pot" statement.
3. Replace the deleted statement with **frmSlideDesigns.Show**.
4. Save your work.
5. Run the PPTpresentation macro, specify the franchise Outline file and key **Your Name** as the presenter.
   ➤ *When the input box closes, the Custom dialog box is presented and you are able to preview each of the approved design options for your presentation.*
6. Select the design option you like best.
7. Click the Exit button to close the dialog box.
8. Save the new presentation and name it SlideShow2.

CONCLUSION

As you can see VBA applications for PowerPoint are designed to support the development of new slideshows. Unlike Word and Excel VBA applications that often help users with day-to-day activities by automating repetitious tasks, PowerPoint applications focus on creating development tools that work behind the scenes. After completing this chapter you should walk away with a greater appreciation of the flexibility and power of VBA when it is used someone who understands what it can do.

KEY TERMS

collection
concatenation
empty string
error trapping
focus
label
module
object variable
UserForm

REVIEW QUESTIONS

On a blank sheet of paper provide a short answer for the following questions.

1. Define the key terms.
2. How is PowerPoint different from Microsoft Word and Excel in its use of VBA?
3. How does PowerPoint identify the starting point of a new slide in a Word outline file?
4. When is a file's path property set?
5. Why do productivity procedures developed for PowerPoint always have to be saved in a presentation?
6. What is one difference between Public and Private procedures?
7. Identify three different unexpected user actions that error-handling code should take into consideration.
8. What is the three-step process for coding an error trap?
9. What statement activates VBA's error trapping resources?
10. How do you create identifiable markers in a procedure?
11. List two properties of VBA's error object.
12. How do you test for an empty string?
13. What is the concatenation operator?
14. Why is it an advantage to use an object variable over just referencing an object in context?
15. What key word must be used when assigning an object to an object variable?
16. Give an example of a PowerPoint collection.
17. Define a situation where you would need a custom dialog box.
18. How do identify the control in a dialog box that has the focus?

CHECK YOUR UNDERSTANDING

Indicate the correct term or choose the correct answer for each item.

1. The ___Exit Sub___ statement must always precede a procedure's error handling code.
2. strUserResponse = ___""___ assigns an empty string to the variable.
3. strName = "Alice" ___&___ "Miller" concatenates the two literal strings and assigns them to the variable.
4. The ___Set___ statement is used to assign object variables.
5. VBA procedures are stored in a ___module___ .
6. Which Project window button would you use to display a UserForm?
   a. Toggle Folders
   c. Object View
   b. Code View
   d. Insert UserForm
7. Which of the following statements correctly assigns a presentation to the presentation object variable prsWordOutline?
   a. prsWordOutline = appPPT.Presentations.Open(strFileName)
   b. Let prsWordOutline = appPPT.Presentations.Open(strFileName)
   c. preWordOutline SetTo appPPT.Presentations.Open(strFileName)
   d. Set prsWordOutline = appPPT.Presentations.Open(strFileName)

8. Which statement correctly identifies the location of the error handling code for On Error GoTo Error_Trap?
   a. Error_Trap
   b. Error_Trap:
   c. Error_Handler:
   d. ErrorTrap:
9. Which of the following is a difference between Public and Private procedures?
   a. All macros are Public procedures.
   b. Private procedures can be executed directly from an application.
   c. Private procedures are listed in the Macros dialog box.
   d. All macros are Private procedures.
10. Which of the following would *not* be a PowerPoint collection?
   a. Design Templates
   b. Slides
   c. Presentations
   d. Shapes

EXERCISES

Complete the following exercises.

Last Step

The Second Look Books' franchise team has authorized an additional design template "Digital Dots". Add an option button to the frmSlideDesigns UserForm and code its click event to apply the new design. Add an option button to a form from the ToolBox in the same way that you added the command buttons in chapter 2. Make sure that the Approved Designs frame is selected when you add the new option button. The new button must reside inside this frame so it functions as part of the existing set of buttons. Once the new button is in the form, set the following properties:

(Name)	= optDigitalDots
AutoSize	= True
Caption	= Digital Dots
Value	= False

Code the new button's click event with the same Call statement used to code the other buttons, except pass the Digital Dots filename to the ApplyDesign procedure. Finally, reposition the four buttons so they are evenly spaced. Save the presentation and then test your new design option.

Debug

The following procedure was written to apply the Digital Dots graphic design template to all the slides in the second presentation of the current collection. It reset only the first slide's template to the Beam design. Four code errors prevent it from executing.

```
Dim appPwrPt as PowerPointApplication
Set appPwrPt = PowrPoint.Application

With appPPT.Presentations(2)
    .ApplyTemplate File "Digital Dots.pot"
    .Slides(1).ApplyTemplate FileName: "Beam.pot"
End With
```

Internet

Locate a Web site that uses a PowerPoint Web presentation. Critique the effectiveness of both the site and PowerPoint as a useful Web presentation tool. *Hint: the MSDN site has several PowerPoint presentations than can be downloaded.*

New Task

Modify the PPTpresentations macro so that the SLB official logo (booklogo.gif) is inserted in the first slide of a presentation if no presenter's name is indicated. Currently the string "SLB Franchise Department" is used when no name is available. To successfully accomplish this, the first slide must be configured as a Title Only layout. The logo, a copy of which is located in the SLBpresentations folder, can then be inserted into the slide. Remember, the macro recorder is an excellent way to create code that can be cut and pasted into other macros.

Discussion

What other tasks do you feel would be worthwhile automating for PowerPoint developers?

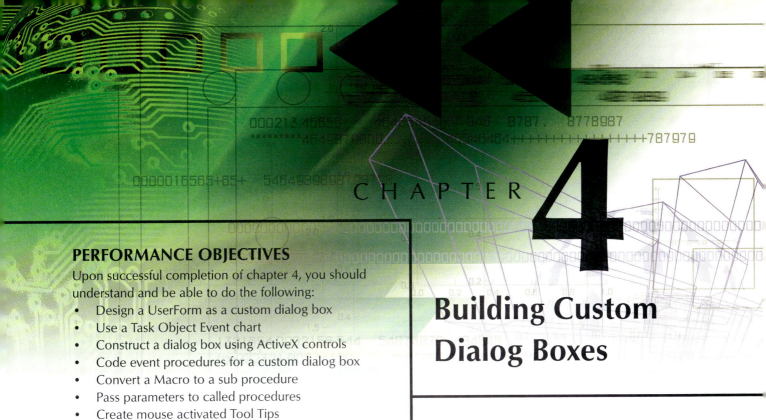

CHAPTER 4

Building Custom Dialog Boxes

PERFORMANCE OBJECTIVES

Upon successful completion of chapter 4, you should understand and be able to do the following:

- Design a UserForm as a custom dialog box
- Use a Task Object Event chart
- Construct a dialog box using ActiveX controls
- Code event procedures for a custom dialog box
- Convert a Macro to a sub procedure
- Pass parameters to called procedures
- Create mouse activated Tool Tips

Businesses often find that information contained in spreadsheets is easier to analyze when presented graphically. Excel's Chart Wizard is an easy-to-use tool that develops professional looking charts from worksheet data. Once created, the chart maintains a **dynamic reference** to the data it presents. This means that there is a real-time link between the worksheet data and the chart, resulting in the chart being updated automatically if the data changes.

At Second Look Books the Sales Analysis chart in figure 4.1 is used to provide a visual image of sales data. This chart and the 2003 sales data from which it is generated are often printed. On many occasions store management needs to print multiple copies of the sales data and chart. If you need three copies of the sales data and one copy of the analysis chart, you need to independently select and print each worksheet. A user-friendly solution to situations like this that have several alterative actions is a dialog box containing appropriate controls, like check and spin boxes. Visual Basic for Applications provides an object called a *UserForm* that enables you to design a custom dialog box. Once created, the dialog box can be coded to perform whatever task you want supported.

SALES ANALYSIS CHART SHEET

Second Look Books' management uses the Sales Analysis chart, seen in figure 4.1, to assist them with the ongoing challenge of monitoring sales levels. This chart provides an illustration of customer buying patterns for each sales category.

1. Launch Excel and, if necessary, close the New Document Task Pane.
2. Open c4-chart.xls, which you downloaded to your student data disk or, if you prefer, you may continue working with the sales.xls workbook from chapter 2.
3. Enable the macros.
4. If you are using c4-chart.xls, key **Prepared by Your Name** in cell A2 after *Sales Analysis*.
5. Save the worksheet as chart.xls.
6. Click on the Sales Analysis tab.
7. If necessary, close the Chart toolbar.
   ➤ *The chart should look similar to figure 4.1.*

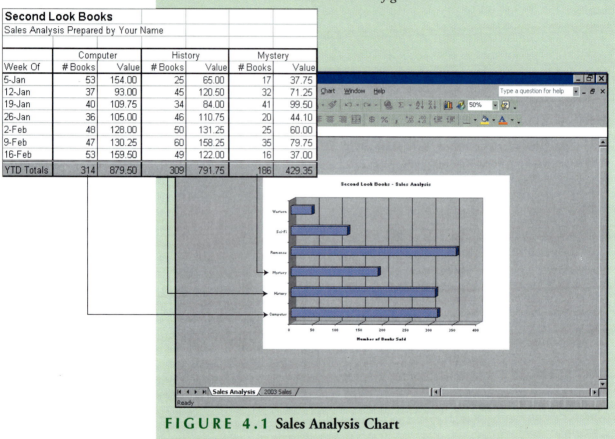

Second Look Books
Sales Analysis Prepared by Your Name

	Computer		History		Mystery	
Week Of	# Books	Value	# Books	Value	# Books	Value
5-Jan	53	154.00	25	65.00	17	37.75
12-Jan	37	93.00	45	120.50	32	71.25
19-Jan	40	109.75	34	84.00	41	99.50
26-Jan	36	105.00	46	110.75	20	44.10
2-Feb	48	128.00	50	131.25	25	60.00
9-Feb	47	130.25	60	158.25	35	79.75
16-Feb	53	159.50	49	122.00	16	37.00
YTD Totals	314	879.50	309	791.75	186	429.35

FIGURE 4.1 Sales Analysis Chart

ADDING A USERFORM

Up until this point, procedures such as the InsertNewRow macro and PrintYTD sub procedure have been created that made the Sales worksheet more convenient to use. The bookstore manager wants to make printing up-to-date worksheets and charts easier. At first, additional controls to the Print report and Print Chart buttons were considered. However, providing the ability to print multiple copies, in varying numbers, of either or both worksheets would require too many embedded controls. When a task requires multiple controls it is best to package them in a dialog box. To accomplish this, add a UserForm to the project and develop it into a custom dialog box.

Designing a Custom Dialog Box for Printing

The first step in designing a custom dialog box is to create a sketch of the interface (see figure 4.2). The second step is to prepare an outline that defines every task the dialog box must accomplish. Once the tasks are defined, objects (controls) are selected that logically support each task. Finally, events are chosen for those objects that must trigger an action. For every event selected to trigger an action, a procedure will be coded. The Task Object Event chart shown in figure 4.3 is typically referred to as a **TOE chart**. It provides a useful overview of the form's functional design.

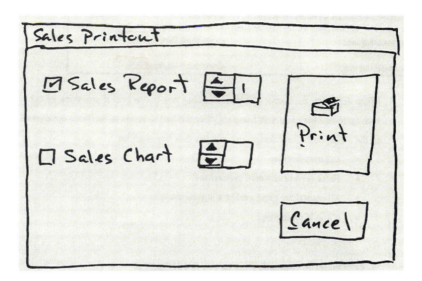

FIGURE 4.2 Sketch of Proposed Custom Dialog Box

Task	Object	Event
Identify which worksheets to print	2 Check Boxes	Click
Select the number of copies to print	2 Spin Buttons	Change
Display the number of copies selected	2 Labels	None
Print worksheets	Command Button	Click
Close dialog box	Command Button	Click

FIGURE 4.3 Task Object Event (TOE) Chart

To provide the necessary printing features, the custom dialog box must accomplish the following four tasks:

- Select either or both worksheets for printing.
- Define the number of copies to be printed.
- Signal the printing process to begin.
- Cancel the printing option.

When designing the layout of a custom dialog box it is helpful to think of the UserForm as a canvas upon which to bring together the best controls to facilitate the overall functionality of the dialog box. Good design incorporates four key qualities:

- It is informative.
- There is an uncluttered appearance.
- All objects are organized in a logical manner.
- It is self-prompting.

Inserting a UserForm into a Project

A UserForm is inserted by the Visual Basic Editor using the Insert menu or the UserForm button. When a form is inserted, a Forms folder is placed in the project to store the form (see the Project Explorer window in figure 4.4). As with other objects, the form is given a default name. Assuming the form is the first for the project, the default name is UserForm1. The form also has a set of properties that can be set from the Properties window in Design mode or with code during the Run mode. Like other objects, a UserForm has a number of events it can recognize.

1. Make sure the worksheet with the Sales Analysis chart is active.
2. Click Tools, point to Macro, and then click Visual Basic Editor.
   ➤ *The Visual Basic Editor opens.*
3. Maximize the Editor, if necessary.
4. Use either the toolbar buttons or the View menu to open the Project Explorer and Properties windows if they are not open (see figure 4.4).
5. From the Insert menu, select UserForm.
   ➤ *A UserForm is created and your screen should look similar to figure 4.4.*

ALTERNATIVE

Use the Insert UserForm button.

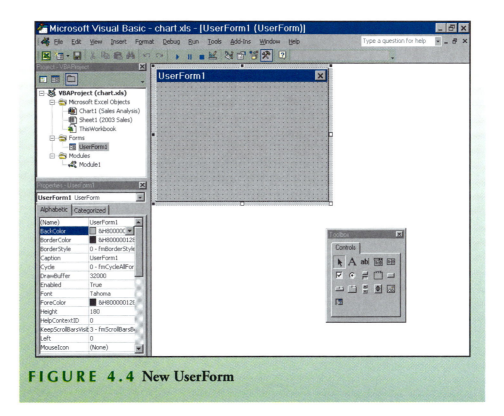

FIGURE 4.4 New UserForm

Setting UserForm Properties

Before placing any controls on the UserForm, four properties need to be modified; Name, Caption, Height, and Width. The name and caption properties should be familiar from the previous chapter. When sizing objects, like the print button in chapter 2, the mouse is typically used to drag the handles to the desired size and location. However, an object's height and width properties provide a more precise alternative for sizing the object. The default height of the UserForm is 180 points and the width is 240 points. A **point** is a standard unit of measurement used in the printing industry. Each point represents 1/72 of an inch. Therefore the form is 180/72" (2.5") high and 240/72" (3.33") wide. To provide the desired layout of the dialog box the size of the UserForm must be altered.

TIP

If the Toolbox disappears from view, click the UserForm window and the Toolbox will reappear.

1. Confirm that the Properties window references the UserForm.
2. Using the Properties window modify the default settings of the following UserForm properties:

(Name)	**frmPrint**
Caption	**Sales Printout**
Height	**140**
Width	**205**

➤ *The form changes in size and the Title bar displays the new caption.*

Adding Check Boxes

Using the sketch from figure 4.2 as a guide, you will place eight controls on the form. These controls are found in the Toolbox. The Toolbox is similar to the one you used to embed the command button control into the 2003 Sales worksheet in chapter 2 and can be seen in figure 4.5.

The check box and option button controls give the user a Yes/No choice for a specific option. If multiple check boxes are present the user can select all, any, or none of the boxes. The ability to have several check boxes in a group selected at the same time is how check boxes differ from option buttons. A group of option buttons can only have one option selected at a time. If another option button is selected, the active button is deselected.

Since users will be given the choice of printing both worksheets, the custom dialog box needs one check box for each worksheet. The 2003 Sales worksheet is the most frequently printed, so it will be the default selection when the UserForm is opened.

Before the check boxes can be placed on the form, the Toolbox needs to be opened if it is not already. This is done by clicking on the UserForm Window, giving it the focus. The View menu or the Toolbox button can be used to return focus back to the Toolbox. Placing the mouse pointer over a button in the toolbar and then pausing causes a tool tip to appear that identifies the tool as shown in figure 4.5.

ALTERNATIVE

Click the Toolbox button.

TIP

If the Toolbox option is not enabled in the View menu, the UserForm is not selected.

PITFALL

Accidentally double-clicking in the UserForm opens the Code window and creates a default sub procedure. To return to the UserForm, click the Object View button in the Project window.

1. If necessary, open the <u>V</u>iew menu and then select Toolbo<u>x</u>.
    ➤ *The Toolbox opens similar to the one shown in figure 4.5.*
2. Click on the Check Box control button in the Toolbox.
    ➤ *The button appears depressed.*
3. Move the mouse pointer into the form.
    ➤ *The mouse pointer becomes a crosshair with an image of the check box control.*
4. Click and drag to open a check box similar in size to the one shown in figure 4.5.
    ➤ *CheckBox1 appears on the form.*

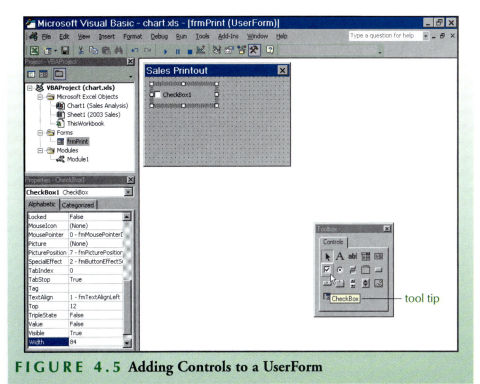

FIGURE 4.5 Adding Controls to a UserForm

AutoSize and Value Properties

Four properties of each check box must be set: Name, AutoSize, Caption, and Value. Of these four only AutoSize and Value are new properties. Controls used to output data, such as labels, typically have an AutoSize property. This property, when set to True, automatically resizes the display area of the control to fit the caption. Controls that toggle a feature on and off, like a check box or an option button, use the Value property to identify if a control has been selected. Setting a check box's Value property to True causes a check mark to appear in the box, providing a visual indication that the option is selected.

1. Confirm that the Properties window references CheckBox1.
2. Set the following properties of the check box:

Appearance	(Name)	**chkSalesReport**
	Caption	**Sales Report**
	Value	**True**
Behavior	AutoSize	**True**

Next Step 4-1

1. Add the check box for the Sales Chart worksheet using figure 4.2 as a model.
2. Set the following properties of the check box:

(Name)	**chkSalesChart**
Caption	**Sales Chart**
Value	**False**
AutoSize	**True**

3. Save the workbook.

Using a Spin Button and a Label for Selection

In the normal course of business it is not uncommon to need up to three additional copies of the Sales Analysis. Adding the spin button as seen in figure 4.7 offers the user an easy way to select the number of copies to print. The label control is included to display the currently selected number of copies.

PITFALL

Be careful not to select the scroll bar control by mistake.

1. Add a spin button to the immediate right of the Sales Report check box as shown in figure 4.6. ⬍
2. Add a label right of the spin button similar to figure 4.6. Ⓐ
3. Select the spin button control and open the Properties window.
   ➤ *List box displays properties for SpinButton1.*

Value, Max, and Min Properties

The Value, Max, and Min properties of the spin button significantly reduce the amount of VBA code necessary to make the button work. The Value property sets the starting value. The Max and Min properties can be used to prevent the user from printing less than one or more then four copies of the Sales Analysis. Spin buttons may be displayed in either a vertical or horizontal orientation.

1. Set the following properties for SpinButton1:

Appearance	(Name)	**spnSalesReport**
	Orientation	**0-fmOrientationVertical**
	Value	**1**
Scrolling	Max	**4**
	Min	**1**

The label control is used to provide output to the user and the PrintYTD printing procedure.

2. Select the Label control.
3. Set the following properties for the label:

Appearance	(Name)	**lblSalesReport**
	Caption	**1**
	SpecialEffect	**2-fmSpecialEffectSunken** (select from the SpecialEffect properties list box)
Behavior	TextAlign	**2-fmTextAlignCenter**

These two controls will be coded to work together as a set related to the Sales Report check box. The spin button's Value property and the label control's caption were set to 1 because the Sales Report check box is presented as the default selection when, the Value property is set equal to True.

Sizing Control Groups

The sizing of controls is typically done using the object sizing handles or the Height and Width properties. Once sized, the controls can be dragged and dropped into position or placed with the Top and Left properties. Often controls are positioned as a set, such as the spin button and label control. In these instances, uniform sizing and alignment is critical to the visual presentation of the controls.

The Format menu in Visual Basic's Editor (see figure 4.6) has sizing and alignment tools specifically designed for this task. The first step is to select all the controls you want to coordinate. Select one of the controls by clicking on it, hold down the Ctrl key, and then click on the other controls in the group to select the set. You will notice that the first control selected has unfilled handles and the others have solid handles. The control selected with the unfilled handles is used as the sizing and alignment reference. This reference can be changed to any of the controls in the set by clicking on the desired control, with the Ctrl key released. The selected set will not be released until you click on an object not included in the set with the Ctrl key released or by pressing the Esc key. You can also select a group of objects by simply clicking and dragging around them with the Select Objects tool from the Toolbox. When you do this a selection box, a dashed line box, appears around the objects.

TIP

If an undesired object is selected, simply deselect it by clicking on the object while the Ctrl key is being held down.

1. Click on the Sales Report check box.
   ➤ *The control is selected with unfilled handles.*
2. Holding the Ctrl key down, click on the spin button, then the label, and then release the Ctrl key.
   ➤ *The label control is selected with unfilled sizing handles while the spin button and check box have solid handles.*
3. Change the reference control to the check box button by clicking on it; do *not* hold down the Ctrl key.
   ➤ *The reference selection, the object with unfilled sizing handles, is changed to the check box.*

4. Click Format, point to Make Same Size, and then click Height as seen in figure 4.6.

➤ *The label control's height property is set equal to that of the check box.*

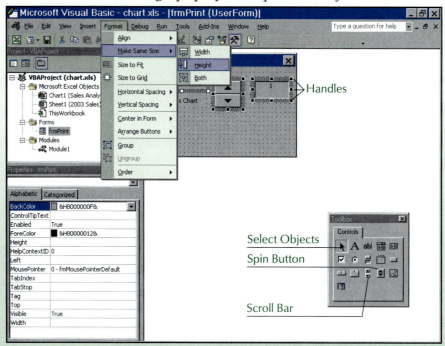

FIGURE 4.6 Control Sizing and Alignment

5. Click Format, point to Align, and then click Tops.

➤ *The three controls' Top properties are set to the same value.*

6. Release the selection by pressing the Esc key.
7. Using your mouse, select the Spin button, adjust its width, and position it next to the check box similar to figure 4.7.
8. Adjust the width of the Label control and position it next to the Spin button.

➤ *The UserForm appears similar to figure 4.7.*

Next Step 4-2

1. Add, size, and align the spin button and label control for the Sales Chart check box using figure 4.7 as a guide.
2. Set the following properties for the spin button:

(Name)	**spnSalesChart**
Orientation	**0-fmOrientationVertical**
Value	**1**
Max	**4**
Min	**1**

3. Set the following properties for the Label control:

(Name)	**lblSalesChart**
Caption	delete caption
SpecialEffect	**1-fmSpecialEffectSunken**
TextAlign	**2-fmTextAlignCenter**

4. Save the workbook.

Adding Command Buttons

The final two controls in the dialog box are the command buttons that print the selected reports or close the dialog box. Both are placed to the right of the label controls as seen in figure 4.7.

1. Place two command buttons on the form in about the same position as shown in figure 4.7.
   ➤ *CommandButton1 and CommandButton2 appear on the form.*
2. Set the following properties of the command buttons:

Appearance		*CommandButton1*	*CommandButton2*
Appearance	(Name)	**cmdPrint**	**cmdCancel**
	Caption	**Print**	**Cancel**
Behavior	Cancel	leave False	**True**
Misc	Accelerator	**P**	**C**
	TabStop	**False**	**False**

3. Size and position the command buttons similar to figure 4.7.

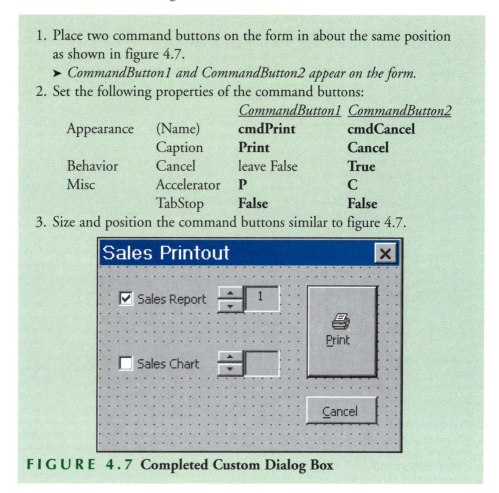

FIGURE 4.7 Completed Custom Dialog Box

Cancel and TabStop Properties

Setting the Cancel property of the Cancel command button to True allows the button's click event to be executed by pressing the Esc key on the keyboard. The Tab key can be pressed to advance the focus from object to object. Setting the TabStop property to False prevents the focus from moving to these buttons if the user presses the Tab key. This way the user will not inadvertently print or cancel if they press the Enter key.

Adding an Icon to a Command Button

Adding the familiar image of a printer to the Print button enhances user recognition and improves the look of the dialog box. The Picture property allows the inclusion of the image and the PicturePosition property provides a variety of placement options.

1. Select the cmdPrint command button in the Properties window.
2. Select the Picture property and click on the Ellipsis button to open the Load Picture dialog box. [...]
3. From the Look in list box, select the disk drive containing your student disk and then open the file Print.bmp.
   ➤ *The Standard printer image appears in the Print button.*
4. Select the PositionPicture property and choose 7 – **fmPicturePositionAboveCenter**.
   ➤ *The Print button looks similar to figure 4.7.*
5. Save the workbook.

Testing the Userform

The UserForm can be tested by running it from the Visual Basic Editor. If everything is correct you should observe the following:

- The Sales Report and Sales Chart check boxes should select and deselect.
- The Spin buttons take the focus when clicked, dotted line appears around the arrowheads, and the buttons appear to depress when clicked.
- The Sales Report label displays a 1 and the Sales Chart label displays nothing.
- Both command buttons visually respond to a mouse click and when the Alt + Accelerator keys are pressed.
- The Cancel button responds to a press of the Esc key.

1. Click the Run Sub/UserForm button.
2. Test the five features of the UserForm listed above.
3. Terminate execution of the UserForm by clicking on the Close button in the Title bar.
   ➤ *The Visual Basic Editor returns.*

If any control fails to work as expected, recheck the control's positioning and properties for necessary corrections and then save and retest.

CODING THE USERFORM

Coding the UserForm is a three part process. Initially, the controls on the form must be coded to function in the way the designers intended. Take a close look at figure 4.7. For the dialog box to work in a manner consistent with other Windows applications, the spin buttons and their associated labels should enable and disable when their related check box is selected or deselected. Once the form controls are functional, user selections must be stored for use in the printing procedure. Finally, VBA code is needed to print the selected reports when the user clicks the Print command button or to close the dialog box if the Cancel command button is clicked.

Up to this point you have only worked in the UserForm design window. The form and all the control objects it contains have events that can be coded. The Code window for the form can be opened in a variety ways. Double-clicking on any object in the form will open the Code window to that object's events. Pressing the F7 key will also open the Code window to the selected object's events, while Shift + F7 returns to the UserForm. Finally, the most versatile technique is to use the Window menu. This menu will give you access to the Forms Design window [Chart.xls – frmPrint(UserForm)], Code window [Chart.xls – frmPrint(Code)], as well as any of the project's modules.

Cancel Command Button

The purpose of the Cancel button is to close the dialog box and not print any copies of either worksheet. Since user selections are only acted upon when the Print command button is clicked, terminating execution of the UserForm will not result in any additional actions.

End Statement versus Unload Method

TIP

The keyword "me" can be used to reference any active object such as unload me.

Termination of a UserForm can be accomplished in two ways. The End statement can execute an immediate and unconditional termination of the form and its related code. The Unload method accomplishes the same task but allows the form to execute any code in its Terminate event prior to close down. Programmers often refer to this as housekeeping. Even though this custom dialog box does not require any housekeeping, the Unload method is the accepted programming practice for form termination. The statement "Unload frmPrint" will be located in the Cancel button's click event. Since you will be testing the UserForm frequently, coding this button early provides an easy way to terminate execution of the form.

1. Open the Code window by double-clicking the <u>C</u>ancel command button.
   ➤ *The Code window opens and a Private sub procedure for cmdCancel_Click() is inserted.*
2. Key the following lines of code:
   'Terminate execution and do not print
   'Prepared mm/dd/yy by Your Name
   '

   Unload frmPrint
   ➤ *CmdCancel_Click procedure matches figure 4.8.*
3. Run the UserForm and test the cancel command button.
   ➤ *The Form closes and control returns to the Visual Basic Editor.*

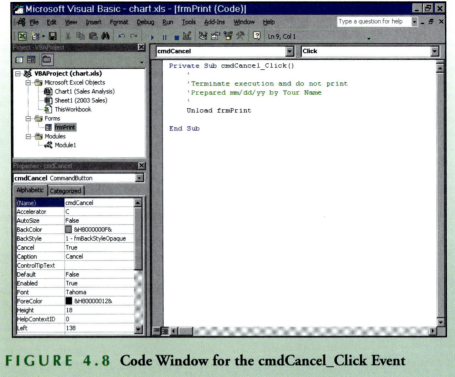

FIGURE 4.8 Code Window for the cmdCancel_Click Event

Coding the Sales Report Check Box

It is not necessary to write any code to select and deselect check boxes since this functionality is built into the control. However, the spin buttons and their associated label controls must be activated or deactivated depending upon the status of the check box.

Enabled Property

Windows typically activates or **enables** features only when the conditions necessary for the feature to function are met. For example, the Paste feature is not enabled until there is something in the clipboard to paste. Likewise, the spin and label controls associated with the form's check boxes should only be enabled when the option is selected. Because the custom dialog box will open with only the Sales Report selected, the spin button and label control associated with printing the Sales Chart should have their Enabled properties set to False. The caption property of the label should also be set to 0 (zero) making the display consistent with the fact that the Sales Chart is not selected for printing. The spin button's value property must stay at 1, its minimum starting value. The coding for each button utilizes an If, Then, Else statement to evaluate the status of the control's Value property.

Value Property

Because the Value property of the chkChartSales is set to False when the dialog box opens, the Enabled property of the Chart Report spin button (spnChartSales) and label control (lblChartSales) need to be changed to False. These properties will switch back and forth between True and False as the associated check box is selected and deselected. Likewise, the Label's default caption will switch between 1 and 0. The changes in these properties will be based on an evaluation of the status of the check box's Value property. For example, if the chkSalesReport's Value property evaluates as not true, both the spin button's and the label's Enabled properties are set to False, the spin button's Value property is set to 1, and the label's caption is set to 0.

TIP

If the Code window opens for some other object, use the Code window's left combo box to select the chkSalesReport object. If the Click event is not selected, choose it from the right combo box.

1. Open the Properties window for the spnSalesChart spin button and set the Enabled property to False.
2. Select the lblSalesChart label control and set its Caption to 0 and Enabled property to False.
3. Open the Code window by double-clicking the Sales Report check box.
   ➤ *The Code window opens for chkSalesReport_Click.*

Using the If, Then, Else Statement

In chapter 1, the If, Then, Else statement was used to manipulate the Font properties used in the logo's header based on the status of a variable. Here this logic will be used to alter Enabled and Caption properties based on the status of a check box's Value property as shown in figure 4.9.

1. Key the following code:

```
'
'Activate/Deactivate print selections
'Prepared mm/dd/yy by Your Name
'
{blank line}
If chkSalesReport.Value = True Then
        spnSalesReport.Enabled = True
        lblSalesReport.Enabled = True
        lblSalesReport.Caption = 1
Else
        spnSalesReport.Enabled = False
        spnSalesReport.Value = 1
        lblSalesReport.Enabled = False
        lblSalesReport.Caption = 0
End If
```
   ➤ *Your screen should look similar to figure 4.9.*
2. Save the workbook and then run the UserForm to test the check box's click event code.

➤ *The spin button and label control associated with the Sales Report check box enable and disable.*

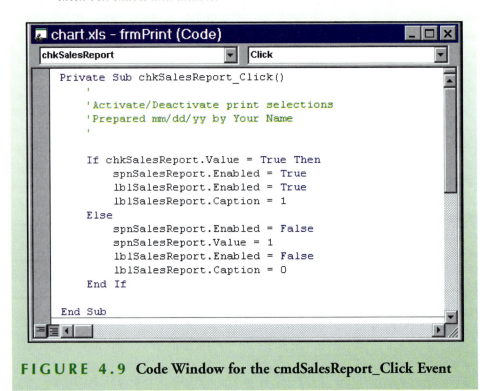

FIGURE 4.9 Code Window for the cmdSalesReport_Click Event

Coding the Sales Report Spin Button

A spin button has three events that are typically used to detect a click on its arrowheads: SpinUp, SpinDown, and Change. The Change event is the simplest of the three and appropriate for our application of the control.

1. Click the spin button associated with the Sales Report.
   ➤ *Handles appear around the spin button.*
2. Press F7.
   ➤ *The Code window opens.*
3. If the Change event is not the current selection, select it now.
   ➤ *The combo box indicates the Change event and the Sub/End Sub statements appear in the Code window.*

Change Property

A spin button's Change event is recognized by Visual Basic when either of the control's arrowheads is clicked. The code for this event, seen in figure 4.10, sets the lblSalesReport caption property to the current numeric setting of the spin button's Value property. The value property can be increased to a maximum value of four or decreased to a minimum value of one as the user clicks the control's arrowheads. These limits were set at design time using the control's Max and Min properties. By displaying the setting of the Value property in lblSalesReport the user has a visual reference of the number of copies being requested for printing.

The spin button's event procedures are automatically defined as private by Visual Basic because they can only be executed from the UserForm they are located within.

1. Key the following remarks and code for the spin button's Change event.

   '

   'Select the number of Sales Report copies to print
   'Prepared mm/dd/yy by Your Name

   '

   {blank line}
   lblSalesReport.Caption = spnSalesReport.Value
   ➤ *The code should resemble figure 4.10.*
2. Save the workbook.
3. Test the spin button.
   ➤ *The values 1-4 are displayed in the label.*

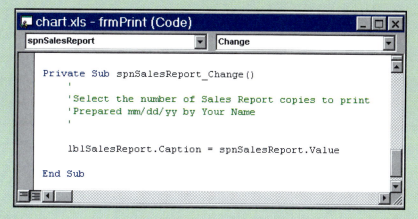

FIGURE 4.10 Code Window for the spnSalesReport_Change Event

Next Step 4-3

Code the Sales Chart check box and spin button and label control as follows:

1. The spin and label controls should enable and disable when the check box is checked and unchecked.
2. The label control's caption is 0 when disabled.
3. The label control's caption displays the spin button's Value property when enabled.
4. Save the workbook and then test the code; repeat as necessary until correct.

PASSING PARAMETERS TO PROCEDURES

Now that the user can elect to print multiple copies of the sales data, it is necessary to communicate this to the PrintYTD procedure in Module1. The best way to handle the communication is with a variable of the integer type. You will add the variables intCopiesReport and intCopiesChart to the UserForm. These variables will provide the resource necessary to pass data to the print procedures contained in Module1. The use of variables opens the door to logic errors if care is not exercised. If in coding the variable data assignment you were to misspell its name, Visual Basic would create a new variable with the altered spelling. This new variable would contain the value 0, thus resulting in no copies of the selected report being printed.

Option Explicit and Dim Statements

To avoid these common mistakes, the Option Explicit statement is used. Its presence in the general declarations area of the form forces the programmer to declare all variables with a Dim statement before the VBA compiler will accept the variable in other parts of the code. A Dim statement defines both the variable's name and type as shown in figure 4.11. As a result, any misspelled variables will be caught by the Visual Basic compiler at run time.

1. Open the Code window and then select the (General) object, and the (Declarations) event.
2. Key the following code:
    Option Explicit
    Dim intCopiesReport As Integer
    Dim intCopiesChart As Integer

Name and Type	Use
Dim intCopiesReport As Integer	Whole numbers only
Dim strCustomerName As String	Text
Dim dtmInvoice As Date	Valid date
Dim curBalanceDue As Currency	Financial data
Dim sngDiameter As Single	Single precision floating point numbers
Dim blnActive As Boolean	True/False

FIGURE 4.11 **Common Variable Naming Conventions**

Initialization

Good programming practice dictates that each variable be assigned its expected initial value. This process is called **initialization**. In the case of intCopiesReport the initial value assigned to it is 1, and the value assigned to intCopiesChart is 0. Initialization is a good example of variable **assignment** where a variable is set to a specific value. This is accomplished using the equal sign (=). For example, the statement *intCopiesReport = 1* assigns the value one to the variable intCopiesReport.

ACTIVATE EVENT

Initialization of form variables is located in the UserForm Activate event procedure. Any code in this event is executed only when the UserForm opened and before control is turned over to the user. A common naming convention used with variables is to precede the name with a three letter tag (all lowercase) that identifies the variable type. Figure 4.11 shows some typical applications of this naming convention.

1. Change to the UserForm object and the Activate event.
2. Key the following code:

   '

   'UserForm variable initialization

   '

   intCopiesReport = 1
   intCopiesChart = 0
   ➤ *Your screen should look similar to figure 4.12.*

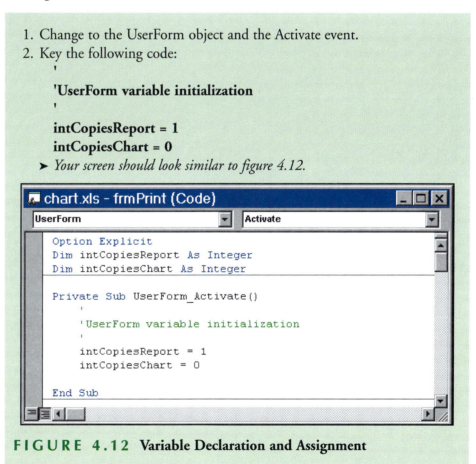

FIGURE 4.12 **Variable Declaration and Assignment**

   A Click event procedure for the Print command button needs to be coded. This procedure first assigns the number of copies of the Sales Report and Chart to the variables intCopiesReport and intCopiesChart. The assignment statement will use the Val function to insure that the data passed to the PrintYTD procedure by the Call statement is numeric.

VAL FUNCTION

Data stored in the Caption property of a Label or the Text property of a text box is often used by other procedures. In this situation, the data passed to the PrintYTD procedure must be numeric since it represents the number of copies to print. One potential problem arises from the fact that a number stored in a text box or label is actually the text representation of the value. As such, if it is used in a situation that interprets it as a number its numeric value is zero regardless of the number it represents. In other words the text value "1" is treated the same way as "one". Both text values have no numeric value. The Val function is used to convert numbers stored as text into a numeric value.

1. Open the Click event of the cmdPrint command button.
2. Key the following code:

```
'
'Print User selected Reports and Charts
'Prepared mm/dd/yy by Your Name
'
'Assign number of Reports & Charts to their respective variable
'
intCopiesReport = Val(lblSalesReport.Caption)
intCopiesChart = Val(lblSalesChart.Caption)
{blank line}
```

PASSING DATA IN A CALL STATEMENT

As you learned in chapter 2, Call statements are used to transfer program control to another procedure. Once the called procedure terminates execution, control is transferred back to the procedure that initiated the call. Therefore, we can use an If statement to determine if the variable intCopiesReport holds a value greater than 0. When it executes, the PrintYTD sub procedure in Module1 is called and the number of copies to print is passed to it. Passing a parameter is accomplished by including a reference to the data in parentheses following the name of the procedure being called, for example Call PrintYTD(intCopiesReport). After the PrintYTD procedure concludes, execution is then passed back to the Print button's Click event procedure. Execution of this procedure continues at the line of code following the Call statement. The same process of evaluation and printing is then applied to intCopiesChart.

Once the chart printing has been initiated, calling the Cancel button's Click event will terminate the dialog box. Good programming strives to have a single point of termination. Though you could simply add the statement "Unload frmPrint" to this procedure that would create two termination points. Calling the Cancel button's Click event is the VBA equivalent of clicking the button. Thus the statement "Call cmdCancel_Click" causes the Cancel button to think it has been clicked, thus it will evacuate the Click event's associated code.

1. Continue coding the cmdPrint Click event.

   'Check for Sales Reports to print
   If intCopiesReport > 0 Then
         'Print indicated number of copies
         Call PrintYTD(intCopiesReport)
   End If
   {blank line}
   'Check for Sales Charts to print
   {blank line – this code will be added later}
   'Close the dialog box
   Call cmdCancel_Click

2. Carefully check your code against figure 4.13.

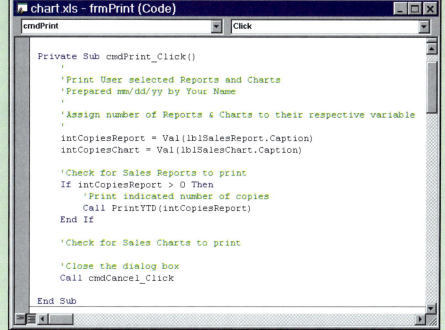

```
chart.xls - frmPrint (Code)

cmdPrint                              Click

Private Sub cmdPrint_Click()
    '
    'Print User selected Reports and Charts
    'Prepared mm/dd/yy by Your Name
    '
    'Assign number of Reports & Charts to their respective variable
    '
    intCopiesReport = Val(lblSalesReport.Caption)
    intCopiesChart = Val(lblSalesChart.Caption)

    'Check for Sales Reports to print
    If intCopiesReport > 0 Then
        'Print indicated number of copies
        Call PrintYTD(intCopiesReport)
    End If

    'Check for Sales Charts to print

    'Close the dialog box
    Call cmdCancel_Click

End Sub
```

FIGURE 4.13 Code Window for the cmd_Print_Click Event

Passing Data to Sub Procedures

The final step for sales report printing is to modify the PrintYTD sub procedure in Module 1 to accept and use the passed data. The PrintYTD procedure requires two modifications so it can receive and use the data passed to it from the custom dialog box. First, a local variable must be declared for the procedure. Then the PrintOut method's Copies parameter is set equal to that variable. A **local variable** differs from other variables in that it is a data storage location that is only active while the code is running.

Local variables are typically used to receive data passed from another procedure and therefore are only necessary during the procedure's execution. One way of defining a local variable is to declare its name and data storage type inside the parentheses of the Sub statement (Public or Private). Special care needs to be taken to insure that the variable type matches the data being passed to the procedure. As mentioned earlier, we intend to pass the number of copies to print as an integer. This then requires a numeric variable to receive the data. An integer variable is used because this value will always be a whole number.

1. Select Module1 from the Project Explorer window.
   ➤ *Module1 procedures are displayed in the Code window.*
2. Select the PrintYTD() sub procedure.
   ➤ *The code is displayed in the Code window.*
3. Position the insertion pointer between the parentheses at the end of the Public Sub PrintYTD() statement.
4. Key **intNumberOfCopies As Integer**.
   ➤ *The statement reads Public Sub PrintYTD(intNumberOfCopies As Integer) as shown in figure 4.14.*
5. Delete the 1 after the equal sign in the Selection.PrintOut Copies:=1 statement and key **intNumberOfCopies**.
   ➤ *The statement reads Selection.PrintOut Copies:=intNumberOfCopies (see figure 4.14).*

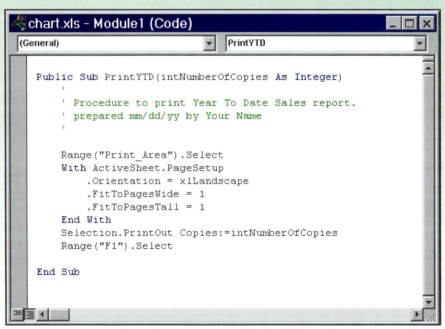

```
chart.xls - Module1 (Code)

(General)                              PrintYTD

    Public Sub PrintYTD(intNumberOfCopies As Integer)
        '
        ' Procedure to print Year To Date Sales report.
        ' prepared mm/dd/yy by Your Name
        '

        Range("Print_Area").Select
        With ActiveSheet.PageSetup
            .Orientation = xlLandscape
            .FitToPagesWide = 1
            .FitToPagesTall = 1
        End With
        Selection.PrintOut Copies:=intNumberOfCopies
        Range("F1").Select

    End Sub
```

FIGURE 4.14 Modifications to PrintYTD Procedure

If you are working with your file from chapter 2, you must edit the code for any custom print buttons you added to the worksheet as follows: **Call** *PrintYTD*(**1**). This change passes the value 1 to the procedure since it now expects an integer value. Your worksheet print buttons still provide a quick way to print a single copy of the 2003 Sales worksheet data.

These two modifications enable the PrintYTD procedure to receive an integer value passed by a call statement. Because macro procedures cannot accept passed data, the PrintYTD procedures life as a macro ends. PrintYTD is now a general sub procedure.

6. Save the workbook.
7. Activate the Excel window.
   ➤ *The Excel window opens.*
8. Click <u>T</u>ools, point to <u>M</u>acro, and then click <u>M</u>acros.
   ➤ *The Macro dialog box no longer references PrintYTD.*
9. Close the dialog box.
   ➤ *The dialog box closes.*

ACTIVATING THE USERFORM FROM THE WORKSHEET

All that is left to do is write the code that will run the UserForm. The most logical way for the user to access the custom Print dialog box is with a macro. This macro can be assigned a shortcut key such as Ctrl + Shift + P, for Print.

1. If necessary, return to Excel and the 2003 Sales worksheet.
2. Click <u>T</u>ools, point to <u>M</u>acro, and then click <u>R</u>ecord New Macro.
   ➤ *The Record Macro dialog box opens.*
3. Name the macro CustomPrint and assign the keyboard shortcut Ctrl + Shift + P.
4. Click OK.
   ➤ *The macro recorder activates.*
5. Stop recording.

SHOW METHOD

To run a UserForm, it first must be loaded into memory and then run. The easiest way to do this is using the Visual Basic's Show method. When the Show method is invoked it will load the UserForm into memory and then run the form.

1. Click <u>T</u>ools, point to <u>M</u>acro, and then click <u>M</u>acros.
   ➤ *The Macro dialog box opens.*
2. Select the CustomPrint macro and then click the <u>E</u>dit button.
   ➤ *The Visual Basic Editor opens the Code window for the UpdateChart macro.*
3. In a new line, key the statement **frmPrint.Show**
4. Save the project.
5. Return to the 2003 Sales worksheet and then run the CustomPrint (Ctrl + Shift + P) macro.
   ➤ *The Custom dialog box opens.*
6. Select 2 copies of the Sales Report only.
   ➤ *The selected reports print.*

Next Step 4-4

1. Return to Excel and record a macro named PrintChart that prints the Sales Analysis chart.
   (Hint: Printing charts is no different than printing worksheet data. Select the sheet containing the chart and then choose the Print option from the File menu and print the active sheet.)
2. Convert the PrintChart macro into a sub procedure by having it accept the number of copies to print as an integer. This variable should determine the number of copies to print.
3. Return to the Visual Basic Editor and the frmPrint UserForm. Open the cmdPrint_Click procedure.
4. Duplicate the If statement that evaluates intCopiesReport and calls the PrintYTD procedure under the remark 'Check for Sales Chart to print.
5. Modify the code to evaluate intCopiesChart and call PrintChart.
6. Save the workbook.
7. Test the UserForm.
8. Debug and resave if necessary.

MAKING THE CUSTOM DIALOG BOX MORE USER FRIENDLY

User friendly interfaces incorporate pop-up labels, called **tool tips**, that define the task accomplished by an object (Print sales chart) or report the status of a control (selected or deselected). The check boxes and the Print button in the UserForm will benefit from this added level of help.

ControlTipText Property

Most ActiveX controls have a ControlTipText property. When text is assigned to this property it appears on the screen as a tool tip when the user pauses the mouse pointer over the control. Because of the ease in adding this feature many programmers overuse it. Good UserForm development with well-positioned and captioned controls do not require tool tips for every control. The custom dialog box you just finished could, however, benefit from some tool tips similar in function to the tool tip provided for the Design/Run Mode button used in chapter 2. Since the check boxes select and/or deselect printing, it would be helpful if they had a tool tip indicating what action a click will have. Both command buttons would also benefit from a little more information. The Cancel button should indicate that no printing will occur and the Print button should tip the user if nothing is selected to print.

The easiest of the tool tips to program is the one for the Cancel button since it only requires adding the desired text to the control's ControlTipText property.

1. Open the Visual Basic Editor and select the frmPrint UserForm.
2. Select the Cancel button and open the Properties window.
3. Select the ControlTipText property and key **Close dialog box and DO NOT print**.
4. Run the form and position the mouse pointer over the Cancel button.
   ➤ *The "Close dialog box and DO NOT print" tool tip is displayed.*
5. Click the Cancel button.
   ➤ *The form closes and returns to the Visual Basic Editor.*

Next Step 4-5

From the Properties window set the following default tool tips for the check boxes:

chkSalesReport	Deselect
chkSalesChart	Select

Because the check boxes already have conditional statements that evaluate their status, the tip property can be reassigned from its default status within that code (see figure 4.15).

1. Select the code for the chkSalesReport_Click event procedure and add the following code shown in bold. Use figure 4.15 as a model.
   ```
   If chkSalesReport.Value = True Then
           {existing code}
           chkSalesReport.ControlTipText = "Deselect"
   Else
           {existing code}
           chkSalesReport.ControlTipText = "Select"
   End If
   ```
2. Make the same modification to the chkSalesChart_Click procedure. Remember to change the control name.
3. Test the code. The altered tool tip will not appear until you run the code and move the mouse pointer off the control and then back onto it.

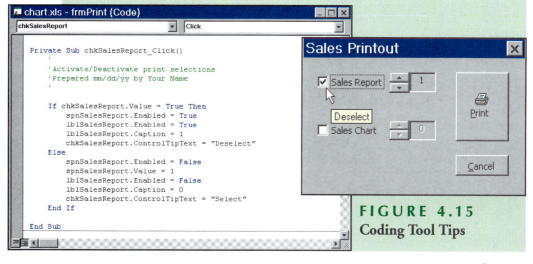

FIGURE 4.15
Coding Tool Tips

assignment
dynamic reference
enable
initialization
local variable
point
TOE chart
tool tip

REVIEW QUESTIONS

On a blank sheet of paper provide a short answer for the following questions.

1. Define the key terms.
2. Why is the relationship between a chart and the worksheet data it illustrates called a dynamic reference?
3. What conditions indicate the need for a custom dialog box?
4. How does the creation of a TOE chart benefit the VBA programmer?
5. What are the key qualities of a good UserForm design?
6. Compare the Option Button control to the check box control.
7. What is the relationship of the TabStop property to the focus?
8. Identify three different ways to open the Code window when using the Visual Basic Editor.
9. What are two ways to close a UserForm using code and how are they different?
10. What are the three key properties of a spin button?
11. How does the Option Explicit statement prevent logic errors in code?
12. What character is used to assign data to a variable?
13. How do local variables differ from variables declared in a UserForm's general declaration area?
14. What VBA method is used to display a custom dialog box?
15. Identify two ways tool tips improve the user friendliness of custom dialog boxes.

CHECK YOUR UNDERSTANDING

Indicate the correct term or choose the correct answer for each item.

1. The VBA _UserForm_ object is used to create custom dialog boxes.
2. _local variables_ are active only when the associated procedure is running.
3. Pausing the screen pointer over a program control often results in the display of a _tool tip_.
4. Pressing the _F7_ function key opens the Code window.
5. A program variable is assigned a starting value during _initialization_.
6. How is a TOE chart used by a VBA programmer?
   a. It displays all the colors used in a dialog box.
   b. It identifies controls to be used in a dialog box.
   c. It automatically generates dimensions of a dialog box.
   d. It sets program variables used within a dialog box.
7. Which of the following symbols is used to assign data values to a variable?
   a. =
   b. @
   c. #
   d. >

8. What key on the keyboard is used to change an object's focus?
   a. Alt
   b. Ctrl
   c. Backspace
   d. Tab
9. In what type of situations are custom dialog boxes needed?
   a. single action is required
   b. color displays are necessary
   c. several different actions are possible
   d. non-graphical applications
10. What VBA method is used to display a custom dialog box?
   a. Display
   b. Show
   c. Project
   d. Set

EXERCISES

Complete the following exercises.

Last Step

The tool tip for the Print button is the last step to complete the custom Sales Printout dialog box. The code to manipulate the tool tip for the Print button must be added to the conditional evaluation of each check box in the chkSalesReport_Click and chkSalesChart_Click event procedures.

1. Use the Visual Basic Editor to update the code in chkSalesReport_Click to do the following:
   a. If the Sales Report check box is selected (chkSalesReport.Value = True) then the Print button's tool tip is turned off by setting cmdPrint.ControlTipText = ""
   b. Else if the Sales Chart check box is also deselected (If chkSalesChart.Value = False)
      then the Print button's tool tip should be *No reports selected* (cmdPrint.ControlTipText = "No reports selected")
2. Make the same modification to the chkSalesChart_Click procedure. (No tool tip if either check box is selected or set the tool tip to *No charts selected* when both check boxes are deselected.)
3. Save the workbook.
4. Test and debug if necessary.
5. Print a copy of the UserForm and the code from all its procedures.

Debug

Custom dialog boxes are used in a computer equipment purchase request document created with Microsoft Word. When the person clicks an [Order Printers] button in the document, a VBA UserForm presents the available options. The user may select any, none, or all of the listed printers and a total price will appear as selections are made. In its current state the code crashes. However, once you correct the problem(s) causing the crash you will discover that if you change your mind and deselect a printer, the price is not appropriately adjusted down.

The following code is contained in a UserForm named frmPrinterOrder:

```
Dim curTotalPrinterCharge as Currency

Private Sub frmPrinterOrder_Activate()
curTotalPrinterCharge=0
End Sub

Private Sub chkCanonBubbleJet_Click()
    If chkCanonBubbleJet.Value = True Then
        curTotalPrinterCharge = curTotalPrinterCharge + 149
        Call DisplayTotalPrice (curTotalPrinterCharge)
    End If
End Sub

Private Sub chkLexmarkLaser_Click()
    If chkLexmarkLaser.Value = True Then
        curTotalPrinterCharge = curTotalPrinterCharge + 389
        Call DisplayTotalPrice (curTotalPrinterCharge)
    End If
End Sub

Private Sub chkHPPhotoSmart_Click()
    If chkHPPhotoSmart.Value = True Then
        curTotalPrinterCharge = curTotalPrinterCharge + 179
        Call DisplayTotalPrice (curTotalPrinterCharge)
    End If
End Sub

Private Sub DisplayCurrentPrice(Dim curPrice As Currency)
    lblTotalPrinterCharge.Caption = curPrice
End Sub
```

Internet

Adding icons to command buttons provides the designer with the ability to incorporate internationally recognized symbols to the user interface. Use your favorite search engine to locate a source for small bitmap images that can be used as a command button's picture property. These bitmaps should not exceed 5KB in size. Print at least three of these icons and the URL of the Web site where you found them. If you feel creative, you can use the Paint program that comes with Windows to create your own icons.

New Task

Using a blank worksheet, develop a custom dialog box that will provide easy data entry of department name, report title, and manager's name. Then, upon the user's command, the company name, the current date, and the user-entered data is inserted into cells A1–A5 of the currently active Excel worksheet.

Cell A1	Acme, Inc.	(text is set to 20 point bold)
Cell A2	Department	(text is set to 14 point)
Cell A3	Report Title	(text is set to italic)
Cell A4	current date	
Cell A5	prepared by - Manager's Name	

Hint: Using the Macro Recoder is an easy way to discover correct code syntax.

Discussion

How will dialog boxes change when voice input becomes a common user interface? Will there be a new meaning to the term *dialog box* when we talk to our computers?

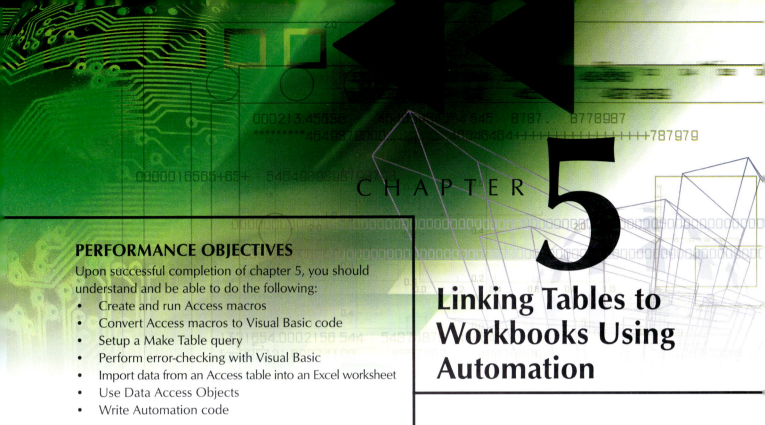

CHAPTER 5

PERFORMANCE OBJECTIVES

Upon successful completion of chapter 5, you should understand and be able to do the following:

- Create and run Access macros
- Convert Access macros to Visual Basic code
- Setup a Make Table query
- Perform error-checking with Visual Basic
- Import data from an Access table into an Excel worksheet
- Use Data Access Objects
- Write Automation code

Linking Tables to Workbooks Using Automation

Microsoft's Office Professional supports the storage and retrieval of large volumes of data through the Access database software. The forms, reports, and macros developed using Access utilize Visual Basic for Applications code. In this chapter, you will see the similarities between the VBA code used by Word, Excel, PowerPoint, and Access. You will start by creating an Access macro that prints a report. Then you will expand upon the InsertNewRow macro created in chapter 2 to transfer data from an Access table to an Excel worksheet.

The Sales Analysis worksheet you modified in chapter 2 used data stored in Access tables. The tables maintained in Second Look Books' Access database are used throughout this chapter.

SECOND LOOK BOOKS' DATABASE

The inventory database slb-inv.mdb should have been downloaded to your student data disk. Currently, it contains four tables, three queries, and one report.

TIP

If Access appears on your taskbar, click on it.

1. Open Access.
2. Click File and then Open.
    ➤ *Access displays the Open dialog box.*
3. Select *slb-inv* found on your student data disk and then click Open.
    ➤ *The slb-inv : Database window opens.*
4. If necessary, click the Tables button in the Objects bar (see figure 5.1).
    ➤ *The slb-inv : Database window should look similar to figure 5.1.*

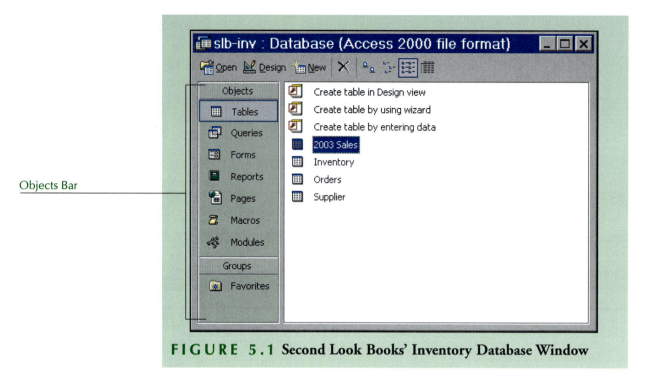

Objects Bar

FIGURE 5.1 Second Look Books' Inventory Database Window

The three tables, 2003 Sales, Inventory, and Supplier, are the backbone of Second Look Books' database. While a real used book store would use a more complex design, these tables utilize Access' relational database management features. As shown in figure 5.2, the book's ISBN number serves as the common field that links data from the 2003 Sales and Inventory tables. This link relates 2003 Sales data with the book's title, author, classification, and cost found in the Inventory table. The Supplier ID links this data to the Supplier table which contains the name and address of the wholesaler who originally supplied the book to Second Look Books.

Weekly Sales by Classification

The 2003 Sales and Inventory tables as shown in figure 5.2 contain the data you used in chapter 2 to analyze weekly sales by classification (see figure 5.9). Classifications fall into one of six categories:

- C for computers
- H for history
- M for mystery
- R for romance
- S for science fiction
- W for western

ISBN	Price	Sales Date	
156324-6961	$1.00	1/19/03	
8306321-4-X	$2.00	1/19/03	2003 Sales
0019-283195X	$3.00	1/19/03	
1-5561519-8-5	$3.00	1/19/03	
0345-336291	$1.00	1/19/03	
155876-1306	$3.00	1/19/03	
0019-2828266	$1.00	1/19/03	
08108-25163	$2.50	1/19/03	
1880505-177	$2.50	1/19/03	
0910959-781	$1.00	1/19/03	
1352871-2-X	$3.00	1/19/03	
1-5561519-8-5	$3.00	1/19/03	

Link

ISBN	Book Title	Author	Classification	Supplier ID	Cost	
0006-1012238	Fatal Convictions	Geller, Shari	M	3000	$0.20	
0006-1012262	Final Judgement	Easterman, D.	M	3000	$0.30	Inventory
0006-1012289	Secret Affair	Bradford, Bar	M	3000	$0.25	
0006-1095168	96 Tears	Swanson, Doug	M	3000	$0.20	
0006-4471705	Bad Sign	Royce, Easton	M	3000	$0.30	
0013-7495730	Colonial America	Reich	H	2000	$0.35	
0014-0257454	The Crusades	Jones, Terry	H	2000	$0.60	
0019-2828266	The War of the Worlds	Wells, H. G.	S	1000	$0.50	
0019-283195X	The Invisible Man	Wells, H. G.	S	1000	$0.30	

Supplier Name	Address	City	State/Province	Postal Code	Supplier ID	Telephone	
Moonbeam Books	1946 Briarwood Avenue	Troy	MI	48084	1000	800.555.7812	
Blue Spruce Resellers	71 Black Rock Canyon Road	Hailey	ID	83333	2000	800.555.1282	Supplier
The Deer Stalkers	3956 Circle Drive	London	ON	NOL1SO	3000	800.555.2711	
Jayhawk Books	1173 Mississippi	Lawrence	KS	66046	4000	800.555.9867	

FIGURE 5.2 **Second Look Books' Tables**

You will use the Weekly Sales by Classification query (see figure 5.3) that came with the SLB Inventory database to identify the number of books sold by classification each day. This select query uses a parameter, Starting Date, that identifies the first day in the week you are analyzing. Access uses the starting date to determine the seven days to include in the result of a query. A query result is called a **dynaset** and can contain data fields from one or more tables. The dynaset in figure 5.3 used 1/5/03 as the starting date and reported sales by classification for the first full week of sales in 2003.

1. Click the Queries button on the Objects bar.
   ➤ *Access displays SLB queries.*
2. Select Weekly Sales by Classification and then click Open.
   ➤ *The Enter Parameter Value dialog box opens similar to figure 5.3.*
3. Key **1/5/03** and then press Enter.
   ➤ *Access displays the Weekly Sales by Classification dynaset shown in figure 5.3.*

This query does three things:
- Organizes sales into related classifications.
- Provides a count of books sold each day by classification.
- Computes the total price paid for books sold each day by classification.

ALTERNATIVE

Click the Design View button.

4. Click View and then Design View.
   ➤ *The Query design is displayed as shown in figure 5.3.*

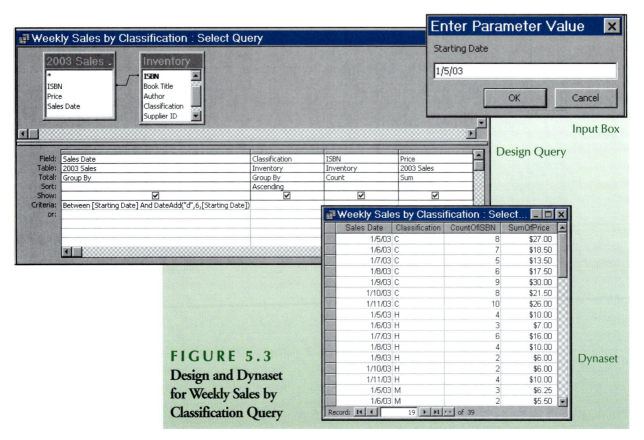

FIGURE 5.3
Design and Dynaset for Weekly Sales by Classification Query

Look in the criteria row under the Sales Date field of the Query design window in figure 5.3 to see the selection logic used in this query. The selection criterion *Between [Starting Date] And DateAdd("d",6,[Starting Date])* adds a record to the dynaset when the sales date falls between the starting date you entered and a date six days later. The DateAdd function adds six days to the starting date to compute the last acceptable day. As you can see in figure 5.3, entering a starting date of 1/5/03 results in a sales summary by classification of all sales from 1/5/03 to 1/11/03.

Next Step 5-1

Use the Run button to practice executing the query several times using different starting dates. Acceptable dates range from 1/2/03 to 3/2/03. You must return to the Design view before running the query again. When finished, close the Design view window using the File menu or Close button.

Sales by Classification Report

The Sales by Classification report is based on the Weekly Sales by Classification dynaset. This report groups sales data for each book classification into a single report line that totals the number of books and sales prices. Since the Weekly Sales by Classification query identifies a week's worth of sales, each line of the report reflects sales for seven days. The starting date is printed in the report header. Before previewing and printing the report, customize the report header to include your name.

1. Select the Reports button, choose Sales by Classification, and then click the Design button.
   ➤ Access displays the Report design as shown in figure 5.4.
2. Click after *Your Name* in the Report Header, click again, and then use the Backspace key to delete the text.
3. Key your name after the text Prepared by.
4. Click View and then Print Preview.
   ➤ The Enter Parameter Value dialog box opens.
5. Key **1/5/03** and then press Enter.
   ➤ Access displays the report as it will appear when printed (see figure 5.4).

ALTERNATIVE

Click the Print Preview button.

Verify that your name is spelled correctly and that the report looks like the one in figure 5.4. If not, make corrections before continuing. You are not going to print the report at this time. Instead, you are going to write a macro to do the task, convert the macro to VBA code, and then modify the code to allow users to print as many copies as needed.

6. Save the changes.
7. Close the Sales by Classification report.
   ➤ Access displays the slb-inv: Database dialog box similar to figure 5.1.

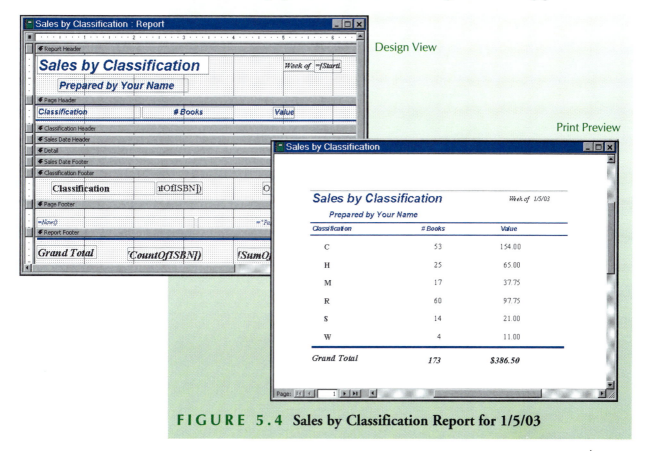

FIGURE 5.4 **Sales by Classification Report for 1/5/03**

DATABASE MACROS

While procedures using VBA code are replacing Access macros, there are still reasons why you might create a new macro using Access' Macro Design window:

- It is quick and easy for a new user to automate simple details like opening forms or printing reports.
- It is the only way to automate some actions that occur when a database first opens.
- It does not require an understanding of VBA syntax and methods.
- Like the macro recorder feature in Word and Excel, developers can get a head start on coding by using the Design window for initial module design. They can then modify the converted macro instead of starting from scratch.

You are going to create a macro that opens the Sales by Classification report and prints it. The Macro design window is easy to use and a good way to identify actions to modify as VBA code.

1. Click Macros on the Objects bar and then click <u>N</u>ew.
   - ➤ *Access opens a Macro design window.*
2. Click the down-pointing triangle in the first cell in the Action column.
   - ➤ *A list box of available Access commands opens.*
3. Scroll down the list and select *OpenReport.*
   - ➤ *Access displays empty input boxes for the Action Arguments associated with the OpenReport command.*
4. Click in the Report Name text box.
   - ➤ *A down-pointing triangle appears.*
5. Click the down-pointing triangle and then select *Sales by Classification.*
   - ➤ *Sales by Classification is displayed as shown in figure 5.5.*
6. Click in the View text box, click the down-pointing triangle, and then select *Print Preview.*
   - ➤ *Print Preview is displayed as shown in figure 5.5.*

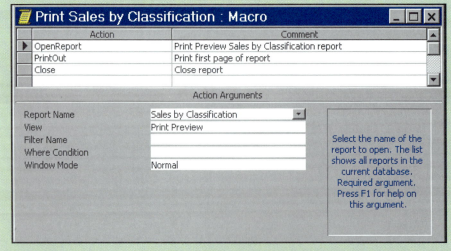

FIGURE 5.5 **Print Sales by Classification Macro**

Now, run the Print Sales by Classification macro.

1. Close the Macro design window.
   - ➤ *Access displays the slb-inv : Database dialog box.*
2. With the Print Sales by Classification macro selected, click the Run button.
   - ➤ *The Enter Parameter Value dialog box opens.*
3. Key **1/12/03** and then press Enter.
   - ➤ *Access prints the Sales by Classification report for the week starting 1/12/03.*

CONVERTING MACROS TO VBA CODE

While the reasons for customizing Access applications with macros still exist, developers now create procedures that utilize VBA code instead. Once you become comfortable writing and modifying VBA code, you should convert any macros you currently use into VBA modules. There are several reasons why:

- VBA code will be easier for you and others to maintain.
- VBA procedures and functions are available for use by other Office applications software.
- Error messages can be detected and handled in a user-friendly manner.
- There is more control over operating system actions, such as running other Windows or DOS-based applications.
- Arguments used by VBA procedures/functions are **dynamic**, meaning that they can change, while those used in macros are **static**, meaning that they cannot change, during execution. The macro you just created always prints one copy of the report. Once converted to VBA, you will modify the code to allow the user to change the number of copies argument as the code executes.

With the additional wizards installed, Access even provides a menu option that converts designated macros into VBA code. To get started, you will convert the Print Sales by Classification macro into a Visual Basic module. Then you can customize it by using the Modules design window. You will use the design window to add an input box that gives the user a choice of how many copies of the report to print. The Modules design window works just like the Visual Basic Editor used in earlier chapters.

TIP

Converting Access macros to VBA code uses a wizard which may not be installed on your PC. The Control Panel's Add/Remove Programs option is used to install the additional wizards.

1. With the Print Sales by Classification macro highlighted, click <u>T</u>ools.
   ➤ *The Tools menu opens.*
2. Point to <u>M</u>acro and then click Convert Macros to Visual <u>B</u>asic.
   ➤ *Access opens Convert macro: Print Sales by Classification dialog box.*
3. Confirm that the errorhandling and comment check boxes are checked and then click the <u>C</u>onvert button.
   ➤ *After waiting, a Conversion Finished message box is displayed.*
4. Click OK.
   ➤ *The Visual Basic Editor opens.*
5. From the Editor's Project window, click Converted Macro- Print by Sales Classification and then the View Code button as shown in figure 5.6.
   ➤ *Displays VBA code for the converted macro Print Sales by Classification (see figure 5.6).*

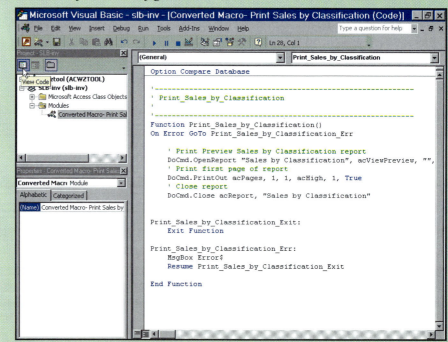

FIGURE 5.6 VBA Code for Converted Macro- Print Sales by Classification

EDITING VBA CODE USING ACCESS

The modifications to be made to the original macro code are identified in figure 5.7. The new VBA code does the following: the variable, intCopies, is dimensioned as an integer (whole number) and is then set equal to the input value the user enters from the keyboard in response to the input box prompt—How many copies? The variable intCopies then replaces the number of copies argument in DoCmd.PrintOut. This argument is located before the text True in the command line and presently has a default value of 1.

1. Click in the blank remark line under Print Sales by Classification, press Tab, and then key **Modified mm/dd/yy by your name.**
   ➤ *Fill in the appropriate information for the date and name categories.*
2. Create a blank line under the Function statement and key **Dim intCopies As Integer.**
   ➤ *Your code should look similar to figure 5.7.*

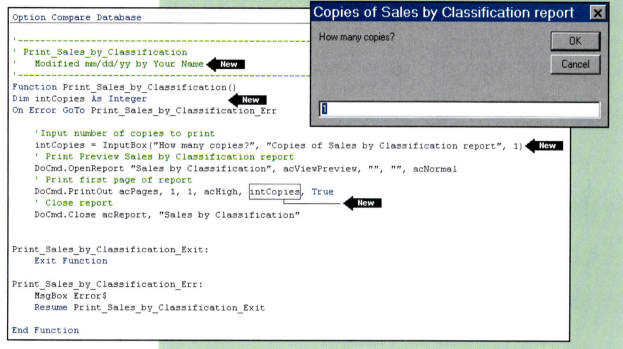

FIGURE 5.7 Code with InputBox Function

InputBox(prompt, title, default) Function

You have already used the InputBox function to accept keyboard input. In this situation, the user is prompted to enter the number of copies of the report. One copy is the default entry. Setting the default entry is an optional argument used by the InputBox function. Others allow the user to position the message box on the screen using X and Y coordinates and identifies a related help screen. You will use three InputBox arguments:

1. Prompt (How many copies?)—appears in the input box.
2. Title (Copies of Sales by Classification report)—appears in Title bar of the input box.
3. Default Input Value (1)—appears as a highlighted entry (see figure 5.7).

1. Create a blank line under the On Error command, press the Tab key, and then key the following statements:

   'Input number of copies to print
   intCopies = InputBox("How many copies?", "Copies of Sales by Classification report", 1)

ALTERNATIVE ▶

Press F5 or click the Run Sub/UserForm button.

2. In the DoCmd.PrintOut line replace the 1 in front of True with **intCopies**.
   ➤ *Your code should look similar to figure 5.7.*
3. Click <u>R</u>un and then Run Sub/UserForm.
   ➤ *Access executes the code and displays the Copies of Sales by Classification report input box.*
4. Key **2** and then press Enter.
   ➤ *The Enter Parameter Value dialog box opens.*
5. Key **1/19/03** and then press Enter.
   ➤ *Access prints two copies of the Sales by Classification report for the week starting 1/19/03.*
6. If the module executes without errors, save it. Otherwise, debug the code using figure 5.7 as a guide.
7. Close the Visual Basic Editor.
   ➤ *Access displays the slb-inv : Database dialog box.*

MAKE TABLE QUERY

We use computers because they help us get things done faster and with fewer errors. For instance, it would be desirable to use an Excel sub procedure to transfer the sales by classification data from the slb-inv database directly into the Sales Analysis worksheet. Doing so would speed up worksheet preparation and eliminates data entry errors that occur when manually entering data.

You will use a Make Table query to establish a new table called Weekly Sales in the SLB Inventory database. Since you want to use the most up-to-date sales data, the Make Table query is based upon the Weekly Sales by Classification dynaset (see figure 5.3). Like the Sales by Classification report, you can use the daily sales data to total the number of books and purchase prices by classification (see figure 5.8).

1. Click the Queries button on the Objects bar and then click <u>N</u>ew.
   ➤ *Access opens the New Query dialog box.*
2. Select the Simple Query Wizard option and then click OK.
   ➤ *The first of a series of Simple Query Wizard windows opens.*
3. From the Tables/Query list box select *Query: Weekly Sales by Classification.*
4. Click the button containing the greater than symbol (>) to move *Classification, CountOfISBN,* and *SumOfPrice* to the Selected Fields area.
5. Click the <u>N</u>ext button.
   ➤ *The next Simple Query Wizard window asks about detailed and summary data.*
6. Choose the Summary option button and then click the Summary <u>O</u>ptions button.
   ➤ *The Summary Options dialog box opens.*
7. Click the Sum check box for CountOfISBN and SumOfPrice and then click OK.

8. Click the Next button.

➤ *The next Simple Query Wizard window asks for a query title.*

9. Key **Weekly Sales Query** in the text box and click the Finish button.

➤ *Access runs the query and displays the Enter Parameter Value box.*

10. Key **1/5/03** and then press Enter.

➤ *Access displays a dynaset that contains the same data found in figure 5.8.*

11. Close the query results and then click the Design view button.

➤ *The Query design window is displayed as shown in figure 5.8.*

12. Click Query and then Make-Table Query.

➤ *The Make Table dialog box opens.*

13. Key **Weekly Sales** in the Table Name text box and then click OK.

➤ *The query is turned into a Make Table query.*

14. Run the query.

➤ *Access runs the query and displays the Enter Parameter Value box.*

15. Key **1/5/03** and then press Enter.

➤ *A message box appears that tells you 6 rows are being pasted to the table.*

16. Click Yes.

➤ *A new Weekly Sales table is created.*

17. Save the changes.

18. Close the Query design window.

19. Click the Tables button on the Objects bar and then open the Weekly Sales table.

➤ *The table should look similar to figure 5.8.*

TIP

After the query is run the first time, a message box asking if you want to overwrite the old version of the Weekly Sales table appears. Click Yes to continue.

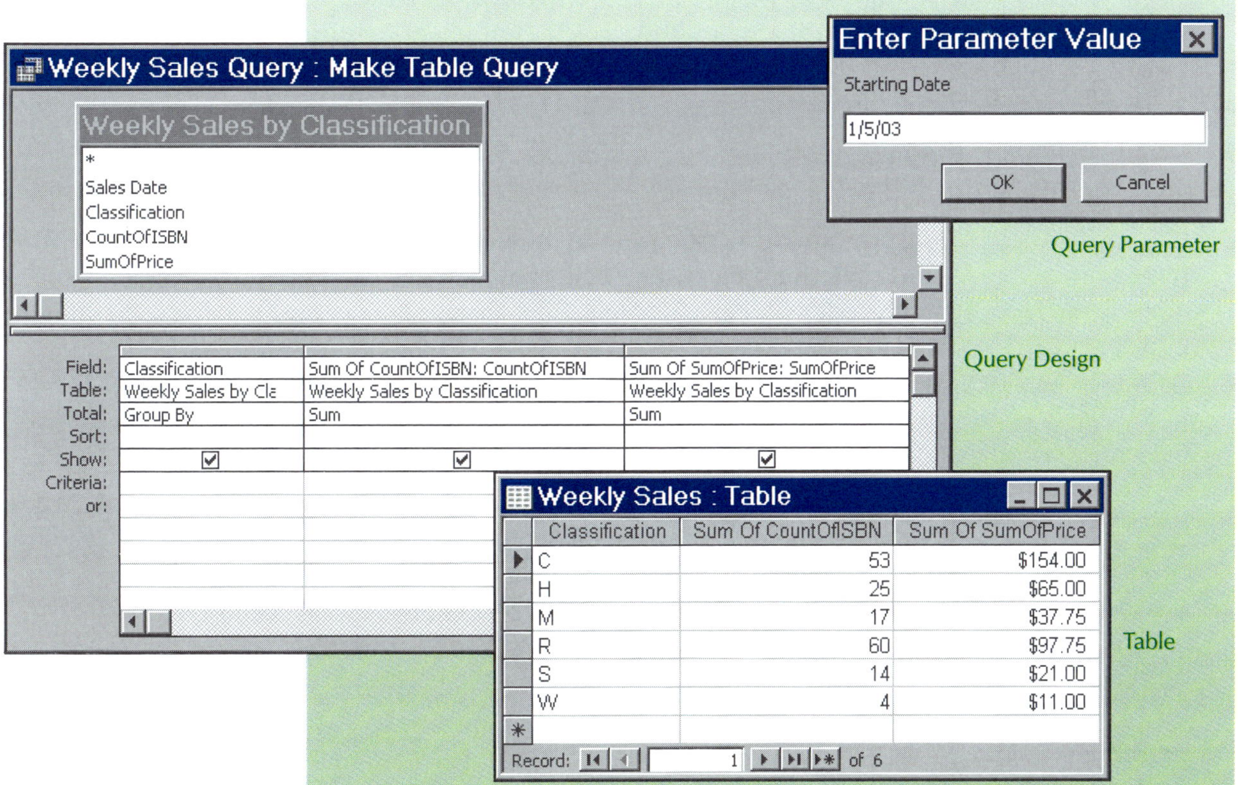

FIGURE 5.8 Weekly Sales Query and Table

IMPORTING DATA USING EXCEL MACROS

With the Weekly Sales Query saved as part of the SLB inventory database, Access should be closed to free computer memory. Next, open Excel to create a macro which imports data from the Weekly Sales table (see figure 5.8) into the Sales Analysis worksheet (see figure 5.9). Remember your macro security level needs to be set to medium as discussed in chapter 1.

ALTERNATIVE

If you completed the Sales workbook in chapter 2 or the Chart workbook in chapter 4, you can use either as an alternative to c5-sales.xls, just remember that the 2003 Sales worksheet should be active.

1. Close the Weekly Sales table.
2. Click File and then Exit.
   ➤ *The Access application window closes.*
3. Open Excel.
4. Open the c5-sales.xls workbook you downloaded to your student data disk.
   ➤ *Excel displays the macro warning message.*
5. Click the Enable Macros button.
   ➤ *Excel opens the c5-sales or selected alternative workbook.*
6. Edit cell A2 by adding **Prepared by Your Name** after the text Sales Analysis if it is not already there.
   ➤ *The worksheet should look similar to figure 5.9.*
7. Save the workbook as AutoSale.

	A	B	C	D	E	F	G	H	I	J	K	L	M	N	O
1	**Second Look Books**														
2	Sales Analysis Prepared by Your Name														
3															
4		Computer		History		Mystery		Romance		Sci-Fi		Western		Totals	
5	Week Of	# Books	Value	# Books	Value	# Books	Value	# Books	Value	# Books	Value	# Books	Value	# Books	Value
6	5-Jan	53	154.00	25	65.00	17	37.75	60	97.75	14	21.00	4	11.00	173	386.50
7	12-Jan	37	93.00	45	120.50	32	71.25	40	68.75	17	31.00	10	28.50	181	413.00
8	19-Jan	40	109.75	34	84.00	41	99.50	26	41.50	19	34.00	9	28.00	169	396.75
9	26-Jan	36	105.00	46	110.75	20	44.10	73	123.00	14	32.00	2	8.00	191	422.85
10	2-Feb	48	128.00	50	131.25	25	60.00	57	96.25	23	35.50	7	23.50	210	474.50
11	9-Feb	47	130.25	60	158.25	35	79.75	40	66.50	14	24.25	9	29.50	205	488.50
12	16-Feb	53	159.50	49	122.00	16	37.00	57	92.25	20	34.50	3	10.00	198	455.25
14	YTD Totals	314	879.50	309	791.75	186	429.35	353	586.00	121	212.25	44	138.50	1327	3,037.35

FIGURE 5.9 Sales Analysis Worksheet

The Excel InsertAccessData procedure will run the query and then transfer the results from the Weekly Sales table to a new worksheet. You will use some of the cell selection commands from chapter 2 to arrange the data to be compatible with the Sales Analysis worksheet. Once the data is imported into the temporary worksheet, it is checked for missing data and copied to the Sales Analysis worksheet. After copying the data to a new row, the temporay worksheet is removed from the workbook.

This programming task is complex enough to benefit from coding in stages. Creating and testing the ImportAccessData procedure can be broken down into five steps:

1. Create the ImportAccessData procedure that calls the InsertNewRow macro (see chapter 2), adds a temporary worksheet, checks for errors, deletes the temporary worksheet, and exits the procedure.
2. Run the Weekly Sales Query from InsertAccessData.
3. Use ImportAccessData to import data from the Weekly Sales table into the temporary worksheet.

4. Create a procedure that checks for a missing classification; for example, no science fiction sales for a week.
5. Move the imported data into a single row in the 2003 Sales worksheet.

Developing the code in stages will allow you to test small pieces of the final code before continuing to the next stage. Trying to write all the code at one time could result in an overwhelming number of interacting errors that would be hard to debug.

Create ImportAccessData Procedure

The easiest way to get started is to use the VB Editor to insert a new procedure into Module1. This module currently contains the InsertNewRow and PrintYTD procedures.

ALTERNATIVE

Press Alt + F11 to open the Editor.

1. Click Tools, point to Macro, and then click Visual Basic Editor.
   ➤ *The Visual Basic Editor window opens.*
2. Open the Project Explorer window.
3. If necessary, open Module1 in the Modules folder by double-clicking the icon.
   ➤ *The Editor displays the Code window containing InsertNewRow and PrintYTD procedures.*
4. Close the Project Explorer window.
   ➤ *Only the Code window is displayed.*
5. Click Insert and then Procedure.
   ➤ *The Editor displays the Add Procedure dialog box similar to figure 5.10.*
6. Key **ImportAccessData** in the Name text box and then press Enter.
   ➤ *The Sub and End Sub statements for the ImportAccessData procedure are added to the module.*

FIGURE 5.10 Add Procedure Dialog Box

TIP

Include 'remarks and {blank lines} as indicated.

7. Key the following code between the Sub and End Sub statement, using figure 5.11 as a guide.

```
'Input sales data from Weekly Sales table in SLB-inv.mdb
'Prepared mm/dd/yy by Your Name
'
Dim shtTempSheet As Worksheet
{blank line}
On Error GoTo Error_Handler
{blank line}
'Start Sub
Call InsertNewRow
Set shtTempSheet = Worksheets.Add 'Insert temporary worksheet
shtTempSheet.Name = "Imported Sales Data"
'Rename worksheet tab
{blank line}
```

The next three statements identify routines that are added next. Programmers often include labels or remarks without related code during the first programming stages. They do this in order to identify where important tasks fit into the program logic before the code is written. *Labels*, like Run_Query:, identify points in the procedure where you can transfer control. A label always ends with a colon. For example, one of the Error_Handler's routines shown in figure 5.11 resumes program execution at Run_Query. The two remarks that follow identify points in the code to which we will need to refer.

8. Key the following code:

```
Run_Query:
{blank line}
'Copy table to temp worksheet
{blank line}
'Move data to Sales worksheet
{blank line}
```

DISPLAYALERTS PROPERTY

Program code often includes a housekeeping routine that closes files, deletes temporary workspaces, and generally cleans up before execution stops. This macro uses Exit_Sub as the housekeeping routine. All you need it to do right now is delete the temporary worksheet named Imported Sales Data. Excel usually displays a message box asking the user to confirm the deletion. Setting the application's DisplayAlerts property to False turns off this alert.

ON ERROR GOTO STATEMENT

The Error_Handler is the last routine in ImportAccessData. This routine is executed when a run time error occurs. The On Error GoTo statement at the beginning of ImportAccessData sends control to the Error_Handler when an error is encountered. A variety of run time errors are possible. For instance, renaming the new worksheet Imported Sales Data when a worksheet with that name already exists will generate a run time error. This error is flagged as error 1004. Thorough and creative testing will identify several errors for which you should account in the Error_Handler code. The error number assigned to the problem can be referenced from the Err objects Number property (Err.Number). This number or its related error message can be displayed using the MsgBox Err.Number or MsgBox Err.Description statements.

SELECT CASE STATEMENT

Unlike the error handling in chapter 3, you are now looking for specific errors. When these errors are trapped, code in the error handler will attempt to correct the problem so the procedure can continue rather than abort execution. If you were looking for a single error number, an If statement would be used. However, error handling routines traditionally use a Select Case statement because a single statement can identify different actions for many error conditions. This statement starts by identifying a variable to examine. Err.Number is used in figure 5.11. Any number of "Case Is =" clauses allows a programmer to identify a variety of cases (error conditions) and the resulting actions that need to take place. Like an If statement, a Case statement has an Else clause that allows a programmer to control what happens when specific error numbers are not found. You will display the context sensitive error message as part of the Case Else condition (see figure 5.11). An End Select statement identifies the last line of the Select Case logic.

1. Finish coding this procedure by keying the following statements:

   Error_Handler:
         Select Case Err.Number
         Case Is = 1004 'Temporary worksheet already exists
               ActiveSheet.Delete 'Remove new worksheet
               Worksheets("Imported Sales Data").Activate
               Resume Run_Query
         Case Else
               MsgBox Err.Description 'Display error message
               Resume Exit_Sub
         End Select
   {blank line}

   ➤ *The ImportAccessData macro should look like figure 5.11.*

2. Save the worksheet.

```
Public Sub ImportAccessData()
'Input sales data from Weekly Sales table in SLB-inv.mdb
'Prepared mm/dd/yy by Your Name
'
Dim shtTempSheet As Worksheet

On Error GoTo Error_Handler

'Start Sub
Call InsertNewRow
Set shtTempSheet = Worksheets.Add 'Insert temporary worksheet
shtTempSheet.Name = "Imported Sales Data" 'Rename worksheet tab

Run_Query:

'Copy table to temp worksheet

'Move data to Sales worksheet

Exit_Sub:
    Application.DisplayAlerts = False 'Turn off messages
    Worksheets("Imported Sales Data").Delete 'Remove temporary worksheet
    Application.DisplayAlerts = True 'Turn on messages
    Exit Sub

Error_Handler:
    Select Case Err.Number
    Case Is = 1004 'Temporary worksheet already exists
        ActiveSheet.Delete 'Remove new worksheet
        Worksheets("Imported Sales Data").Activate
        Resume Run_Query
    Case Else
        MsgBox Err.Description 'Display error message
        Resume Exit_Sub
    End Select

End Sub
```

FIGURE 5.11 ImportAccessData Macro (Stage 1)

Next Step 5-3

The error number associated with not having your data disk ready in the disk drive is 3043. Using figure 5.11 as a guide, add a Case Is = option in the Select Case statement that does the following when this error occurs:

1. Displays an error message.
2. Resumes execution at the Run_Query routine.

Save changes when you are done.

Testing ImportAccessData

If the Excel and VB Editor are tiled horizontally, you can use the F8 key to watch the code execute in Excel. Do not forget you can also halt execution by clicking on the Reset button on the toolbar or by clicking Run and then Reset. Resetting the procedure clears all program variables and forces the Editor to start from the beginning the next time the procedure is run.

TIP

The active window will be placed at the top of the screen when the windows are tiled horizontally.

TIP

If more than two windows are horizontally tiled, close the extra window(s) and repeat the last two actions.

TIP

After corrections are made, reset the procedure before running it.

1. Except for Excel and the Visual Basic Editor, close all programs listed on the taskbar.
   ➤ *Only the Excel and Visual Basic buttons appear on the taskbar.*
2. Right-click on an open area of the taskbar.
   ➤ *The taskbar's shortcut menu opens.*
3. Select the Tile Windows Horizontally option.
   ➤ *The Excel and VB Editor windows are tiled horizontally on the screen.*
4. Save the worksheet.
5. Click on the first line of the ImportAccessData procedure you just created.
   ➤ *Insertion point is blinking somewhere in the first line.*
6. Use the F8 key to execute the procedure one line at a time.
7. If any line causes execution to jump to the Error_Handler, double-check the line's syntax with figure 5.11 and make necessary changes until it works.
8. Delete the new row in the 2003 Sales worksheet by right-clicking on the row header and then clicking Delete.
   ➤ *Worksheet should look similar to figure 5.9.*

Next Step 5-4

The Error_Handler routine needs to be tested. To test if it handles the presence of an Imported Sales Data worksheet, do the following:

1. Create a new worksheet and rename the tab *Imported Sales Data*.
2. Make the 2003 Sales Data worksheet active.
3. Run the ImportAccessData macro.

(continued)

TIP

To eliminate the need for the user to respond to the Delete Worksheet prompt, turn the DisplayAlert property to True and False like you did in the End_Sub routine.

If the Error_Handler is working properly, running the macro should: create a new worksheet; generate an error when it tries to rename the worksheet; drop down to Error_Handler; identify the error as Error.Number = 1004; prompt user to delete the new worksheet; delete it; activate the Imported Sales Data worksheet; and resume execute at the Run_Query routine.

IMPORTING ACCESS DATA INTO EXCEL

There are a variety of ways to import data organized and saved by other application software. This occurs because several object libraries (see figure 5.12) support database objects that are compatible with Access databases. To a great degree, the object library determines the program logic and syntax used to transfer the data. To start, you are going to reference the Data Access Object (DAO) library. DAO objects include database and recordset objects you can use to transfer data from the Weekly Sales table to Excel's Imported Sales Data worksheet.

1. If necessary, delete any blank rows in the 2003 Sales worksheet.
   ➤ *Worksheet should look similar to figure 5.9.*
2. In the Editor window, click <u>T</u>ools and then <u>R</u>eferences.
   ➤ *A list of object libraries similar to figure 5.12 opens.*
3. If necessary, select *Microsoft DAO 3.6 Object Library*.
4. Press Enter or click OK.

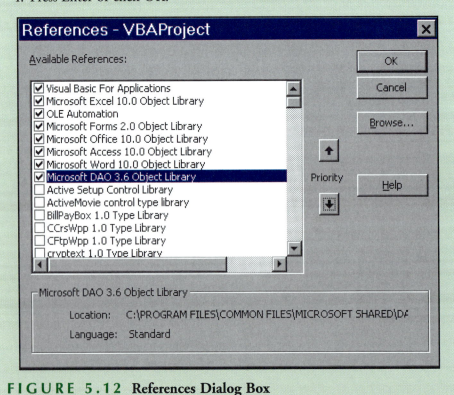

FIGURE 5.12 **References Dialog Box**

Data Access Object (DAO) Library

DAO objects are designed to link Office applications with Access and other database management software. As illustrated in figure 5.13, the hierarchy of DAO objects starts with a **database engine** object. The engine is the software that handles the exchange of data from one application to another. Microsoft's Office applications use the Jet database engine. Other database engines, generally referred to as **open database connectivity (ODBC) data sources**, also supply database objects. For example, an Oracle database is an ODBC data source. For our purposes, the default Jet database engine used by Access *.mdb* files is the one to use.

DBEngine objects are assigned workspaces (see figure 5.13), which are temporary areas where the Jet database engine or an ODBC data resource handles data. Exiting or logging off the software eliminates the associated workspace. While you will be using the default workspace, more sophisticated applications set up data security using Workspace properties. Several Workspaces can be active at the same time.

Coding resumes in the ImportAccessData procedure with two new Dim statements that identify Database and Recordset objects. Recordset objects are used to manage data at the record level. You will use the standard Visual Basic tags of *dtb* for databases and *rst* for recordsets. As shown in figure 5.13, the database object dtbSLBinv is assigned to slb-inv.mdb from your data disk. Data from the Weekly Sales table is assigned to the record set rstSalesByClassification.

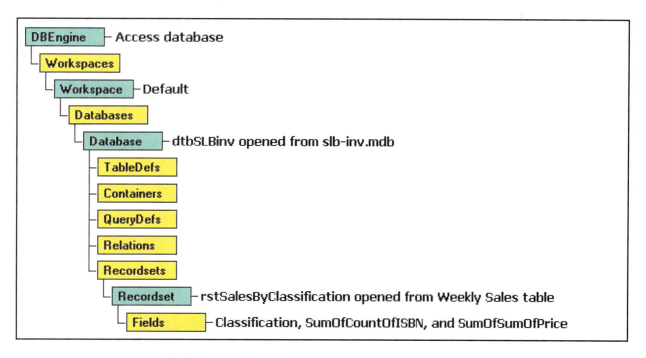

FIGURE 5.13 Hierarchy of Data Access Objects (DAOs)

1. Create a blank line under the Dim shtTempSheet As Worksheet statement.
2. Key the following statements:
   Dim dtbSLBinv As DAO.Database
   Dim rstSalesByClassification As DAO.Recordset

DAO Code

The DAO code that makes up the Copy Table To Temp Worksheet routine is straightforward. Once the database is opened and assigned to the dtbSLBinv object, you will assign the Weekly Sales table to the rstSalesByClassification record set. While the record set could contain any number of records, we know it contains six records with three fields—Classification, SumOfCountOfISBN, and SumOfSumOfPrice (see bottom of figure 5.8). In spreadsheet terminology, rstSalesByClassification is a block of data six rows by three columns.

PITFALL

If you do not reference the correct drive and path location of where you stored the slb-inv.mdb database, the statement that assigns the database to the dtbSLBinv object variable will fail.

1. Click in the blank line under the 'Copy Table To Temp Worksheet remark.
2. Key the following statements after pressing Tab once:
   Set dtbSLBinv = OpenDatabase("a:slb-inv.mdb")
   Set rstSalesByClassification = dtbSLBinv.OpenRecordset ("Weekly Sales")
   ➤ *The code should look similar to the top lines in figure 5.14.*

The next line of code copies the record set to the active cell (A1) in the temporary worksheet. As a result, the first record is inserted into the first three columns of row 1, the second record into row 2, and so on, as shown in figure 5.14.

3. Finish the routine by keying the following:
   ActiveCell.CopyFromRecordset   rstSalesByClassification
   rstSalesByClassification.Close
   dtbSLBinv.Close
   {blank line}
4. Save the worksheet.

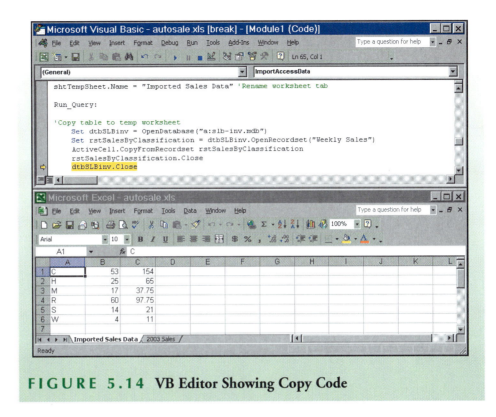

FIGURE 5.14 VB Editor Showing Copy Code

Ctrl + Alt + Delete Keys

To test the new objects and routines, you should continue to use the F8 function key to test the code line by line. This way you can reset the macro if you find an error. When accessing data disk files, this is especially important because a variety of situations could lock up the computer and force you to close Excel. In this type of emergency you use the *three-finger salute*—hold down the Ctrl and Alt keys and then press the Delete key. This key combination displays the Close Program dialog box. You can use it to end any tasks, like Excel, that have stopped responding.

> **TIP**
>
> If a new line causes the execution to jump to the Error_Handler, double-check the line's syntax at the top of figure 5.14 and make necessary changes.

1. Use the F8 key to execute the macro one line at a time until you get to the dtbSLBinv.Close statement as shown at the top of figure 5.14.
   - ➤ *The Imported Sales Data worksheet contains data from Weekly Sales tables as shown at the bottom of figure 5.14.*
2. Use the F8 key to finish executing the macro.
3. Print the code from the current module.
4. Delete the new row in the 2003 Sales worksheet.
   - ➤ *The worksheet should look similar to figure 5.9.*

Move Data to Sales Worksheet

Nothing new appears in the Move Data To Sales Worksheet routine. This code copies data from the temporary worksheet into the 2003 Sales worksheet. Two new variables, intRow and vntDataRange, are dimensioned at the beginning of the procedure.

Linking Tables to Workbooks Using Automation | **141**

1. Create a blank line under the Dim rstSalesByClassification As Recordset statement.
2. Key the following statements:

    Dim vntDataRange As Variant
    Dim intRow As Integer

Since the variable vntDataRange is a variant, when it is set equal to the cell range A1:C6 the compiler automatically sets the data into a two-dimensional array with six rows and three columns. After making 2003 Sales the active worksheet, a For/Nest loop moves the book count *vntDataRange (intRow,2)*, and sales value *vntDataRange (intRow,3)* to the selected cell.

3. Click in the blank line under the Move Data To Sales Worksheet remark.
4. Key the following statements after pressing Tab once:

    'Check for No Sales call will go here
    Range("A1:C6").Select
    vntDataRange = Selection
    {blank line}
    Worksheets("2003 Sales").Activate
    For intRow = 1 To 6
        ActiveCell.Value = vntDataRange(intRow, 2)
        Selection.Offset(0, 1).Select
        ActiveCell.Value = vntDataRange(intRow, 3)
        Selection.Offset(0, 1).Select
    Next intRow
    {blank line}

5. Save the worksheet.
6. Use the F8 function key to run the ImportAccessData macro line by line. Correct any errors you find using figure 5.15 as a guide.
    ➤ *Since the Weekly Sales table contains data from 1/5/03, check to see if the new line matches the original worksheet data for 1/5/03.*
7. Run the PrintYTD macro.
    ➤ *The printer outputs the current copy of the Sales Analysis worksheet.*
8. Delete row 13 with 23-Feb sales data.
    ➤ *The worksheet should look similar to figure 5.9.*

USING AUTOMATION CODE

The basic routines to import Access data are in place. However, the ImportAccessData macro does not provide the most up-to-date sales data. To be functional, the macro needs to run the Weekly Sales Query to update the Weekly Sales table before importing the data. Since running an Access query requires code that executes database methods, you could use the DAO object library. However, you will do it using Office's Automation code and Access library objects.

1. In the Editor window click <u>T</u>ools and then <u>R</u>eferences.
   ➤ *A list of object libraries similar to figure 5.12 opens.*
2. If necessary, select the *Microsoft Access 10.0 Object Library.*
3. Click OK.

Object Linking and Embedding

Automation code is based on **object linking and embedding** (**OLE**) standards for interchanging objects between different application software. In earlier Microsoft products, Automation was referred to as *OLE Automation.* OLE relationships between the software that created the object (the **server**) and the software that it is transferred to (the **client**) gave rise to one usage of the term client/server. You will find that objects are exchanged between applications in one of three ways:

1. *Copying.* A duplicate of the original object is pasted into the client document. Changes to the original object have no impact on the duplicate. No information is maintained about the original object or the server software—think of a photocopy.
2. *Embedding.* A duplicate of the original object is inserted in the client document with information about the server software. Changes to the original object have no impact on the duplicate. However, the duplicate object can be independently modified by the server software—think of an executable video file.
3. *Linking.* A designated area of a client document is exposed to the original object. Changes to the original object are shown in the client document. In some cases, the client software gives the user a choice of whether or not to show the changes—think of an Internet hypertext link.

Automation code links the macro to Access in order to execute the Weekly Sales Query object.

Application Objects

The focus of Automation code is the Application object. Once a Dim statement assigns an Application object to a specific software package (like Word, Excel, or Access), it can create or manipulate all the objects associated with the application. The assigned software actually runs in the background and appears in the taskbar.

GetObject Function

The GetObject and CreateObject functions actually open or establish new tables, queries, and other Access objects in real time. You will use the GetObject function to open the slb-inv database. The DoCmd object provides a variety of methods to execute Access commands. The related Automation code allows the programmer to initiate actions just like he or she does by clicking on menu options when the Access application window is open.

1. Add the following statement under the other Dim statements:
   Dim acsAccess As Access.Application
2. Click on the blank line under the Run_Query routine.
3. Key the following statements after pressing Tab once:
   Set acsAccess = GetObject("a:slb-inv.mdb")
   acsAccess.DoCmd.OpenQuery ("Weekly Sales Query")
   acsAccess.DoCmd.Close   acQuery, "Weekly Sales Query"
   acsAccess.CloseCurrentDatabase
   {blank line}
   ➤ *Your program code should look similar to figure 5.15.*

Quit Method

Since the macro runs Access, you need to exit it as part of the Exit_Sub housekeeping. The Quit method initiates the shutdown of Access. The acExit intrinsic constant calls for exiting Access without saving any objects. In addition, good coding practice dictates that you release the references held by the object variables from memory by assigning them to Nothing.

1. Create a blank first line in the Exit_Sub routine.
2. Key the following statements:
   acsAccess.Quit acExit
   Set shtTempSheet=Nothing
   Set dtbSLBinv=Nothing
   Set rstSalesByClassification=Nothing
   Set acsAccess=Nothing
3. Save the worksheet.

If you step through the procedure rather than run it, the Enter Parameter Value input box will activate under the Editor. Though it appears the procedure is locked up, it is merely waiting for you to respond to the Parameter input box. Hold down the Alt key and press the Tab key until the Access – Enter Parameter Value appears. Release and respond to the input box.

4. Run the ImportAccessData macro using 2/23/03 as the starting date query parameter. Correct any errors you find using figure 5.15 as a guide.
   ➤ *The 2003 Sales worksheet should look similar to figure 5.15. Note that no books with a Western classification were sold the week of February 23rd.*

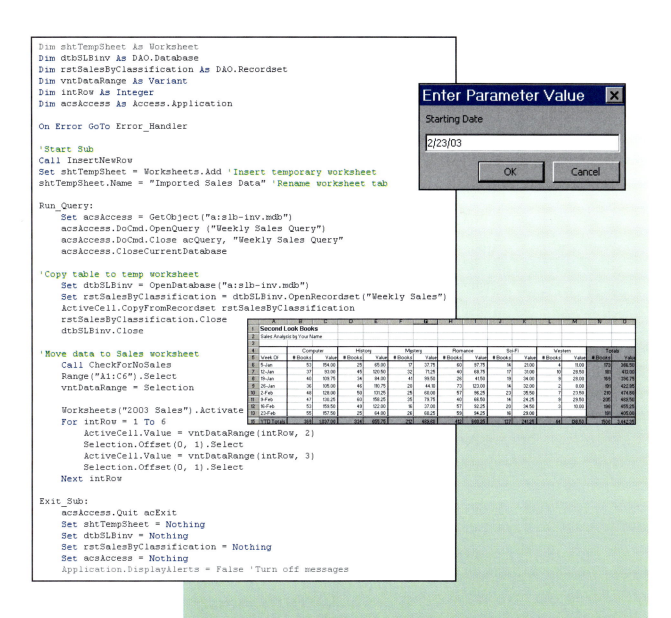

```
Dim shtTempSheet As Worksheet
Dim dtbSLBinv As DAO.Database
Dim rstSalesByClassification As DAO.Recordset
Dim vntDataRange As Variant
Dim intRow As Integer
Dim acsAccess As Access.Application

On Error GoTo Error_Handler

'Start Sub
Call InsertNewRow
Set shtTempSheet = Worksheets.Add 'Insert temporary worksheet
shtTempSheet.Name = "Imported Sales Data" 'Rename worksheet tab

Run_Query:
    Set acsAccess = GetObject("a:slb-inv.mdb")
    acsAccess.DoCmd.OpenQuery ("Weekly Sales Query")
    acsAccess.DoCmd.Close acQuery, "Weekly Sales Query"
    acsAccess.CloseCurrentDatabase

'Copy table to temp worksheet
    Set dtbSLBinv = OpenDatabase("a:slb-inv.mdb")
    Set rstSalesByClassification = dtbSLBinv.OpenRecordset("Weekly Sales")
    ActiveCell.CopyFromRecordset rstSalesByClassification
    rstSalesByClassification.Close
    dtbSLBinv.Close

'Move data to Sales worksheet
    Call CheckForNoSales
    Range("A1:C6").Select
    vntDataRange = Selection

    Worksheets("2003 Sales").Activate
    For intRow = 1 To 6
        ActiveCell.Value = vntDataRange(intRow, 2)
        Selection.Offset(0, 1).Select
        ActiveCell.Value = vntDataRange(intRow, 3)
        Selection.Offset(0, 1).Select
    Next intRow

Exit_Sub:
    acsAccess.Quit acExit
    Set shtTempSheet = Nothing
    Set dtbSLBinv = Nothing
    Set rstSalesByClassification = Nothing
    Set acsAccess = Nothing
    Application.DisplayAlerts = False 'Turn off messages
```

FIGURE 5.15 VBA Code for New ImportAccessData Routines and Related Excel Worksheet

Checking for No Sales

The data from the week of February 23rd highlighted a flaw in the program design. Up until now there has been at least one book sold each week in every classification. The underlying assumption was that there would always be six rows of data in the Weekly Sales table listed in alphabetical order (CHMRSW). Row 1 always contained the Computers sales data, row 2 the Horror book sales, and so on. But what would the Move Data To Sales Worksheet routine do if the store did not sell any computer books one week?

We could add the code that corrects this problem to the Move Data To Sales Worksheet routine. Instead, we thought it would make sense to use the code in an independent procedure and have you create the CheckForNoSales procedure as part of Next Step 5-5.

Mid(String, Start, Length) Function

The CheckForNoSales procedure inserts a row and the words "No Sales" for any classification missing from the Weekly Sales table. To accomplish this task you will use one of VBA's built-in functions. A *function* is a procedure that can return a value based on the data provided in its arguments. The Mid function is used to compare the expected value in the string constant strClassification with the first value in each row. This function dissects the string by extracting a selected number of characters from it. As the For/Next statement increments intCounter, the Mid function dissects the string "CHMRSW" one character at a time. The third argument dictates how many characters are examined in the string. If it is set to 1, one character is used.

Consider the situation mentioned above where the store does not sell any computer books for a week. When the For/Next loop starts at 1, the Mid function examines the string "CHMRSW" and identifies the first character as C. The Weekly Sales table does not have any data for computer sales, so row 1 starts with Horror book sales data. Since "C" does not equal "H", the Else option within the If statement inserts a new row and sets the first cell's value to "No Sales".

Next Step 5-5

1. Create a new procedure in Module 1 named CheckForNoSales that uses the following code:

```
Dim intCounter As Integer
Dim strClassification As String
strClassification = "CHMRSW"
Range("A1").Select
For intCounter = 1 To 6
    If Mid(strClassification, intCounter, 1) = ActiveCell.Value Then
        Selection.Offset(1, 0).Select
    Else
        Selection.EntireRow.Insert
        ActiveCell.Value = "No Sales"
        Selection.Offset(1, 0).Select
    End If
Next intCounter
```

2. Replace the remark 'Check for No Sales call will go here with **Call CheckForNoSales** (no period at end).
3. Save the worksheet.
4. Run the ImportAccessData macro procedure from Excel using 3/2/03 as the starting date.
5. Print the code for the ImportAccessData and CheckForNoSales procedures.
6. Run the PrintYTD procedure.
7. Exit Excel.

automation
client
database engine
dynamic
dynaset
object linking and
   embedding (OLE)
open database con-
   nectivity (ODBC)
   data sources
server
static

REVIEW QUESTIONS

On a blank sheet of paper provide a short answer for the following questions.

1. Be able to define each of the key terms.
2. What are four reasons for automating tasks using an Access macro?
3. Why would a programmer convert Access macros to VBA code?
4. What Access feature must be installed before converting Access macros to VBA code?
5. Which function is used to let users enter data as a procedure executes?
6. Why do programmers develop complex code in stages?
7. Why would a programmer include a label or remark statement without the related code?
8. How do you turn warning messages off and on?
9. Why is a Select Case statement used instead of an If statement in an error handling routine?
10. How do you stop a procedure while it is executing?
11. What determines the logic and syntax of code used to transfer data between applications?
12. What database engine is used by Microsoft Office applications?
13. Why would you use the "three finger salute"?
14. How are copying, embedding, and linking different?
15. What Automation statement is used to open an existing object?
16. How do you use Automation code to exit an open application?
17. What does the Mid function do?

CHECK YOUR UNDERSTANDING

Indicate the correct term or choose the correct answer for each item.

1. The location of code to be added at a later date in a procedure is typically identified by a _Comment_ or _label_.
2. Application-generated message boxes that require a user to confirm an action can be prevented with the application object's _Display Alerts_ property.
3. The _Select Case_ statement is used in error handling when many different types of errors are possible.
4. The _object library_ determines the program logic and syntax used to transfer the data.
5. The _Ctl Alt Del_ key combination enables you to break out of a faulty procedure that has locked up your computer.
6. Which of the following is a toolbar option that stops the execution of a procedure?
   a. Close
   b. Exit
   c. Reset
   d. PgDn key

7. The result of an Access query is called a(n)
   a. procedure.
   b. dynaset.
   c. module.
   d. object library.
8. Which of the following is a Visual Basic code label?
   a. 'Start Sub
   b. Exit Sub
   c. Error_Handler
   d. Run_Query: p. 134
9. What of the following database engines is used by Office applications?
   a. Jet
   b. Black Beauty
   c. Oracle 9
   d. Access
10. The Microsoft standard for interchanging objects between different applications software is
   a. ODBC.
   b. OLE.
   c. PARAM.
   d. PATH.

EXERCISES

Complete the following exercises.

Last Step

As you know, it is possible that the temporary "Imported Sales Data" could be left in the worksheet. This is why the error handler has code to take care of this potential problem. If this situation occurs, the error handler's code removes the newly created sheet and makes the leftover Imported Sales Data sheet active. This works fine provided there is not any leftover data in the Imported Sales Data sheet. To absolutely assure that the incoming data does not get mislocated or contaminated, the error handling code must do the following after making Imported Sales Data the active sheet:

1. Select the cell range from A1:C6 and clear it.
2. Make cell A1 the active cell.

Print out the new code after it has been tested and is working correctly.

Debug

The programmer who wrote the error handling code in this procedure has made significant errors that result in both syntax and logic problems that must be corrected. Identify and correct all coding errors found below the note.

```
Private Sub ImportFile()

    On Error Goto Error_Handler
    {code staements}

    Open_File:
    {code statements}
```
(NOTE: All errors occur below this point in the Sub procedure.)

```
    'Exit_Sub

    'Error_Handler
    Select Case Number
    Case Is = 53 'File Not Found
        MsgBox "The requested file is not present"
        Goto Open_File:
    Case Else
        MsgBox Err.Description
        Goto Exit Sub:
    End Select

End Sub
```

Internet

In this chapter we used the DAO library to link an Excel workbook to a database created and maintained by Access. While this object library is more than sufficient to link any Office application with an Access database, Office applications now support ActiveX Data Objects (ADO) that can be used to establish links between these applications and a variety of databases. Use the Internet and your favorite search engine to find out more about ADO. In particular, find out what types of data, besides Access databases, are handled by this new interface.

New Challenge

A serious error can occur in the ImportAccessData procedure when the Cancel button is used. If you have not discovered it yet, run the macro and when the Enter Parameter Value input box appears click the Cancel button. The [Microsoft Excel – AutoSale] button in the taskbar and the Microsoft Excel Title bar will start to alternately flash. If you click on the 2003 Sales worksheet tab you will force the error to be displayed and handled. Although the temporary worksheet has been deleted, a new blank row has been inserted into the 2003 Sales worksheet. Both problems must be corrected. First identify and trap the canceled operation error and then delete the inserted row from the 2003 worksheet. Print out the new code after it has been tested and is working correctly.

Discussion

Most Microsoft Office users do not have the skills necessary to accomplish even the simple automation task presented in this chapter. Do you feel that the automation resources in the Office Suite provide a significant enough productivity tool to warrant increased training of Office users or the hiring of VBA programmers in an organization?

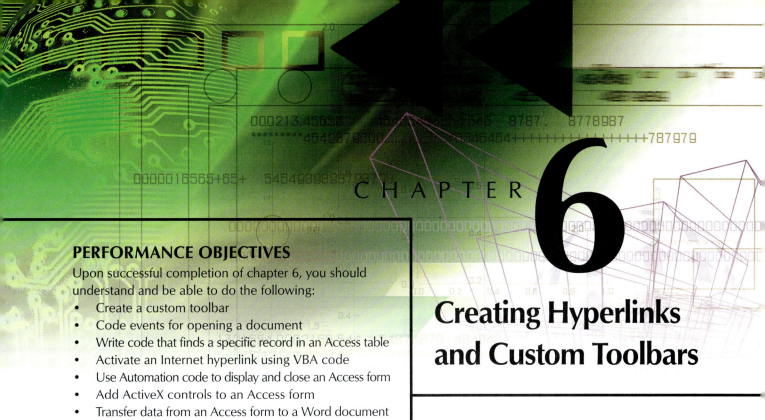

CHAPTER **6**

PERFORMANCE OBJECTIVES

Upon successful completion of chapter 6, you should understand and be able to do the following:

- Create a custom toolbar
- Code events for opening a document
- Write code that finds a specific record in an Access table
- Activate an Internet hyperlink using VBA code
- Use Automation code to display and close an Access form
- Add ActiveX controls to an Access form
- Transfer data from an Access form to a Word document
- Insert a formula into a Word table
- Clear cells in a Word table using VBA code

Creating Hyperlinks and Custom Toolbars

In the last chapter of this book, you will use VBA to integrate data from an Access database within a Word document. Chapter 1 started with Word when you added the Second Look Books logo to a document using the InsertLogo macro. From there you created code that aided in the development of PowerPoint presentations and manipulated Excel worksheets and charts, as well as Access tables. You have also copied data from a table to worksheet cells. It is now time to link Access tables and forms to a Word document.

For a bookstore to be successful, it continuously needs to be purchasing new books. At Second Look Books this is the store manager's job. Book ordering decisions require knowledge of the books the store recently sold along with information about newly published books. The manager sets aside time each week to review sales data and order books from each of the store's four book suppliers. The Internet is used to keep up-to-date on book reviews and new book lists.

BOOK ORDERING DOCUMENT

You are going to use a Word document similar to figure 6.1. It is designed so the manager can send the book order by mail or fax. When this book order document is opened, the user is asked to enter the supplier's identification number. This number is used to incorporate data from the slb-inv database's Supplier table into the document.

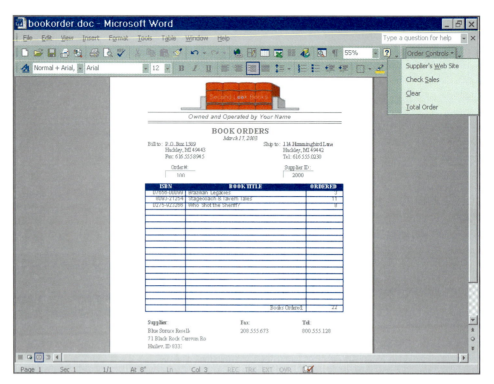

FIGURE 6.1 Second Look Books' Word Document for Book Ordering

A custom toolbar is found in the top right corner of figure 6.1. The Total Order menu option activates a VBA procedure that computes the total number of books ordered. The result is displayed in the last cell of the book order table. In figure 6.1, the number of books ordered is 22. The Clear option erases any orders currently in the order table. If the manager wants to look at the sales data of books purchased from the supplier, the Check Sales option is activated. Clicking the Supplier's Web Site option links the manager to the supplier's Internet Web site.

OPEN BOOK ORDERS

A partially complete book ordering document named c6-order.doc should have been downloaded to your student data disk. You are going to modify it to look like figure 6.1 using the following steps:

1. Run Word.
2. Open c6-order.doc from your student data disk.
   ➤ *This document contains macros.*
3. Add your name as the owner and operator.
4. Replace the date under the Book Orders heading with today's date.
5. Save this document on your student data disk as bookorder.

Take a close look at the book order document you just opened. When compared to figure 6.1, it is missing the custom toolbar with order controls and information about the supplier and the number of books ordered.

TIP

If Word appears in your taskbar, click it to activate the Word application window.

152 | Chapter 6

OPEN DOCUMENT PROCEDURE

A book order is sent to a specific supplier. Therefore, the user is going to enter the supplier's identification number when the book order is opened. The supplier ID is then used to retrieve the supplier's name, address, telephone, and fax number from the Suppliers table in the slb-inv database. This data is inserted into the document as shown in figure 6.1. All of these activities can be accomplished through an Open event procedure that is available with every Office XP application. The code associated with a document's Open event is executed when Word initially displays the document.

You will create the Open event procedure for bookorder.doc using the Visual Basic Editor to insert VBA code.

1. Click Tools, point to Macro, and then click Visual Basic Editor.
   ➤ *Word opens the Visual Basic Editor's code window.*
2. Use the Project Explorer to verify that you are viewing code for ThisDocument within the Bookorder project as shown in figure 6.2.
3. If necessary, maximize the code window.

Before going any further, verify that all the object libraries you need are available and active on your computer system.

4. Click Tools and then References.
   ➤ *The Editor opens the References dialog box that lists available active object libraries with a check mark as shown in figure 6.2.*
5. Verify that your computer has all the references shown in figure 6.2 checked.
6. Click OK.
7. Close the Project Explorer window.

PITFALL

Unexpected errors can result if these object libraries are not in use. Notify your instructor if your computer is missing a reference to any of the available active libraries shown in figure 6.2.

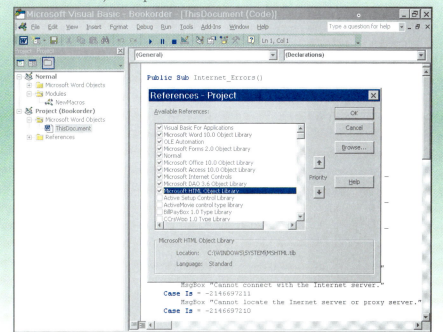

FIGURE 6.2 List of Available Object Libraries for Word

TIP

The Visual Basic Editor automatically creates Sub and End Sub codes for an object's default event, in this case the document's New procedure. However, this procedure is not necessary when ordering books and should be deleted.

The code currently displayed in the code window is an error handling routine you will use later in this lesson.

8. Click the down-pointing triangle in the Object box (see figure 6.3) and then select *Document* from the drop-down list.
   ➤ *New appears in the Procedure box and the sub procedure Document_New() is added to the code window.*
9. Click the down-pointing triangle in the Procedure box and select *Open* from the drop-down list as shown in figure 6.3.
   ➤ *Open appears in the Procedure box and the sub procedure Document_Open() is added to the code window.*
10. Highlight and delete the two lines associated with the Document_New() sub procedure.

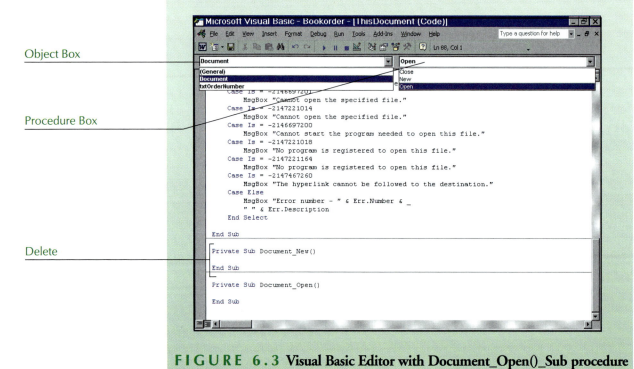

Object Box

Procedure Box

Delete

F I G U R E   6 . 3 **Visual Basic Editor with Document_Open()_Sub procedure**

Data Access Objects

To fill in the supplier data, the slb-inv database is opened. You must first define the data access objects and other variables needed to import data from an Access database. In addition, it is time to set up the error handling and exiting routines found in every data access procedure and function as shown in figure 6.4.

1. Place the insertion point in the blank line under Private Sub Document_Open() and add the following remarks:

```
'Input Supplier ID and
'update order entry with supplier data
'from the Supplier table in the slb-inv database.
'

'Prepared  mm/dd/yy by Your Name
'
```

{blank line}

2. Dimension the following variables:

```
Dim dtbSLBinv As DAO.Database
Dim rstSupplierData As DAO.Recordset
Dim vntSupplierData As Variant
```

{blank line}

3. Under the Dim statements enter the following statements:

```
On Error GoTo Error_Handler
```

{blank line}

```
Exit_Sub:
        Exit Sub
```

{blank line}

```
Error_Handler:
Select Case Err.Number
        Case Is = 432
                MsgBox "File does not exist."
                Resume Exit_Sub
        Case Else
                MsgBox "Error number - " & Err.Number & _
                " " & Err.Description
                Resume Exit_Sub
End Select
```

➤ *The code should look similar to figure 6.4.*

4. Save the code.
5. Use the F8 key to step through the code.

➤ *The procedure code terminates when it executes the Exit Sub statement.*

6. Correct any coding mistakes, if necessary, and resave.

PITFALL

Programmers often use the underscore (_) character to break long lines of code into multiple lines. Failure to place this character after a normally occurring blank space in the statement will result in an error.

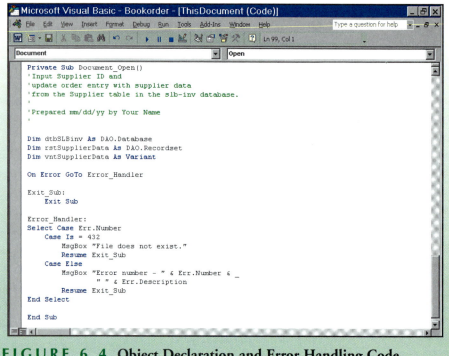

```
Microsoft Visual Basic - Bookorder - [ThisDocument (Code)]

File  Edit  View  Insert  Format  Debug  Run  Tools  Add-Ins  Window  Help       Type a question for help

                                                              Ln 99, Col 1

Document                              Open

Private Sub Document_Open()
'Input Supplier ID and
'update order entry with supplier data
'from the Supplier table in the slb-inv database.
'
'Prepared mm/dd/yy by Your Name
'

Dim dtbSLBinv As DAO.Database
Dim rstSupplierData As DAO.Recordset
Dim vntSupplierData As Variant

On Error GoTo Error_Handler

Exit_Sub:
    Exit Sub

Error_Handler:
Select Case Err.Number
    Case Is = 432
        MsgBox "File does not exist."
        Resume Exit_Sub
    Case Else
        MsgBox "Error number - " & Err.Number & _
               " " & Err.Description
        Resume Exit_Sub
End Select

End Sub
```

FIGURE 6.4 Object Declaration and Error Handling Code

Seeking the Supplier ID

An InputBox function is used to prompt the user to enter the Supplier ID. The Supplier ID is used in several procedures and must be declared in the general declarations to ensure it has wide availability. Local variables declared in a procedure are only available to the code in the procedure where they were declared. These variables are destroyed when the procedure in which they were declared ends and are recreated every time the procedure is executed. When the InputBox's Cancel button is clicked on, the input value is set to " " (empty string). Since the Supplier ID is the primary key for the Supplier table, it can be used to locate matching supplier data within the table. A **primary key** is a special field in a table that uniquely identifies a record. In the following VBA code, you will set the recordset rstSupplierData equal to the data found in the Supplier table (see figure 6.5). The recordset's Index property uses the table's primary key, Supplier ID, to find a matching record. Searching through the recordset is accomplished using the Seek method.

1. Open the code window's Object box (see figure 6.3) and select *(General)*.
   ➤ *The Procedure box displays (Declarations).*
2. Key **Dim strSupplierNumber as String** (no period at the end).
3. Press Enter.
4. Insert a second blank line under the On Error statement and add the following code starting on the second blank line:
   Get_Supplier_Data:
       strSupplierNumber = InputBox("Supplier ID", "Order Entry")
       If strSupplierNumber = " " Then 'Cancel pressed
           Exit Sub

```
End If
Set dtbSLBinv = OpenDatabase("a:\slb-inv.mdb")
Set rstSupplierData = dtbSLBinv.OpenRecordset("Supplier")
rstSupplierData.Index = "PrimaryKey"
rstSupplierData.Seek "=", strSupplierNumber
```

Primary Key

Supplier ID	Supplier Name	Address	City	State/Province	Postal Code	Telephone	Fax	Internet Address
1000	Moonbeam Books	1946 Briarwood Avenue	Troy	MI	48084	800.555.7812	248.555.2199	file:moonbeam.htm
2000	Blue Spruce Resellers	71 Black Rock Canyon Road	Hailey	ID	83333	800.555.1282	208.555.6734	file:b-spruce.htm
3000	The Deer Stalkers	3956 Circle Drive	London	ON	NOL1SO	800.555.2711	519.555.7921	file:dstalker.htm
4000	Jayhawk Books	1173 Mississippi	Lawrence	KS	66046	800.555.9867	607.555.1082	file:jayhawk.htm

Supplier Table

Supplier ID	ISBN	Book Title	Author	Classification	Cost
3000	0006-1012238	Fatal Convictions	Geller, Shari	M	$0.20
3000	0006-1012262	Final Judgement	Easterman, D.	M	$0.30
3000	0006-1012289	Secret Affair	Bradford, Bar	M	$0.25
3000	0006-1095168	96 Tears	Swanson, Doug	M	$0.20
3000	0006-4471705	Bad Sign	Royce, Easton	M	$0.30
2000	0013-7495730	Colonial America	Reich	H	$0.35
2000	0014-0257454	The Crusades	Jones, Terry	H	$0.60
1000	0019-2828266	The War of the Worlds	Wells, H. G.	S	$0.50
1000	0019-283195X	The Invisible Man	Wells, H. G.	S	$0.30

Inventory Table

FIGURE 6.5 Matching Records in the Inventory and Supplier Tables

Rows(Row Numbers) Method

Once the Seek method has found a matching Supplier ID, you can assign related fields to a variant variable. A variant is used because it automatically becomes an array to accommodate the number of fields found in the record. The GetRows method's argument indicates how many rows are assigned to the variant. You will use 1 as the argument since you want only the record found by the Seek method.

1. Open the code window's Object box and then select *Document*.
2. Enter the following code in the Get_Supplier_Data routine after the Seek statement:
   vntSupplierData = rstSupplierData.GetRows(1)
3. Close the database when exiting the procedure by adding the following statement between the Exit_Sub: label and the Exit Sub statement
   rstSupplierData.Close
   dtbSLBinv.Close
   ➤ *Check your code against figure 6.8.*
4. Save the code.

Adding Access Data to a Word Document

After the Supplier's record is found, the name, address, telephone number, and other data are inserted into the book order. This is accomplished by adding labels to the document and assigning each database field to the related label's caption.

1. Activate Word by clicking on the appropriate button on the taskbar.
   ➤ *Word displays the book order document.*
2. If necessary, activate the <u>R</u>uler using the <u>V</u>iew menu.
3. Move the insertion point under S in Supplier ID and then click.
   ➤ *The insertion point is flashing at the 4 3/8" tab under the Supplier ID.*
4. If necessary, display the Control toolbox by clicking <u>V</u>iew, pointing to <u>T</u>oolbars, and then clicking Control Toolbox.
   ➤ *The control toolbox opens as shown in figure 6.6.*
5. Click the Label button in the Control toolbox. [A]
   ➤ *A new label appears in the document under Supplier ID.*

The location of the insertion point determines where the new label is placed within the document. The label also takes on the font properties assigned to the insertion point's current location.

6. Confirm the location of the label you just added using figure 6.6 as a guide.

The new label sits in the same line on the form as the text box under Order #. Currently the caption for the new label is Label1 (or the next default number).

7. Right-click the new label.
   ➤ *Word displays a shortcut menu as shown in figure 6.6.*
8. Select <u>F</u>ormat Control from the menu.
   ➤ *The Format Object dialog box opens similar to the one shown in figure 6.6.*
9. Click the Layout tab and then select <u>I</u>n line with text Wrapping style if it is not currently selected.
   ➤ *This allows the label to hold its place in the existing line of text.*
10. Click OK.

TIP

If the label is not in the correct location, click <u>E</u>dit and click Undo OCXLabel to remove the label, reposition the insertion point in the correct location, and then reinsert the label.

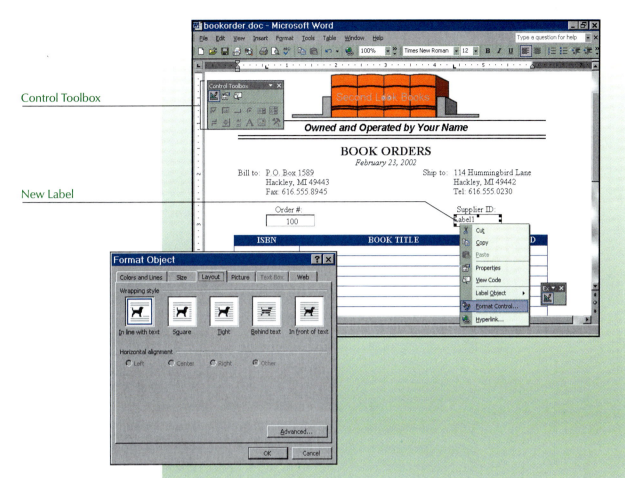

Control Toolbox

New Label

FIGURE 6.6 **Inserting a Label in a Word Document**

11. Right-click on the label and select the <u>P</u>roperties option.
    ➤ *The Properties dialog box opens.*
12. Using figure 6.7 as a guide, make the following changes to the label's properties:

    (Name) = **lblSupplierNumber**
    Caption = delete current Caption Label1
    SpecialEffect = 2 - fmSpecialEffectSunken
    TextAlign = 2 - fmTextAlignCenter
    WordWrap = False

13. Check that the font being used is a regular 12 point Times New Roman font.
14. Exit Design view.
15. Save the document.

PITFALL

On occasion some system configurations will not change the name property of the label. If your system displays the message "No Current Record," use the default name as the label's name property. Remember to always reference the default name rather than lblSupplierNumber.

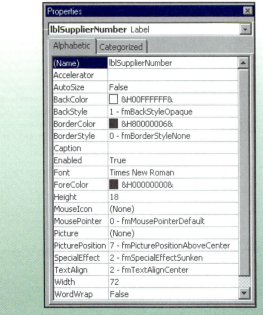

FIGURE 6.7 Properties for Supplier Number Label

Assigning Captions to Labels

When the Bookorder document is opened, the caption of the lblSupplierNumber label will be assigned the requested Supplier ID. The Supplier ID and other fields from the Supplier table are organized within the variant vntSupplierData. The array values for these data are arranged as follows:

- Supplier ID = vntSupplierData(0,0)
- Name = vntSupplierData(1,0)
- Address = vntSupplierData(2,0)
- City = vntSupplierData(3,0)
- State/Province = vntSupplierData(4,0)
- Postal Code = vntSupplierData(5,0)
- Telephone Number = vntSupplierData(6,0)
- Fax Number = vntSupplierData(7,0)
- Web site URL = vntSupplierData(8,0)

You will need to add the appropriate labels to the BookOrder document and assign the related captions to vntSupplierData. The code below assigns the supplier number to the new label's caption. Similar code is required to complete Next Step 6-1, which has you add the remaining supplier data to the book order.

TIP

If you were unable to change the name of the label you will assign Label1.Caption = vntSupplierData(0,0).

1. Activate the Visual Basic Editor.
2. Create a blank line under the GetRows statements and key the following:
   lblSupplierNumber.Caption = vntSupplierData(0,0)
3. Save the document and code.
4. Run the code from the code window entering **1000** when prompted for the Supplier ID number.
   ➤ *The supplier number 1000 should appear in the book order – you will need to switch to the Bookorder window to verify.*

No Matching Record

Since it is possible for the user to enter an invalid Supplier ID, the error handling routine needs to account for such a situation.

1. Add the following condition to the Select Case statement:
   Case Is = 9

          MsgBox "Matching Supplier Number not found."

          Resume Get_Supplier_Data
2. Save the code.
   > ➤ *The code should look similar to figure 6.8.*
3. Run the code entering **5000** as the Supplier ID number.
   > ➤ *The Matching Supplier Number not found message should appear.*

```vba
Private Sub Document_Open()
'Input Supplier ID and
'update order entry with supplier data
'from the Supplier table in the slb-inv database.
'
'Prepared mm/dd/yy by Your Name
'

Dim dtbSLBinv As DAO.Database
Dim rstSupplierData As DAO.Recordset
Dim vntSupplierData As Variant

On Error GoTo Error_Handler

Get_Supplier_Data:
    strSupplierNumber = InputBox("Supplier ID", "Order Entry")
    If strSupplierNumber = "" Then 'Cancel pressed
        Exit Sub
    End If
    Set dtbSLBinv = OpenDatabase("a:\slb-inv.mdb")
    Set rstSupplierData = dtbSLBinv.OpenRecordset("Supplier")
    rstSupplierData.Index = "PrimaryKey"
    rstSupplierData.Seek "=", strSupplierNumber
    vntSupplierData = rstSupplierData.GetRows(1)
    lblSupplierNumber.Caption = vntSupplierData(0, 0)

Exit_Sub:
    rstSupplierData.Close
    dtbSLBinv.Close
    Exit Sub

Error_Handler:
Select Case Err.Number
    Case Is = 9
        MsgBox "Matching Supplier Number not found."
        Resume Get_Supplier_Data
    Case Is = 432
        MsgBox "File does not exist."
        Resume Exit_Sub
    Case Else
        MsgBox "Error number - " & Err.Number & _
            " " & Err.Description
        Resume Exit_Sub
End Select

End Sub
```

FIGURE 6.8 VBA Code for Open Document Procedure

Next Step 6-1

1. Using the bottom of figure 6.1 as a model, add labels for the supplier's name, address, telephone number, and fax number. Remember, you must be in the Design view to add objects to a document and it is always wise to place the insertion point before adding the object. Use the Visual Basic Editor to assign the related captions to data in vntSupplierData. To simplify adding the city, state/province, and postal code, create one label called lblSupplierAddress2. Set the caption of this label to vntSupplierData(3,0) & ", " & vntSupplierData(4,0) & " " & vntSupplierData(5,0). The ampersand concatenates the data to create a complete address line. All the labels should use a regular 12 point Times New Roman font. Turn the Autosize property to True and the WordWrap property to False.
2. Exit Design view.
3. Close the Control Toolbox.
4. Save the document.
5. Run the code entering **2000** as the Supplier ID number and compare the results to figure 6.1.

ADDING LINKS TO INTERNET SITES

The Internet provides up-to-date information about new books being published. Web sites maintained by publishers and suppliers are used by Second Look Books' store manager when ordering books. Each Web page is found on the Internet using its unique **URL** (**Uniform Resource Locator**), sometimes called the Web address. For example, the home page of the publisher for this textbook has the URL http://www.emcp.com/index.php. To help the store manager find new books to order, you are going to write VBA code that links the book ordering document to the supplier's Web site.

The URLs you will be using identify Web pages that you downloaded to your student data disk. Since we could not anticipate in which disk drive your data disk would be, the URLs found in the Supplier table under InternetAddress (see figure 6.9) assume the default disk drive. If your data disk is always in drive A, file://a:/moonbeam.htm would be a more specific URL for Moonbeam Books. Any active URL can be used in this field. For instance, if the computer you are using has access to the Internet, you could use http://www.emcp.com/visualbasic/moonbeam.htm to access Moonbeam Books' Web site.

Supplier ID	Supplier Name	Telephone	Fax	Internet Address
1000	Moonbeam Books	800.555.7812	248.555.2199	file:moonbeam.htm
2000	Blue Spruce Resellers	800.555.1282	208.555.6734	file:b-spruce.htm
3000	The Deer Stalkers	800.555.2711	519.555.7921	file:dstalker.htm
4000	Jayhawk Books	800.555.9867	607.555.1082	file:jayhawk.htm

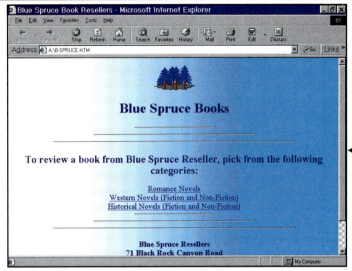

FIGURE 6.9 Suppliers URLs with Web Page

Identifying the URL

As shown in figure 6.9, the Internet Address field in the Supplier table contains the URL for each book supplier. You need to assign the Internet address to the string variable strSupplierURL. However, you want to avoid rewriting code that opens the slb-inv database again to find the supplier's Internet address. The best time to assign the supplier URL to a variable would be during the Document_Open procedure. The variable strSupplierURL can be assigned to the Internet Address at the same time the document's label captions are assigned to other supplier data. Since strSupplierURL is used in another procedure, it is declared in general declarations.

1. Activate the Visual Basic Editor.
2. Open the Object box and select *(General).*
   ➤ *The Procedure box displays (Declarations).*
3. Key **Dim strSupplierURL as String** (do not include a period).

Assigning the Internet Address to the variable strSupplierURL as part of the Get_Supplier_Data routine (Document_Open procedure) makes future references to the address easier. You will be adding VBA code at a point in the routine where data from the Supplier table has already been assigned to the variant vntSupplierData. The actual Internet address is found in vntSupplierData(8,0).

4. Open the Object box and select *Document*.
   ➤ *The Procedure box displays Open.*
5. Create a blank line at the bottom of the Get_Supplier_Data routine found in the Document_Open procedure and key the following:
   strSupplierURL = vntSupplierData(8, 0)

Opening a Browser Window

Next, you need to write the code that opens the supplier's Web page. Your computer system must have an Internet browser such as Netscape's Navigator or Microsoft's Internet Explorer (shown in figure 6.9) for this code to work. Error checking in this situation can be tricky because you have to deal with all the potential problems associated with a computer network. To help with this task, we have included the general procedure Internet_Errors. This VBA code is one long Case statement that checks for a variety of network-related errors.

   Consider this procedure the foundation from which to build you own customized error-handling routine. The Case Else alternative displays the error number (Err.Number). Whenever you encounter error numbers that fall through the checks within Internet_Errors, you should add new Case Is checks.

1. Click Insert and then Procedure.
   ➤ *The Editor opens the Add Procedure dialog box.*
2. Key **WebLink** in the Name text box.
3. Verify that the Sub and Public options are selected.
4. Click OK.
   ➤ *The Editor adds the first and last statements of the WebLink procedure to the code window.*
5. Key the following code within the WebLink procedure:
   'Open Internet Page in a separate window.
   'Prepared mm/dd/yy by Your Name
   {blank line}
   On Error GoTo Error_Handler
   {blank line}
   Error_Handler:
     Call Internet_Errors

FollowHyperlink (Address, NewWindow) Method

The FollowHyperlink method downloads the page description from the Internet address and displays the information in a new window on your screen. Since the Web data you will be using resides on your student data disk, you are technically opening, not downloading, the Web page using ActiveDocument as an object. A valid URL is required and set equal to Address. Our situation calls for using the optional NewWindow parameter. When NewWindow is set to True, it opens the Web page in a new browser window. The FollowHyperlink method offers other optional parameters you will skip over at this time: SubAddress, AddHistory, ExtraInfo, Method, and HeaderInfo.

1. Create a blank line after the On Error GoTo statement and key this code:

   ActiveDocument.FollowHyperlink Address:=strSupplierURL, NewWindow:=True
   Exit Sub
   ➤ *The WebLink procedure should look similar to figure 6.10.*

FIGURE 6.10 VBA Code for WebLink Procedure

```
Public Sub WebLink()
'Open Internet Page in a separate window.
'Prepared mm/dd/yy by Your Name

On Error GoTo Error_Handler

ActiveDocument.FollowHyperlink Address:=strSupplierURL, NewWindow:=True
Exit Sub

Error_Handler:
    Call Internet_Errors

End Sub
```

TIP

If you get a *Web site not found* message, try running the Open Document procedure again. Since the Internet address from your student data disk does not contain a disk drive designation or path, it is possible that the default drive has changed.

2. Use the Visual Basic Editor to run the Document_Open event for Supplier 2000. This will establish an initial value for strSupplierURL.
3. Save the code.
4. Test and debug WebLink.
   ➤ *Close the Internet window by clicking the Close button.*

CUSTOM TOOLBARS AND MENUS

Up until now you have employed keyboard shortcuts or command buttons to activate VBA code. However, Second Look Books' book ordering introduces a situation where creating a custom toolbar and menus is superior to the control options used in previous lessons. In particular, keyboard shortcuts are not intuitive and they can override pre-assigned key combinations users rely on. While command buttons with descriptive captions are easy to use, they are not very professional looking in a document of this nature.

Adding a Custom Toolbar

You are going to create a custom toolbar with menu options that open a Web site, clear old orders from the form, total order amounts, and check the database for previous sales. Each of these activities represents a VBA procedure, like the WebLink sub procedure you just wrote.

1. Activate Word and the Bookorder document.
2. Click View, point to Toolbars, and then click Customize.
   ➤ *Word displays the Customize dialog box similar to the one in figure 6.11.*
3. Select the Toolbars tab and then click the New button.
   ➤ *Word displays the New Toolbar dialog box (see figure 6.11).*
4. Key **Book Ordering** in the Toolbar name text box.
5. Click the down-pointing triangle at the right of the Make toolbar available to list box and select *bookorder.doc*.
   ➤ *The New Toolbar dialog box should look like figure 6.11.*
6. Click OK.
   ➤ *The new toolbar is inserted into the document (see figure 6.11) and a check box for the toolbar is added to the Toolbars list box in the Customize dialog box.*

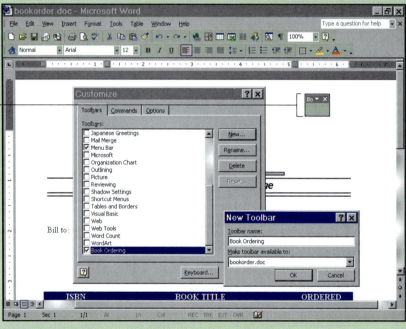

Book Ordering Toolbar

FIGURE 6.11 **Creating a Custom Toolbar**

Adding a Custom Menu

The next step is to add a custom menu to the new toolbar. Menus, like command buttons, have keyboard shortcuts that activate the menu. For example, the underlined F in the File menu indicates the Alt + F keyboard combination will open the File menu. Placing an ampersand (&) in front of one of the letters (or numbers) in the menu name designates that character as the keyboard alternative.

1. Select the <u>C</u>ommands tab in the Customize dialog box as shown in figure 6.12.
2. Scroll to the bottom of the Categories list box and select *New Menu*.
   ➤ *New Menu appears in the Comman<u>d</u>s list box as shown in figure 6.12.*
3. Drag the New Menu option from the Comman<u>d</u>s list box onto the Book Ordering toolbar as shown in figure 6.12.
   ➤ *The pointer changes as New Menu is added to the toolbar.*
4. Right-click on New Menu on the Book Ordering toolbar.
   ➤ *A shortcut menu opens as shown in figure 6.12.*
5. Change the menu name to **Order &Controls** and then press Enter.
   ➤ *Order <u>C</u>ontrols replaces New Menu on the toolbar as shown in figure 6.13.*

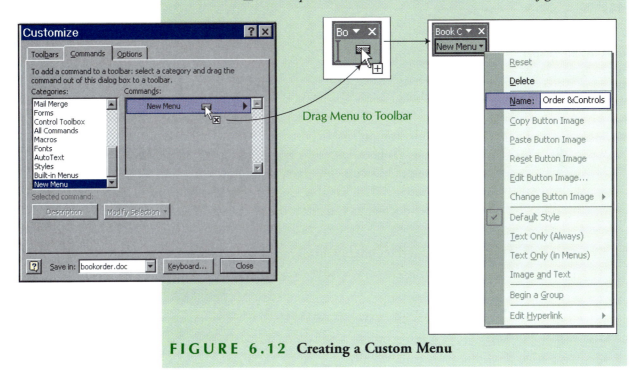

FIGURE 6.12 Creating a Custom Menu

Adding Menu Options

The procedure for adding menu options is almost the same as adding a menu. Menu options are displayed when the user clicks on the Order <u>C</u>ontrols menu. The first menu option, Supplier's <u>W</u>eb Site, executes the WebLink procedure you just coded. Other menu options will be added as you complete this lesson. You will use the Macros option in the Categories list box (see figure 6.13) to select WebLink. Dragging it from the dialog box into the toolbar inserts a new menu option into the related menu.

1. Click the new Order <u>C</u>ontrols menu.
   ➤ *An empty menu options box appears under the menu.*
2. Select *Macros* from the Categories list box.
   ➤ *A list of macros and VBA procedures appears in the Comman<u>d</u>s list box.*

3. Drag Project.ThisDocument.WebLink from the Commands list box to the empty menu option box.
   ➤ *Project.ThisDocument.WebLink appears as the only menu option under the Order Controls menu.*
4. Right-click on the new menu option.
   ➤ *A shortcut menu opens.*
5. Change the option name to **Supplier's &Web Site**.
   ➤ *Supplier's Web Site replaces Project.ThisDocument.WebLink as the menu option name (see figure 6.13).*
6. Select the Options tab in the Customize dialog box and make sure the Show Standard and Formatting toolbars on two rows check box is selected.
7. Drag the Book Ordering toolbar to the right of the Standard toolbar as shown in figure 6.13.
   ➤ *The Order Control menu is docked next to the Standard toolbar.*
8. Close the Customize dialog box.

TIP

On smaller monitors the custom toolbar might appear on a new line.

When you select this menu option, if the Internet_Errors procedure returns a *Web Site Not Found* error it is most likely due to one of two situations. Either the variable strSuppliersURL has lost its data or the location of the Web site's related files has been lost. This is a development related problem and is solved by running the Document_Open procedure from the Editor. This will reestablish the SupplierURL variable and default drive reference. Now switch to the Bookorder document and select the Supplier's Web Site option.

9. Open the Order Control menu and select Supplier's Web Site.
   ➤ *A window opens displaying the supplier's Web page.*

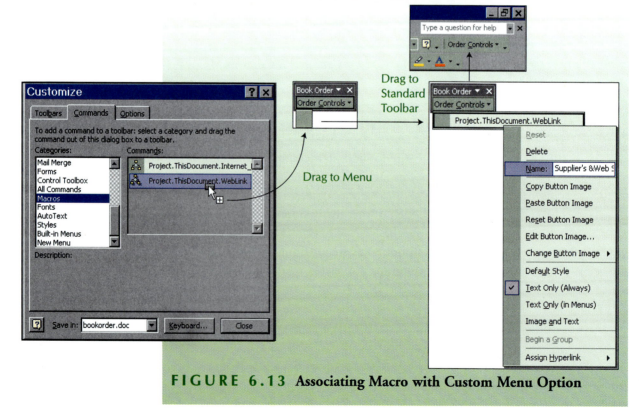

FIGURE 6.13 Associating Macro with Custom Menu Option

Next Step 6-2

1. Locate an ISBN number and associated book title using the active Internet site. Enter this information and an order amount of your choice into the book order.
2. Print the book order.

OPENING AN ACCESS FORM

While the supplier's Web site can provide ideas, Second Look Books' sales are the best indicators of which books to order. You have used this sales data throughout this book. Until now, weekly sales have been organized into sales categories, like History or Science Fiction. In this application, the store manager needs to see weekly sales organized by supplier. The Access form Weekly Sales by Supplier (see figure 6.14) organizes this information. You are going to write code for a new menu option named Check Sales, which displays this form.

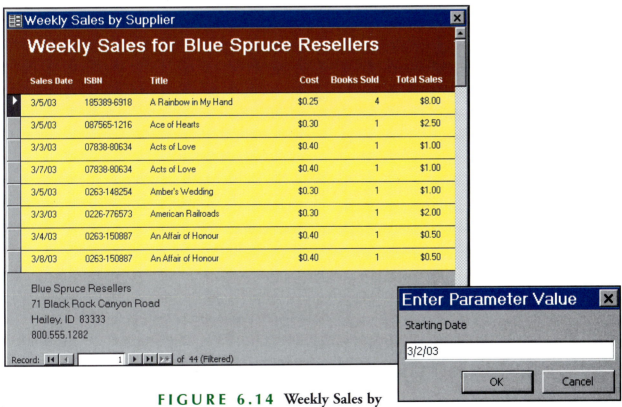

FIGURE 6.14 Weekly Sales by Supplier Form for the Week of March 2nd for Supplier 2000

1. Use the Editor's <u>I</u>nsert menu to create a new public sub procedure called CheckSales.
   ➤ *The Editor displays* General *in the Object box and CheckSales in the Procedure box.*
2. Enter the following statements into the CheckSales procedure:
   'Display Weekly Sales by Supplier form
   'from slb-inv database.
   'Prepared mm/dd/yy by Your Name
   {blank line}
   Dim appAccess As Access.Application
   Dim strWhereCondition As String
   {blank line}
   On Error GoTo Error_Handler
3. Copy the Error_Handler routine you created for the Document_Open procedure and paste it into the CheckSales procedure.
4. Delete the Case Is = 9 condition and its related statements from the Error_Handler.
5. Save the code.

Structured Query Language

SQL stands for **Structured Query Language**. It is an industry-wide syntax standard for accessing database data. The VBA code you just wrote incorporates this SQL condition:

   Where Supplier ID = "strSupplierNumber"

Supplier ID is the field name used for the Supplier's identification number within the Weekly Sales by Supplier query. You used this condition as an argument in the Open Form method to limit the form's display to records with a matching Supplier ID. This eliminates the need for the user to enter the supplier's number as a query parameter.

Access and SQL syntax rules require brackets around Supplier ID because of the embedded space and because the strSupplierNumber must be in quotes. Ampersands are used to concatenate the field name, quotes, and variable into a single value. Double quotes identify textual data and single quotes are used when double quotes are required by the syntax. The argument does not require the inclusion of the word "where," so the argument's final syntax looks like this:

   "[Supplier ID] = '" & strSupplierNumber & "'"

GetObject Function and OpenForm Method

As discussed in chapter 5, Automation code using the Access object library can display a database object. In this case, you want to display the Weekly Sales by Supplier form. The GetObject function opens the slb-inv database. Once a link to the database is established, the OpenForm method opens the Weekly Sales by

Supplier form. The acNormal argument displays the form in the default view rather than in the Preview or Design views. The strWhereCondition is used as the SQL filter that limits the form's output to sales for the current supplier. The syntax for the SQL argument is described in the next section. The form opens in a separate window on top of the document because the acDialog argument opens the form as a modal window. A **modal** window must be closed before you can continue working with the application.

1. Under the On Error statement add the following lines of code. Spaces must always surround the concatenation (&) character.

   Get_Access_Form:
     Set appAccess = GetObject("a:\slb-inv.mdb")
     strWhereCondition = "[Supplier ID] = '" & strSupplierNumber & "'"
     appAccess.DoCmd.OpenForm "Weekly Sales by Supplier", acNormal, , strWhereCondition, , acDialog
   {blank line}
   Exit_Sub:
     appAccess.DoCmd.Close acForm, ("Weekly Sales by Supplier")
     appAccess.CloseCurrentDatabase
     appAccess.Quit
     Set appAccess = Nothing
     Exit Sub
   ➤ *The code should look similar to figure 6.15.*
2. Save the code.
3. Test and debug the code using supplier 2000 and 3/2/03 as a starting date.
4. Use the Close button to close the Weekly Sales by Supplier form.

TIP

If strSupplierNumber has lost its value you need to run the Bookorder's Open_Document event again.

```
Public Sub CheckSales()
'Display Weekly Sales by Supplier form
'from slb-inv database.
'Prepared mm/dd/yy by Your Name

Dim appAccess As Access.Application
Dim strWhereCondition As String

On Error GoTo Error_Handler

Get_Access_Form:
    Set appAccess = GetObject("a:\slb-inv.mdb")
    strWhereCondition = "[Supplier ID] = '" & strSupplierNumber & "'"
    appAccess.DoCmd.OpenForm "Weekly Sales by Supplier", acNormal, , strWhereCondition, , acDialog

Exit_Sub:
    appAccess.DoCmd.Close acForm, ("Weekly Sales by Supplier")
    appAccess.CloseCurrentDatabase
    appAccess.Quit
    Set appAccess = Nothing
    Exit Sub

Error_Handler:
Select Case Err.Number
    Case Is = 432
        MsgBox "File does not exist."
        Resume Exit_Sub
    Case Else
        MsgBox "Error number - " & Err.Number & _
               " " & Err.Description
        Resume Exit_Sub
End Select

End Sub
```

FIGURE 6.15 VBA Code for the CheckSales Procedure

TRANSFERRING DATA FROM FORMS TO DOCUMENTS

The book order is not very easy to fill out. As you discovered during Next Step 6-2, the ISBN number and book title to be ordered from the Supplier's Web site need to be written down, the Web site closed, and then the information input into the book order document. The same is true when using the Weekly Sales by Supplier form. Not only is this process time-consuming, it is prone to error as well.

You can write VBA code to directly transfer data from the Weekly Sales by Supplier form to the order. To do this, you will add the command button, cmdInsertOrder, to the Weekly Sales by Supplier form. The Click event associated with this button will execute the VBA code, which transfers the ISBN number and book title to the Word document.

1. Run Access and open the slb-inv database from your student data disk.
2. Click the Forms button on the Objects bar.
3. Select Weekly Sales by Supplier and click the Design button.
4. If necessary, use the View menu to display the Toolbox.

Insert Command Button

Two command buttons need to be added to the right of the Supplier's address in the form footer as shown in figure 6.16. Do not be surprised when using the Command Button button from the Toolbox when Access evokes the Command Button Wizard. While you are not going to use the Command Button Wizard when designing the Insert Order button, you will use it when inserting the Close button.

1. Click the Command Button button in the Toolbox and then move the mouse pointer to the right of the supplier name in the Form Footer.
   ➤ *The mouse pointer changes into the Insert Command pointer.*
2. Click with the pointer in the Form Footer.
   ➤ *Access displays the Command Button Wizard dialog box.*

3. Click the Cancel button.

> *A command button is inserted into the Form Footer as seen in figure 6.16.*

4. Right-click on the new command button and select <u>P</u>roperties from the shortcut menu.

> *The Properties dialog box opens.*

5. Click on the All tab and make the following changes to the button's properties:

Name = **cmdInsertOrder**

Caption = **Insert Order**

6. Scroll down the properties list and click the On Click option.

> *An insertion point, a down-pointing triangle, and the Ellipsis (…) button appear in the text box.*

7. Click the down-pointing triangle.

> *[Event Procedure] appears in the list box.*

8. Select [Event Procedure].

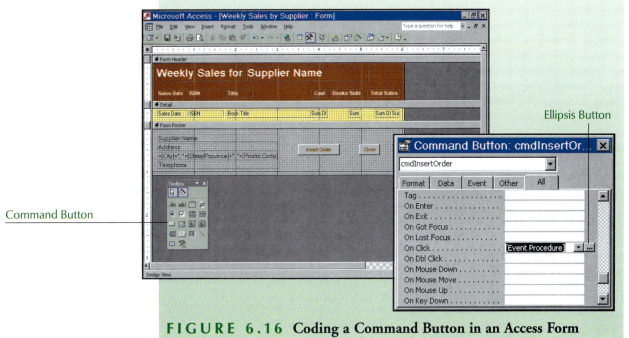

FIGURE 6.16 Coding a Command Button in an Access Form

Coding the Event Procedure

The Click event for cmdInsertOrder is the event procedure you are now going to code. The associated VBA code does three things:

1. Identifies the ISBN number and book title currently selected in the Weekly Sales by Supplier form.

2. If possible, transfers the ISBN and title to an empty row in the bookorder's book list table.

3. Informs users they need to print and clear the form when the table is full of book orders.

   When using Access, you build code for the event procedure using the Ellipsis (…) button.

1. Click the Ellipsis button.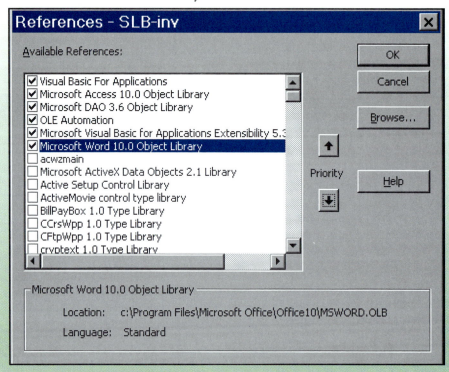
   ➤ *Access displays the VBA Editor window with the new procedure cmdInsertOrder_Click.*

Before you start coding the Click event procedure for the cmdInsertOrder command button, it is essential to confirm that the necessary object library references (see figure 6.17) are active. If the following code is entered prior to the references being defined you may need to reenter the code after the references are activated for it to work correctly.

F I G U R E 6 . 1 7 Object Libraries Used by slb-inv.mdb

2. Click Tools and then References.
   ➤ *The References – slb-inv dialog box opens.*
3. Using figure 6.17 as a guide, confirm that the following references are checked:
   Visual Basic for Applications
   Microsoft Access 10.0 Object Library
   Microsoft DAO 3.6 Object Library
   OLE Automation
   Microsoft Visual Basic for Applications Extensibility 5.3
   Microsoft Word 10.0 Object Library
4. Click OK to close the References dialog box.
5. Enter the following code into cmdInsertOrder_Click:
   'Transfer selected book information
   'from Weekly Sales by Supplier form
   'to bookorder.doc

```
'Prepared mm/dd/yy by Your Name
{blank line}
Dim strISBN As String
Dim strTitle As String
Dim intRow As Integer
Dim frmOrder As Form
{blank line}
On Error GoTo Error_Handler
{blank line}
Exit_Sub:
Exit Sub
{blank line}
Error_Handler:
    Select Case Err.Number
    Case Is = 432 'File does not exist
        MsgBox Err.Description 'Display error message
        Resume Exit_Sub
    Case Else
        MsgBox "Error number - " & Err.Number & _
        " " & Err.Description
        Resume Exit_Sub
    End Select
End Select
```

Referencing an Access Form

The first action within the procedure is to identify the form you want to use. Notice that an exclamation point follows the word Form and that square brackets, not parentheses, enclose the form name. Then the selected ISBN number and book title are assigned to the string variables strISBN and strTitle. Next, focus is returned to Word and the Bookorder document with the Activate method. The integer variable intRow is used when searching for an empty row in the book list table to place the ISBN and title. Since the first row of the table is set aside for the table headings, intRow is set equal to 2.

1. After the On Error statement enter the following code:
   ```
   {blank line}
   Set frmOrder = Forms![Weekly Sales by Supplier]
   strISBN = frmOrder.ISBN
   strTitle = frmOrder.[Book Title]
   Documents("bookorder.doc").Activate
   intRow = 2
   ```

Setting Table Cells Equal to Form Data

The book order's table in bookorder.doc has 20 rows and is designed to hold 18 new book orders. Data in Word tables are referenced just like Excel workbooks by using the intersecting column and row labels as a cell address. In other words the top left cell is A1 with A2 below it and B1 to the right. The first row is reserved for the headings and the last row is set aside to show the total number of books ordered. Therefore, the Find_Empty_Row routine uses a Do While loop to make 19 loops, starting at row 2, looking for an empty row to place the book data. On the 19th try, it drops out of the loop and displays the message *Order form full. Print form and clear it.*

Left (String, Characters) Function

An empty row is identified by a carriage return (ASCII character 13) as the first value in cell 1. You will use the Left function to examine the first character in the selection. When a carriage return (intrinsic constant vbCr) is found as the leftmost character, cell 1 is set equal to strISBN and cell 2 to strTitle. The number of books to order in cell 3 is temporarily set to 1. This number is easily changed afterwards by clicking on it and keying a new value.

1. Enter the following code before the Exit_Sub routine and after the new code you just entered:

```
Find_Empty_Row:
  Do While intRow < 20
    ActiveDocument.Tables(1).Cell(intRow, 1).Select
    If Left(Selection, 1) = vbCr Then 'Look for empty row
      With Documents("bookorder.doc").Tables(1)
        .Cell(intRow, 1).Select
        Selection = strISBN
        .Cell(intRow, 2).Select
        Selection = strTitle
        .Cell(intRow, 3).Select
        Selection = 1
      End With
      Exit Do
    Else
        intRow = intRow + 1
    End If
  Loop
{blank line}
  If intRow >= 20 Then
        MsgBox ("Order form full. Print form and clear it.")
  End If
```

➤ *The code should look similar to figure 6.18.*

2. Save the code.
3. Click on the Weekly Sales by Supplier: Form button on the taskbar.

4. Close the command button properties dialog box.
5. If necessary, reposition the button in the Form Footer as shown in figure 6.16.
6. Click View and then Form View.
7. Select one of the books and then click on the Insert Order button to test the new code. You will have to display bookorder.doc to see the results.

```vba
Private Sub cmdInsertOrder_Click()
'Transfer selected book information
'from Weekly Sales by Supplier form
'to bookorder.doc
'Prepared mm/dd/yy by Your Name

Dim strISBN As String
Dim strTitle As String
Dim intRow As Integer
Dim frmOrder As Form

On Error GoTo Error_Handler

Set frmOrder = Forms![Weekly Sales by Supplier]
strISBN = frmOrder.ISBN
strTitle = frmOrder.[Book Title]
Documents("bookorder.doc").Activate
intRow = 2

Find_Empty_Row:
    Do While intRow < 20
        ActiveDocument.Tables(1).Cell(intRow, 1).Select
        If Left(Selection, 1) = vbCr Then 'Look for empty row
            With Documents("bookorder.doc").Tables(1)
                .Cell(intRow, 1).Select
                Selection = strISBN
                .Cell(intRow, 2).Select
                Selection = strTitle
                .Cell(intRow, 3).Select
                Selection = 1
            End With
            Exit Do
        Else
            intRow = intRow + 1
        End If
    Loop

    If intRow >= 20 Then
        MsgBox ("Order form full. Print form and clear it.")
    End If

Exit_Sub:
    Exit Sub

Error_Handler:
    Select Case Err.Number
    Case Is = 432 'File does not exist
        MsgBox Err.Description 'Display error message
        Resume Exit_Sub
    Case Else
        MsgBox "Error number - " & Err.Number & _
            " " & Err.Description
        Resume Exit_Sub
    End Select

End Sub
```

FIGURE 6.18 VBA Code for the cmdInsertOrder_Click Procedure

The Command Button Wizard

The Command Button Wizard is designed to simplify tasks like adding a Close button to the form.

1. Display the Weekly Sales by Supplier form.
2. Click the Design button.
3. Use the Command Button button to create a new button beside the Insert Order button in the Form Footer as shown in figure 6.16.
   ➤ *Access displays the Command Button Wizard dialog box.*
4. Select Form Operations in the <u>C</u>ategories list box.
5. Select Close Form in the <u>A</u>ctions list box and click <u>N</u>ext.
   ➤ *The next wizard screen lets you choose between descriptive words and icons as a caption.*
6. Click the Text option button.
7. Delete the word *Form* from the text box.
   ➤ *The sample button displays* Close *as a caption.*
8. Click <u>N</u>ext.
   ➤ *The next wizard screen allows you to rename the button.*
9. Key **cmdClose** and then click <u>F</u>inish.
   ➤ *The New Close button is inserted under the Insert Order button.*
10. If necessary, reposition the button in the Form Footer as shown in figure 6.16.
11. Save and test the code.
12. Close Access when you are confident the new procedures are working correctly.

CLEARING OLD ORDERS

For various reasons, old orders have to be cleared from the list of orders table. VBA code for the new <u>C</u>lear menu option accomplishes this task. In doing so, the column headings in table row 1 and the *Books Ordered* label in cell (20,2) need to be preserved. The code below and in figure 6.19 clears the orders using nested For/Next loops. The outside loop changes the integer intRow from 2 to 19, while the inside loop changes intColumn from 1 to 3. Each completion of a loop allows the table object ActiveDocument.Tables(1).Cell(intRow, intColumn) to be selected and the cell contents deleted. Cell (20,3) contains the Sum function that totals the books ordered. It is independently deleted.

1. Use the Editor to create a public sub procedure named ClearForm.
2. Enter the following code into the new procedure:
   ```
   'Clears orders from Bookorder table
   'Row 1: column headings
   'Rows 2-19: book order (ISBN, book title, number)
   'Row 20: total orders
   'Prepared mm/dd/yy by Your Name
   ```

{blank line}
Dim intRow As Integer
Dim intColumn As Integer
{blank line}
For intRow = 2 To 19
    For intColumn = 1 To 3
        ActiveDocument.Tables(1).Cell(intRow, intColumn).Select
        Selection.Delete
    Next intColumn
Next intRow
ActiveDocument.Tables(1).Cell(20, 3).Select
Selection.Delete

➤ *Code should look similar to figure 6.19.*

3. Save and test the code.

```
Public Sub ClearForm()
'Clears orders from Bookorder table
'Row 1: column headings
'Rows 2-19: book order (ISBN, book title, number)
'Row 20: total orders
'Prepared mm/dd/yy by Your Name

Dim intRow As Integer
Dim intColumn As Integer

For intRow = 2 To 19
    For intColumn = 1 To 3
        ActiveDocument.Tables(1).Cell(intRow, intColumn).Select
        Selection.Delete
    Next intColumn
Next intRow
ActiveDocument.Tables(1).Cell(20, 3).Select
Selection.Delete

'Call Document_Open
End Sub
```

FIGURE 6.19 VBA Code for the Procedure to Clear Order Table

Next Step 6-4

Add to the ClearForm procedure, under the Call Document_Open remark shown in figure 6.19, code that does the following:

1. Use an input box or a message box to display a message that asks if the user wants to enter a different supplier.
2. If the user does, call the Document_Open procedure.
3. After saving and testing the code, add the menu option Clear to the Book Ordering toolbar's Order Control menu. Make C the keyboard alternative. Assign the ClearForm procedure to this new menu option. Save the document and test the menu option to make sure it is working as expected.

COMPUTING AN ORDER TOTAL

When the book order is ready to be sent, the number of books in the order needs to be totaled. Clicking on the Total Order menu option should perform this task. If this situation sounds like a spreadsheet task, it is. By inserting the Sum(Above) function into a formula in table cell (20,3), the orders listed above it are totaled. Any values currently in the cell should be deleted before the computation takes place.

InsertFormula (Formula, NumberFormat) Method

Many formulas inserted into a Word table use the Sum(Above) and Sum(Left) functions. These functions total integer or variant values in the cells above or to the left of the cell with the formula. Blank lines should not occur between orders because the function looks for a blank cell to determine which cell values to use. In other words, book orders above a blank line would not be included in the total. The NumberFormat argument allows you to suppress insignificant zeros or add commas and dollar signs to the results. The online help and the related examples provide a complete list of formatting options.

1. Use the Editor to create a public sub procedure named TotalOrder.
2. Enter the following code into the new procedure:

    '

    'Totals book orders in column 3
    'of the Bookorder table.
    '

    'Prepared mm/dd/yy by Your Name
    '

    {blank line}
    ActiveDocument.Tables(1).Cell(20, 3).Select
    Selection.Delete
    Selection.InsertFormula Formula:="=SUM(ABOVE)", NumberFormat:=" "
    ➤ *The code should similar to figure 6.20.*
3. Save and test the code.
4. Close bookorder.doc.

```
Public Sub TotalOrder()
'Totals book orders in column 3
'of the Bookorder table.
'

'Prepared mm/dd/yy by Your Name
'

ActiveDocument.Tables(1).Cell(20, 3).Select
Selection.Delete
Selection.InsertFormula Formula:="=SUM(ABOVE)", NumberFormat:=""

End Sub
```

FIGURE 6.20 **VBA Code for Procedure to Total Book Orders**

KEY TERMS

modal
primary key
Structured Query
    Language (SQL)
Uniform Resource
    Locator (URL)

REVIEW QUESTIONS

On a blank sheet of paper provide a short answer for the following questions.
1. Be able to define each of the key terms.
2. What procedure executes VBA code before a document file is displayed on the screen?
3. Identify two routines that are found in every automation procedure and function.
4. How is a variable that is declared in a form's general declarations different from one declared in a procedure?
5. What value is returned when an InputBox's Cancel button is clicked?
6. How would you use VBA code to locate a specific record in a database table?
7. What method assigns table data to variable names?
8. Briefly explain one way to add database data to a document.
9. How would you open an Internet page in a separate window using VBA code?
10. How are keyboard alternatives assigned to custom menu options?
11. Explain how a new toolbar is added to a document.
12. How are VBA procedures assigned to create and customize menu options?
13. What function is used to activate a database object?
14. Identify the method that displays a database form on the screen.
15. What special syntax rules are used when referencing a database form?
16. Write a VBA statement that extracts the first three characters from the string variable strTelephone.
17. Identify two functions that are commonly used in Word tables and describe what they do.
18. How do you use VBA code to insert a formula into a Word table?

CHECK YOUR UNDERSTANDING

Indicate the correct term or choose the correct answer for each item.
1. A(n) _modal_ window must be closed before a user can continue working with the related application.
2. Another term used to describe a Web page's Internet address is _URL_.
3. The _primary key_ field in a table uniquely identifies each record.
4. Database data is added to a label in a document by assigning each database field to the related label's _caption_.
5. The _FollowHyperlink_ method downloads a Web page.
6. Which of the following statements correctly opens the Access Inventory form?
   a. Assign frmInventory = Form(Inventory)
   b. frmInventory = Form.Inventory
   c. Set frmInventory = Form![Inventory]
   d. frmInventory is equal Form@{Inventory}

7. Select the statement that correctly defines a letter in a caption as a keyboard alternative.
   a. $Open
   b. #Close
   c. F&ormat
   d. T~able

8. Which of the following methods is used to locate a record in an Access database table?
   a. Find
   b. Seek
   c. Search
   d. Locate

9. What value is returned when an InputBox's Cancel button is clicked?
   a. "0"
   b. "null"
   c. "space"
   d. ""

10. The Open event of a Word document is recognized
    a. when the document is opened or the Open event is called from code.
    b. any time the document is opened or becomes active (gets the focus).
    c. only when the document is opened.
    d. any time the document is selected from the Window menu.

EXERCISES

Complete the following exercises.

Last Step

Add the menu option Total Order to the Book Ordering toolbar's Order Control menu. Make T the keyboard alternative. Assign the TotalOrder procedure to this new menu option. Save the document and test the menu option to make sure it is working as expected.

Create, save, and print book order 502 for Jayhawk Books, supplier ID 4000, that contains the following information. Use sales data for the week of March 2, 2003.

1. Two copies of Eye on India.
2. One copy of Cowboys.
3. Three copies of Incas.
4. One copy of any book listed on the supplier's Web site.

Debug

Listed below is the code contained in the General Declarations area of a Word Document plus portions of two procedures in the same document. The GetRecord procedure obtains the data from the 15 fields in a selected customer record. The PlaceData procedure then inserts the record field data into a table in the Word document. Three code problems arise in the PlaceData procedure. Locate the errors and indicate the recommended corrections.

```
(General)        (Declarations)
Dim vntDataFields As Variant


Public Sub GetRecord()
Dim dtbCustomers As Database
Dim rstCustomerRecord As Recordset
Dim strCustomerNumber as String

Set dtbCustomers = OpenDatabase("file specification")
Set rstCustomerRecord = dtbCustomers.Recordset("table name")
rstCustomerRecord.Index = "PrimaryKey"
rstCustomerRecord.Seek "=", strCustomerNumber
vntDataFields = rstCustomerRecord.GetRows(1)


Public Sub PlaceData()
Dim intRow As Integer
Dim intCell As Integer

intRow = intRow + 1

With Documents("SelectCustomeers.doc").Activate
        For intCells = 1 to 15
                .Cell(intCell, intRow).Select
                Selection = vntDataFields(intCell, 0)
        Next intCell
End With
End Sub
```

Internet

Wizards are popular development tools. They enhance user productivity and in many instances enable users who do not have strong programming skills to add features they typically would have to avoid or work around. In this chapter, you had an opportunity to compare code development from scratch and with a wizard. Using an Internet search engine, explore what is available in the world of third party wizards that are available for Office applications. Identify three add-in wizards you feel would be valuable. Indicate the site where you located these wizards and briefly describe what they provide. Two should relate to Access and one for Word or Excel.

New Challenge

Transferring data from the Weekly Sales by Supplier to the order form has improved the productivity of the ordering process. However, the person building the order still needs to return to the Bookorder document and enter the number of copies they want of each book included in the form. It would be considerably more efficient if this number could be indicated at the time the book is selected and transferred to the order form.

Discussion

With the advent of VBA driven automation, do you feel there is a need to purchase custom written application programs?

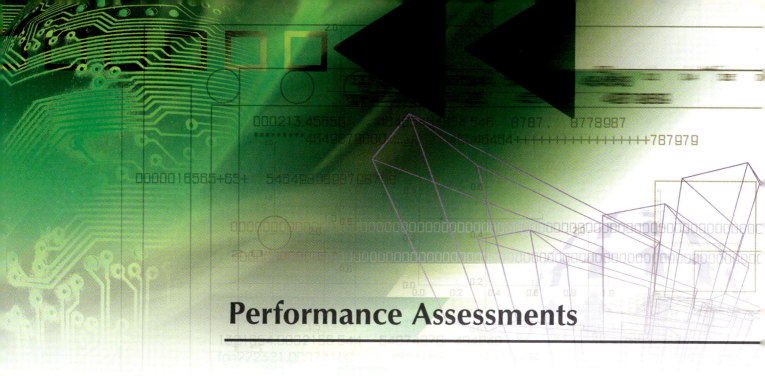

Performance Assessments

PROJECT 1 – MONTHLY FEATURED TITLES LIST

Second Look Books prints a monthly list of books on the shelf in a specific category, such as Westerns. Since this list is three to four pages long the document's header is used to contain the company name (left aligned), user selected category (center aligned), and the words Feature List (right aligned). The footer contains the current date (left aligned) and page number (right aligned).

Header Text – Second Look Books (Bold, 14 point, and Left Align)	Category (Center Align)	Feature List (Right Align)

Footer Text – mm/dd/yy (Regular, 12 point, and Left Align)	Page: # (Right Align)

Create a macro that will set up a Word document that can be used to type selected books for the Monthly Feature List as specified above. The category should be input via an InputBox.

Advanced Step: Develop a UserForm from which the user can select the desired category rather than key it into an InputBox.

PROJECT 2 – SECOND LOOK BOOKS MONTHLY SALES DATA AND ANALYSIS

SLB also monitors their sales revenue by month. The workbook salesbymonth.xls, which you downloaded to your student data disk, is used for this task. The Monthly Sales workbook is different from the Sales workbook for weekly sales in two ways. First, only sales revenues are monitored. Second, the Sales Data worksheet uses the book categories as the row headers.

Look through the SalesByMonth workbook and identify how the column data headers and totals are generated. Then create a macro procedure that will insert a new column with the appropriate header and total for the next month.

Advanced Step: Convert the "Sales By Month Query" found in the slb-inv database to a Make Table Query. Then develop a workbook procedure that will insert the sales data for the month requested, using the query parameter input box to specify the desired month. Your VBA code should insert the data from the resulting table into the "Sales By Month" worksheet. *(Note: The Sales By Month Query expects the month as a numeric value. Sales data only exists for January (1) through March (3).)*

PROJECT 3 – INSERTED CHARTS

SLB franchise owners frequently need to embed a copy of the current Weekly or Monthly Sales Analysis chart into their correspondences. If the workbook with the desired chart is open, this requires a simple copy and paste process that does not require any assistance by VBA. However, if the desired workbook is not open, you will need to open the workbook and select the desired sheet to be able to copy and paste. *(Note: You cannot just insert the workbook because you do not know which sheet is active.)*

Create a VBA procedure that will allow the user to copy and paste either the Weekly or Monthly sales analysis chart into a Word document at the insertion point. This procedure will need to:
- Open the indicated workbook
- Make the chart the active window
- Copy the chart to the clipboard
- Close the workbook
- Paste the chart into the Word document at the insertion point

Advanced Step: Develop a similar procedure to insert a chart into a PowerPoint slide. Before copying the chart, the selected slide's layout should be set to Title and Content and the Content shape selected.

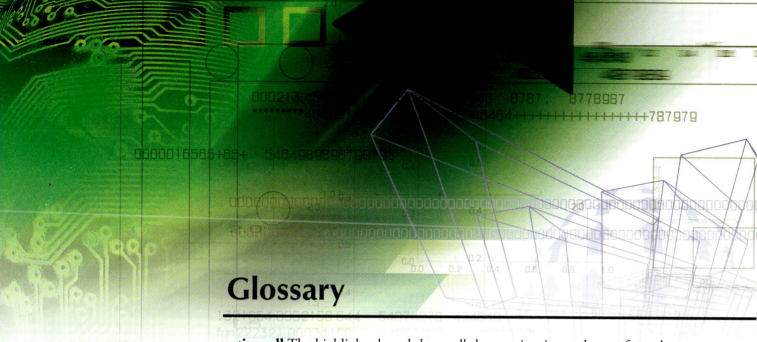

Glossary

active cell The highlighted worksheet cell that receives input data or formula.

ActiveX control A Microsoft sponsored graphic object, such as a command button or check box, which is placed on a document, worksheet, slide show, form, or report to activate a software resource.

antivirus software A computer program that identifies disk files that have been infected with a virus, worm, or other destructive program. In some cases, the antivirus software can delete unwanted programs and repair damaged files.

application software A class of programs that solve specific user-oriented processing problems.

assignment The process of setting a variable to a specific value.

Automation VBA code based on Microsoft's OLE standard. In earlier Microsoft products Automation was referred to as OLE Automation.

backup An extra copy of data or programs on a disk or CD that is kept for use in case the original is destroyed.

bug An error within a computer program.

button A labeled icon which initializes or cancels a program option.

call The process of executing one procedure from another.

cell The intersection of a worksheet column and row, which stores a label, value, or formula.

cell address The column letter and row number of a specific worksheet cell.

click The process of pressing the left mouse button once to select a menu option or icon.

Click-Shift-Click method This process is used to select a sequence of objects by clicking on the first object, holding down the Shift key, and then clicking on the last object in the sequence.

client The software that accepts an object from another application in an OLE relationship.

code A written program instruction.

coding The process of writing a computer program.

collection A set of similar objects, like all the pages in a document, worksheets in a workbook, or slides in a slide show.

compiler A program that translates VBA statements into the computer's binary machine language.

computer A machine that allows input of facts and figures, processes them, and outputs useful information.

computer program A set of instructions you can activate or key into the computer's memory that controls computer operations.

computer system A collection of components (people, procedures, data, software, and hardware) that work together to solve specific problems.

concatenation The process of combining two independent strings of text into one.

context sensitive help screen The information displayed when a Help screen is activated; relates to the program operation currently being used.

control object A graphical feature that contains properties, methods, and events.

database An organized collection of data that can be retrieved and cross-referenced by a computer.

database engine Software that handles the exchange of data from one application to another.

debugging The process of finding and correcting program errors.

default Standard assumptions, like hardware connections and formats, that a computer system uses unless otherwise instructed.

Design mode Control Toolbox status that determines when controls are added to the worksheet or other objects.

desktop The screen layout associated with Windows, which parallels an actual desktop by using icons that represent documents, file folders, calculators, and other office tools.

dialog box A window that prompts the user to enter text, select options from a list, or click on a button to initiate or cancel a program option.

diskette (also known as **floppy disk**) A removable flexible disk used to store computer-readable data.

documentation Written instructions, design diagrams, and support materials for a computer program.

DOS (disk operating system) An early operating system that used command line entries instead of a graphical interface.

double-click The process of pressing the left mouse button twice in quick succession to run a program or activate a program operation.

drag The process of moving an object on the screen by pointing at it and holding down the mouse button while you move it to a new screen location.

dynamic Values change as a VBA procedure executes.

dynamic reference A real time link between a worksheet data and a chart.

dynaset The results of a query.

electronic spreadsheet Software that organizes numbers and associated text into rows and columns for processing and analysis. Financial data, such as budgets and income statements, are often organized in this way.

ellipsis A series of three periods. When found behind a menu option, an ellipsis indicates that additional user input is necessary.

embedding (OLE) A duplicate of an original object is inserted in a client document with information about the server software. Changes to the original object have no impact on the duplicate.

empty string A zero length string that can be tested for with two quotation marks and nothing between them ("").

enable To activate a feature when the conditions necessary for the feature to function are met.

error message A listing of program errors or errors in running an application package. Suggested corrections may be given.

error trapping The process of intercepting errors in order to code corrective actions.

event A user-generated action.

event-driven programming The process of creating interactive programs that respond to user actions in real time.

execute To run a computer program or macro.

export The process of saving data in a file format that enables other software packages to use it.

field A related group of letters, numbers, and symbols; for example, a name or address.

file A group of related records about people, places, things, ideas, or events.

file folder (also known as a **folder**) An icon representing a group of related programs and data files. File folder icons represent a specific disk subdirectory.

filename A unique set of letters, numbers, and symbols that identifies a data file or program.

filename extension A combination of three letters that are added to the end of a filename by an application program.

Focus A property of the active control in a dialog box.

footer A line that appears at the bottom of each document page.

function A set of VBA code that accepts arguments from other procedures and returns some type of data.

graphical interface (sometimes called a **graphical user interface** or **GUI**) An interface that relies on mouse or keyboard input to select menus or buttons, which initiate program options.

handles A set of small squares at each corner and in the middle of each side of a selected object. The object is resized by dragging a handle to a new screen location.

header A line that appears at the top of each document page.

Help screen A description of software features or an explanation of error messages displayed upon demand so the user does not have to refer to a manual.

high-level language A programming language that resembles human language. Programs written in high-level languages, like Visual Basic and VBA, must be translated into the computer's machine language before being used.

icon A picture of item, action, or computer operation.

import The process of adding graphics, images, or text created by other software.

initialization The process of setting a starting value for a program variable.

integer A whole number with no decimal places or decimal point.

integrated development environment (IDE) An interface used by Microsoft applications that standardizes the programming tools for VBA coding and for developing macros.

interactive Direct communication with a computer wherein every request is immediately acted upon.

intrinsic constant A label associated with a specific value from an object library.

iteration The basic structure of a computer program wherein a sequence of instructions is repeated until some processing condition is changed.

keyboard shortcut A combination of keyboard keys assigned to a macro. Pressing these keys at the same time executes the associated macro.

keyword The word associated with specific VBA statements that should not be used in a VBA statement out of context.

kilobyte (K or **KB)** Approximately one thousand bytes of storage or memory.

label A marker that can be included in a procedure and branched to, using a GoTo statement, as part part of the procedure code.

landscape Orientation of a document page where the page is wider than it is tall.

language translator The system program that converts program instructions written in a high-level language into the computer's machine language.

linking The process of exposing the designated area of client document to the original object. Changes to the original object are shown in the client document.

list box Displays a list of options by clicking the down-pointing triangle next to the box.

local variable A data storage location that is only active when the code is running.

logic error A program error that is translatable but does not produce correct results.

logical operator A symbol (<, >, =) indicating which logical operation is to be used in an IF statement.

machine language An operating language unique to each computer that is made up of bits (0 or 1) representing internal electronic switches (off or on).

macro A sequence of instructions that are grouped together to automate a task.

macro virus An unwanted VBA code that is destructive in nature. This type of code can display unwanted messages or erase data.

Maximize button An icon with small window found in the top right corner of the Title bar next to the Minimize button. Clicking the Maximize button expands the related window to fill the screen.

megabyte (MB) One million bytes of storage or memory.

menu A list of program options that allows a user to activate an option by highlighting it or by entering a single letter or number.

menu bar The horizontal area that runs across the top of a window and displays menu titles.

method Identifies preset actions the computer can perform.

Minimize button The icon with an underscore found in the top right corner of the Title bar next to the Maximize/Restore button. Clicking the Minimize button removes a window from the screen, but leaves the related button on the taskbar.

modal window A window that must be closed before a user can continue working with the related application.

module A VBA container displayed in the Visual Basic Editor for macros and other procedures that are not associated with any specific object.

nested statements A set of VBA codes that start and finish within another feature or task. The nesting structure helps assure a beginning and close to the related actions.

numeric data Data containing only numbers (0–9), a decimal point, and positive (+) and negative (-) signs.

object An element of Office applications such as a macro, button, document, paragraph, workbook, or a column of cells or data tables.

object library Contains a variety of elements (objects) commonly used within the related application; for example, document, paragraph, and margin are all objects within the Word object library.

object linking and embedding (OLE) A Microsoft standard for interchanging objects between different applications software.

object variable A user-declared variable that is a named memory location that contains data assoicated with a specific object, like a document or slide show presentation.

open database connectivity (ODBC) data sources A general term used to describe any database engine.

operating system A collection of system programs that oversee the execution of application programs, manage files, and control the computer system's resources such as a monitor, a keyboard, disk drives, or memory.

peripheral Equipment attached to a computer for storing, entering, and outputting data and programs.

personal computer (PC) A computer with a single processor that is designed for use by one person at a time.

pixel A picture element which is one component of an array or matrix of dots that makes up a visual image.

point A standard unit of measurement used in the printing industry where each point represents 1/72 of an inch.

portrait Orientation of a document page where the page is taller than it is wide.

primary key A field in a table that uniquely identifies a record.

private procedure A procedure that can only be executed from the module in which it resides.

procedure A set of VBA code that accomplishes a specific task.

program A set of instructions a computer follows in sequence to control a specific input, processing, output, and storage cycle.

program loop The process of repeating a sequence of statements.

programmer A person who translates users' specifications into computer programs and tests new programs for errors.

project All of the VBA code associated with a specific document or worksheet.

Project Explorer A feaure of the Visual Basic Editor that identifies various objects and modules associated with a project.

prompt A computer generated request for input.

property A feature of an object such as the font used in a document object, the numeric format of a worksheet cell object, or the name assigned to a macro object.

Property window A comprehensive list of an object's properties that can be set at design time.

public procedure A procedure that can be executed from any module in an application.

query A user request to a database management system for information.

range (also called a **block**) A group of continuous worksheet cells in a row, column, or a combination of both.

range name A user-defined name assigned to a single cell or group of cells.

remark A comment added to program code that is not translated by the compiler. These comments are for program documentation.

resolution A measure of graphic image sharpness in bits (pixels) per inch or bits per line. The higher the resolution, the sharper the graphic image.

Restore button The icon with overlapping windows found in the top right corner of the Title bar next to the Minimize button. Clicking the Restore button returns a maximized window back to its original dimensions.

root directory The primary disk directory that is created when the disk is formatted.

Run mode The mode used when the macro's code is executed.

screen pointer An icon, usually an arrow, on a screen that moves when the mouse or some other pointer device is moved. Program options are activated by using a mouse to move the screen pointer over the desired icon and then clicking the mouse button.

selection The process of running one set of program code instead of another set based on the value of a variable.

sequence The basic structure of a computer program whereby instructions are executed in the order they appear in the program.

server The software that creates an object in an OLE relationship.

software Programs or instructions for the input, processing, output, and storage of data.

statement One executable action the computer can perform.

static Values do not change as a VBA procedure executes.

string A value or variable containing text.

Structured Query Language (SQL) An industry-wide syntax standard for accessing database data.

sub procedure A set of VBA code that accepts arguments from other procedures, but does not return any data.

syntax The structure of a VBA statement.

syntax error A spelling error or mistake in the statement's word order that the compiler cannot translate.

systems software Software that controls internal computer activities. Windows is an example of systems software.

table An independent file within a relational database that consists of a matrix of rows and columns into which data is placed.

tag A usually three-letter lowercase prefix to a variable name that identifies the type of data associated with the variable, for example, *int* stands for an integer or whole number.

task Any operation performed by a computer system.

taskbar An area of the Windows desktop that displays buttons for all the currently active programs, the time, and icons for commonly used programs.

test data Sets of data used for program testing that represent all extremes and normal conditions the program would experience.

text box An element that accepts keyboard entries from user. Text boxes are often used within a dialog box.

textual data Any combination of letters, numbers, or special characters such as #, $, %, ,, and so on.

three-finger salute The process of holding down the Ctrl and Alt keys and then pressing the Delete key. This action reboots older PCs or opens the Close Program or Task Manager dialog box on newer PCs.

Title bar The horizontal area across the top of a window that displays the window's title.

TOE chart A Task/Object/Event chart used to give an overview of a form's function design.

toggle The process of switching a value or setting between one of two preset assignments.

tool tip Text that appears on the screen when the screen pointer is paused over a control object.

toolbar A group of buttons that activate different program options.

Uniform Resource Locator (URL) A Web page's Internet address.

update The process of adding, changing, or deleting data in a file or document.

user interface A combination of menu options, buttons, and commands people use when working with a computer program.

UserForm A set of user-created custom dialog boxes that can contain a wide variety of controls and procedures needed to accomplish different variations of a task.

variable A location in the computer's memory where data values are stored and changed as the program executes.

variable name Identifies the memory location assigned to a specific variable.

virus A computer program that invades a computer system by attaching itself to other commonly used programs. Once the virus infects a system, it displays unwanted messages, erases data, or promotes activities that damage hardware.

Visual Basic for Applications (VBA) A programming language that is a part of Microsoft's Office Suite.

Index